THE EVERYWHERE CHRIST

92 Topics from *A Course in Miracles*

Original Author Helen Schucman
Abridgment by Stan Herrmann

Helen Schucman (Author, Editor) and William T. Thetford (Editor)

Abridged by: Stan Herrmann

ISBN: 978-0-578-64762-3

Library of Congress Control Number: 2020904186

Acknowledgments:

Interior and cover design by Rebecca Shaw, www.BrockleyDesigns.com
Interior and cover images by John Greenleaf Maple www.jgmgraphicart.com

Website: www.EverywhereChrist.com

Email: stan@EverywhereChrist.com

18-Steps-2-Peace is a web app to help direct you on a journey of self-discovery.

www.18Steps2Peace.org

Table of Contents with Topic and Page Number

Alphabetical List of Topics with Page Number

Preface

From 1975 through 1995, I was an evangelical Christian. During those years, the churches to which I belonged taught that the Bible was the infallible Word of God, that it was the only "true" spiritual book, and that it was the only way to find God and eternal life. As the years passed, I questioned the literalism of the Bible and recognized its metaphorical language, which allows for a more heart-centered interpretation. So, after twenty years, I left evangelical Christianity. Christianity can be a wonderful spiritual option, just not when it is entrenched in the belief it is the only path. I still support and embrace the universal truths that reside in the Bible. I identify as a follower of the Christ that is within everyone and is everywhere.

In the years after my departure, I studied many other types of spiritual writings and practices. In 2012, I discovered a book called *A Course in Miracle*s (*ACIM*). At first, I found the book awkward and difficult to read, so I put it on my bookshelf. About a year later, I made a more focused commitment to understand this book. This time, it became clear to me that this book contained divine spiritual wisdom. It has become a supportive guide that continues to awaken within me more love, unity, and agency.

Jesus is a perfect role model for demonstrating how to extend love and acceptance to everyone. With this book, my aim is to help us find ways to extend and receive love, to and from others and ourselves, by seeing the Christ everywhere.

ACIM explores spiritual principles about God, the Christ, Heaven, hell, and more that provide a thought-provoking path to higher consciousness. Its poetic and philosophical cadence presents a riddle-like rhythm when reading, and it takes attentive contemplation to find its metaphorical insight while avoiding the constraints of literalism.

In 2016, I published *A Course in Miracles Abridged Edition*, an abridgment of the original *ACIM* textbook. From that book, I grouped ninety-two specific topics into twelve assembled parts. The process involved additional abridgment with careful attention to keeping the poetic flow, maintaining the rhythm, and upholding the accuracy of the spiritual principles of the original text.

This book is not intended to encourage a rigid *ACIM* doctrine, but to increase our encounters with perceptual miracles, which shifts thoughts of fear to ones of love. Perceptual miracles provide the insight to awaken us from the destructive perceptions that we have carried for years so we can experience more joy, peace, and happiness.

Blessings,

Stan Herrmann

Helpful Information Prior To Reading This Book

What Is A Course in Miracles?

ACIM defines miracle as a divine healing of human perception, a change of mind that shifts perception from one of fear and guilt to one of love and forgiveness. This higher level of perception heals the mind from pain and suffering and places it in the service of a higher purpose.

ACIM was scribed as if Jesus were the author. It is not a doctrinal religion and makes no claim of being the only way.

This mystical book is about us, God, the Christ, the Holy Spirit, and the ego, and while this book uses Christian vernacular, it is not fixed in Christian theology. It is a book of symbols, metaphors, concepts, and ideas that, as it is with all sacred literature, are meant to awaken within us higher consciousness.

The author, Helen Schucman, was a clinical and research psychologist and an associate professor of medical psychology at Columbia University's College of Physicians and Surgeons at the Columbia-Presbyterian Medical Center in New York City.

In 1965, to Helen's surprise, she began to recognize a distinct inner voice. Over the next seven years, in a fully conscious state, she wrote down the information she received from this inner voice. Helen could stop writing when interrupted by work or personal affairs and then continue at the next opportunity. Several times a week, Helen met with her medical colleague, Dr. William Thetford, to read aloud her notes so that he could transcribe them on a typewriter. The first edition of *ACIM* was published in 1975.

The power of any spiritual book's authority is in what it says, not in the person who wrote it. The question about any spiritual book is: "What truth is here that will help me express and experience more love and unity?"

ACIM can be misunderstood. Some have tried to make it into a doctrine of absolute truth about reality. How can words, which are symbols and metaphors, be the absolute truth about anything? Words can only help us create or change our perceptions of what we believe about reality. Spirit helps us experience reality.

This book's rhythmic and metaphorical prose is not meant to be a theological blueprint; instead, it is meant to be an inspired spiritual treasure map that helps us find the treasure of our true Selves.

Words are Symbols

Words are a method of communication consisting of spoken sounds or the sounds' written representation. As such, words are symbols (metaphors) and can be affected by factors such as culture, ethnicity, personal bias, idioms, paradigms, semantics, connotations, and context. Nonetheless, words create a remarkable framework when used to share our thoughts and feelings with others.

Words can be powerful. However, the power is not in the words themselves, but rather in what is perceived in the mind. As we use words, we are expressing, creating, and changing our thoughts, which continually build and shape our perceptions (beliefs). Words can be helpful or hurtful depending upon their usage and interpretation.

Even though words are symbols they are valuable. Words can build a dynamic state of mind through reading and talking to others; they can identify areas in our lives we want to preserve, advance, or change. The mind uses words to help us maneuver through this physical world, but words alone are not the end point. Therefore, we want to find the essence that is beyond the surface of the words to connect with the truth within them, as this is vital for a more profound experience when contemplating meaning. Words can point to truth, but they are not the embodiment of truth.

Personal Doctrine

We all build a personal doctrine (our truth) of specific beliefs through the years of our experiences. It is in our best interest to be mindful of what we believe because acting out our beliefs can physically and emotionally affect ourselves and others.

Our personal doctrine is our truth (our beliefs) because we choose to believe in it. Choosing beliefs is extremely important. They are a valuable tool to direct our attentions and intentions.

Beliefs are thoughts in which we to place our faith and trust. Some beliefs are very dominant, some are less prevalent, and others are veiled. Beliefs come from a variety of sources: hypotheses, theories, concepts, religions, traditions, imaginations, intuitions, observable outcomes, scientific conclusions, physical laws, spiritual laws, stories, books, assumptions, experiences, feelings, or simply other people's beliefs; all of which have constraints and strengths in finding our best truth.

All beliefs are relative truth, not absolute, because beliefs are always relative to some frame of reference. Absolute truth just is. Relative truth can point toward absolute truth, but absolute truth does not need a belief to make it true.

For example, what happens when we die? Various beliefs (relative truth) try to answer this question, but no one's belief is the absolute truth about what really happens.

Death's result does not require a belief to direct it. Maybe we go to Heaven. Maybe we get reincarnated. Maybe we become worm food. Any belief about death does not affect what happens but is only an attempt to explain what happens. The absolute truth of death will just happen as it does.

Another example: who is God? We choose our beliefs about who God is by using one or a variety of sources, yet God is as God is. It can be useful and inspiring to contemplate and choose who we think God is, while recognizing this is relative (not absolute) truth.

Our beliefs can be based in love or fear, they can be helpful or hurtful, enlightened or deceitful. This is why it is crucial to be willing to examine and question our beliefs, and to be kind and considerate when we express them through our actions.

Some people adopt truth as it is told to them from a group's established doctrine or ancient writings without prudent consideration of its origin, practical relevance, or the motive behind the people telling it. It is sensible to carefully observe and evaluate the fruits of all beliefs.

When we have beliefs that would cause us to oppress or attack someone or something, it is best if we ask ourselves, "Why do I believe this and where did it come from?" The conviction or confidence in our truth should be questioned, and perhaps, as a result, our truth should be modified.

It is also beneficial to remain open and inclusionary of others who have a different set of beliefs. Having a basic trust and respect for others in their pursuit of truth is an act of love; however, trust and respect for others does not mean we accept or overlook someone's truth that harms or injures. "Love thy neighbor as thyself" as each of us is accountable to ourselves for what we read, hear, see, and do.

Our personal truth will be added to, modified, and abandoned as we have various life experiences. It is not helpful to build a belief system into a strict form of dogma and project it onto others. No one has the completely "true" truth.

Gender Words

The original *ACIM* was written in a similar style as that of Judeo-Christian texts. Like the Bible, it uses patriarchal nouns and pronouns, such as "Father," "Son," "he," "his," "brother," and more.

Words are symbols, and the intention of *ACIM's* words is to encourage us to awaken from separation and join one creation. As we see the world through the eyes of Christ, we will see everyone as equals.

I have therefore taken the liberty of altering the original text from its usage of masculine nouns and pronouns to alternate between feminine and masculine within each set of passages. I substituted the gender nouns and pronouns from "Father" to "Mother," "he" to "she," "him" to "her," "brother" to "sister," and so on, to balance the usage of gender terms within this book. I considered changing the gender pronouns into non-binary nouns; unfortunately, it made the reading of this book difficult.

Gender identification is generally a human distinction. When gender nouns and pronouns are used to refer to God, Christ, and the Holy Spirit, this is not asserting they have gender; rather it is for a metaphorical purpose, as this usage may support a deeper personal connection.

Why Read This Book?

Through years of survival, our ego (lower level consciousness) has adopted many perceptions that cause us to feel afraid and guilty. Now we find reasons to blame ourselves, others, and circumstances for our unhappiness.

This book is a resource for us to identify current beliefs that are rooted in fear and guilt, then to find a way to replace those beliefs with ones that contain love and forgiveness. Use this book for group study or devotional purposes.

At the end of each topic, a section is provided for us to write down the practical truth, practical action, and heartfelt thoughts. This contemplative exercise can help us grow spiritually by increasing awareness of our feelings, thoughts, and actions.

Definitions for Topics

ACIM does not have an official glossary, so I created definitions for most of the topics using the following sources: the original *ACIM* textbook, Dr. Kenneth Wapnick's *Glossary-Index for A Course in Miracles*, and Robert Perry's *Glossary of Terms from* A Course in Miracles.

The definitions were created from the point of view of ACIM to aid in understanding this book's concepts regarding how we can experience more love and less fear.

The full glossary is located at the back of the book.

The Everywhere Christ

This book is not about theology;

it is about perceptions.

Perceptions are weaved into beliefs.

Beliefs can have elements of fear or love.

Fear is from the ego, and love is from the Christ.

Mind and spirit are the keys to undoing egoic beliefs.

Embrace the truth that lifts you higher to Christ consciousness.

Overlook what does not.

May this poetic, symbolic, and deeply contemplative

rendering help awaken within you the love and peace of

the Christ energy that is EVERYWHERE.

Original Author - Helen Schucman

Abridgment Author - Stan Herrmann

PART ONE

www.jgmgraphicart.com

Topics

1. **BODY**
2. **EGO**
3. **MIND**
4. **CHRIST**
5. **ANTI-CHRIST**
6. **HOLY SPIRIT**
7. **SON/DAUGHTER OF GOD**

Note: All chapter and section notations for the passages are referencing a previously published book titled *A Course in Miracles Abridged Edition.*

TOPIC 1

BODY

body: A biological form (a physical instrument) that our mind uses to communicate with the outer world. The body is a means (a device) to connect with all that we encounter while in the physical world of time. The body is neutral and has no opinions or influence of its own. Only the mind assigns meaning to things. The body is important and valuable, as it is the thing we use to extend love and expand the Self. Seeing through the Christ mind will guide us to use the body for its highest purpose.

Ch. 2. Sec. 4.

The **body** is merely part of your experience in the physical world. The **body's** abilities can be, and frequently are, over evaluated. However, it is almost impossible to deny the **body's** existence in this world. Those who do so are engaging in a particularly unworthy form of denial. The term "unworthy" here implies only that this denial is not necessary to protect the mind by denying the unmindful. If one denies this unfortunate aspect of the mind's power, one is also denying the power of the mind itself.

Ch. 6. Sec. 5.

The ego uses the **body** for attack, for pleasure and for pride. The Holy Spirit sees the **body** only as a means of communication, and because communicating is sharing, the **body** becomes communion. Those who communicate fear are promoting attack and attack always breaks communication. Egos do join together in temporary allegiance, but always for what each one can get separately. The Holy Spirit communicates only what each one can give to all. The Holy Spirit never takes anything back, because She wants you to keep what She gives. Therefore, the Holy Spirit's teaching begins with the lesson:

To have, give all to all.

Ch. 19. Sec. 4.

The **body** can bring you neither peace nor turmoil; neither joy nor pain. The **body** is a means, and not an end. The **body** has no purpose of itself, but only what purpose is given to it by the mind. The **body** will seem to be whatever is the means for reaching the goal that you assign to the **body**. Peace and guilt are both conditions of the mind.

Ch. 28. Sec. 6.

The **body** has not judged itself, nor made itself to be what it is not. The **body** does not tell you what its purpose is and cannot understand what the **body** is for. The **body** does not victimize, because it has no will, no preferences and no doubts. The **body** does not wonder what it is. And so the **body** has no need to be competitive. The **body** can be victimized, but cannot feel itself as victim.

The **body** behaves in ways you want, but it never makes the choice. The **body** can but follow aimlessly the path on which it has been set. And if that path is changed, the **body** walks as easily another way. The **body** takes no sides and judges not the road it travels. The **body** perceives no gap, because it does not hate. The **body** can be used for hate, but the **body** cannot be hateful.

The **body** sees and acts for your mind. The **body** hears your mind's voice.

The **body** represents the gap between the little bit of the mind you call your own and all the rest of what is really yours, the Christ mind. You think the **body** is your self, and that, without the **body**, would your self be lost.

Ch. 31. Sec. 3.

The **body** thinks no thoughts. It has no power to learn, to pardon, nor enslave. The **body** gives no orders that the mind need serve, nor sets conditions that the mind must obey.

Learning is all that causes change. And so the **body**, where no learning can occur, could never change unless the mind preferred the **body** change in its appearances, to suit the purpose given by the mind to the **body**. For mind can learn, and there in the mind is all change made.

Discussion notes: Practical Truth • Practical Action • Heartfelt Thought

____

____

____

____

TOPIC 2

EGO

ego: Lower level consciousness that stifles Self awareness. Thoughts and beliefs that are rooted in fear and can produce guilt, arrogance, blame, confusion, stress, and separation. The ego is habitually involved in various struggles and dramas, aggrandizing the little self and its story, which distract us from our real purpose of knowing our true divine Self. The ego is not something to fight against but rather to recognize, be amused by, and not fooled by. Waking up from the ego's deceptions is the pathway to redemption. This frees us to experience peace, joy, and contentment. Desire, motivation, and accomplishments can originate and be pursued through egoistic thoughts or through the higher Self. Our best interest is to listen to and follow our higher Self when determining how to use our intention and attention.

Ch. 4. Sec. 2.

To the **ego**, to give anything implies that you will have to do without what we are giving. When you associate giving with sacrifice, you give only because you believe that you are somehow getting something better, and can therefore do without the thing you give. "Giving to get" is an inescapable law of the **ego**, which always evaluates itself in relation to other **egos**. The **ego** is therefore continually preoccupied with the belief in scarcity that gave rise to it.

Ch. 4. Sec. 3.

It is hard to understand what "The Kingdom of Heaven is within you" really means. This is because it is not understandable to the **ego**, which the ego interprets this statement as if something outside is inside. The word "within" is unnecessary. The Kingdom of Heaven is you.

> *The Kingdom is perfectly united and perfectly protected, and the* ***ego*** *will not prevail against it. Amen.*

It is surely apparent by now why the **ego** regards spirit as its "enemy." The **ego** arose from the separation, and the **ego's** continued existence depends on your continuing belief in the separation. The **ego** must offer you some sort of reward for maintaining this belief.

All the **ego** can offer is a sense of temporary existence. Against this sense of temporary existence spirit offers you the knowledge of permanence and unshakable *being*. No one who has experienced the revelation of the spirit can ever fully believe in the **ego** again. How can the **ego's** meager offering to you prevail against the glorious gift of God?

Ch. 4. Sec. 5.

Thoughts of God are unacceptable to the **ego**, because thoughts of the God clearly point to the nonexistence of the **ego** itself. The **ego** therefore either distorts the Thoughts of God or refuses to accept them. The **ego** cannot, however, make them cease to be.

"Seek and ye shall find" does not mean that you should seek blindly and desperately for something you would not recognize. Meaningful seeking is consciously undertaken, consciously organized and consciously directed by the mind. The goal of meaningful seeking must be formulated clearly and kept in mind. Learning and wanting to learn are inseparable. You learn best when you believe what you are trying to learn is of value to you.

Ch. 4. Sec. 6.

The **ego** does not recognize the real source of "threat," and if you associate yourself with the **ego**, you do not understand the situation as it is. Only your allegiance to the **ego** gives the **ego** any power over you.

The fact that you believe you must escape from the **ego** shows that you want peace and joy; but you cannot escape from the **ego** by humbling it or controlling it or punishing it.

I am teaching you to associate misery with the **ego** and joy with the spirit. You have taught yourself the opposite. You are still free to choose misery or joy, but can you really want the rewards of the **ego** in the presence of the rewards of God?

Your mission is very simple. You are asked to live so as to demonstrate that you are not an **ego**.

Ch. 4. Sec. 7.

The **ego** is the part of the mind that believes your existence is defined by separation.

Everything the **ego** perceives is a separate whole, without the relationships that imply *being*. The **ego** is thus against communication, except insofar as communication is utilized to establish separateness rather than to abolish separation. The communication system of the **ego** is based on its own thought system, as is everything else the **ego** dictates. The

ego's communication is controlled by its need to protect itself, and the **ego** will disrupt communication when it experiences threat.

Ch. 5. Sec. 5.

The **ego** has a purpose, just as the Holy Spirit has. The **ego's** purpose is fear, because only the fearful can be egotistic. The **ego's** logic is as impeccable as that of the Holy Spirit, because your mind has the means at its disposal to side with Heaven or earth, as the mind elects. But again, remember that both the **ego** and the Holy Spirit are in you.

In Heaven there is no guilt. Guilt is always disruptive. Anything that engenders fear, such as guilt and separation, is divisive because guilt and separation obey the law of division. If the **ego** is the symbol of the separation, the **ego** is also the symbol of guilt.

The **ego** is the part of the mind that believes in division. If you identify with the **ego**, you must perceive yourself as guilty. Whenever you respond to your **ego** you will experience guilt, and you will fear punishment. The **ego** is quite literally a fearful thought.

Ch. 11. Sec. Intro.

Either God or the **ego** is insane. If you will examine the evidence on both sides fairly, you will realize that the **ego** is insane and this must be true. Nothing alive is motherless, for life is creation. Therefore, your decision between God or the **ego** is always an answer to the question, "Who is my mother?" And you will be faithful to the mother you choose.

If you made the **ego**, how can the **ego** have made you? The **ego** was made out of the wish of God's Daughter that the **ego** would mother her. The **ego**, then, is nothing more than a delusional thought system in which you made the **ego** your own mother. Make no mistake about this insanity. It sounds insane when this delusion is stated with perfect honesty, but the **ego** never looks on what it does with perfect honesty. Yet that is the **ego's** insane premise, which is carefully hidden in the dark cornerstone of the **ego's** thought system. And either the **ego**, which you made, is your mother, or the **ego's** whole thought system will not stand.

The cornerstone of God's creation is you, for God's thought system is light. The more you approach the center of God's thought system, the clearer the light becomes. The closer you come to the **ego's** thought system, the darker and more obscure becomes the way. Yet even the little spark in your mind is enough to lighten the way. Bring this light fearlessly with you, and bravely hold this light up to the foundation of the **ego's** thought system. Be willing to judge the **ego's** thought system with perfect honesty. Open the dark cornerstone of terror on which darkness rests, and bring darkness out into the light. There you will see that the **ego's** thought system rested on meaninglessness, and that everything of which you have been afraid was based on nothing.

Ch. 12. Sec. 3.

To identify with the **ego** is to attack yourself and make yourself poor. That is why everyone who identifies with the **ego** feels deprived. What he experiences by identifying with the **ego** then is depression or anger, because what he did was to exchange self-love for self-hate, making him afraid of himself. He does not realize this exchange. Even if he is fully aware of anxiety, he does not perceive anxiety's source as his own **ego** identification, and he always tries to handle the anxiety by making some sort of insane "arrangement" with the world. He always perceives this world as outside himself, for this is crucial to his adjustment. He does not realize that he makes this world, for there is no world outside of him.

Everything you perceive as the outside world is merely your attempt to maintain your **ego** identification, for everyone believes that **ego** identification is salvation. You have projected outward what is antagonistic to what is inward, and therefore you would have to perceive your outside world this way. That is why you must realize that your hatred is in your mind and not outside your mind before you can get rid of your hatred; and why you must get rid of your hatred before you can perceive the world as it really is.

Ch. 13. Sec. 7.

The **ego** wants to have things for salvation, for possession is the **ego's** law. Possession for its own sake is the **ego's** fundamental creed, a basic cornerstone in the churches the **ego** builds to itself. And at the **ego's** altar, the **ego** demands you go get all of the things it bids, leaving you no eternal joy in all those things.

Therefore, ask not of your self what you need, for you do not know, and your own advice to your self will hurt you. For what you think you need will merely serve to tighten up your world against the light, and render you unwilling to question the value that this world can really hold for you.

The Holy Spirit knows what you need. For She will give you all things that do not block the way to light. And what else could you need?

Discussion notes: Practical Truth • Practical Action • Heartfelt Thought

TOPIC 3

MIND

mind: (1) The set of cognitive faculties including consciousness, imagination, perception, thinking, judgment, language, and memory. The faculty of a thing's consciousness. It is debatable as to where the mind is and what things influence it. (2) The expression of the self that includes awareness, choice, thought, and emotion.

Ch. 2. Sec. 6.

Everyone experiences fear. Yet it would take very little right thinking to realize why fear occurs. Few appreciate the real power of the **mind**, and no one remains fully aware of the real power of the **mind** all the time. However, if you hope to spare yourself from fear there are some things you must realize, and realize fully. The **mind** is very powerful, and never loses its creative force. The **mind** never sleeps. Every instant the **mind** is creating. It is hard to recognize that thought and belief combine into a power surge that can move mountains. It appears at first glance that to believe such power about yourself is arrogant, but that is not the real reason you do not believe in this power of your **mind**. You prefer to believe that your thoughts cannot exert real influence because you are actually afraid of your thoughts. If you believe that what you think is ineffectual you may cease to be afraid of what you think, but you are hardly likely to respect what you think. There are no idle thoughts. All thinking produces form at some level.

Ch. 3. Sec. 4.

Only your mis-perceptions stand in your way. Without your mis-perceptions your choice is certain. Sane perception induces sane choosing. "Many are called but few are chosen" should be, "All are called but few choose to listen." Therefore, they do not choose right. The "chosen ones" are merely those who choose right sooner. Right **minds** can do this now, and right **minds** will find rest unto their souls.

Ch. 4. Sec. 4.

There is no limit to the power of a Son of God, but he can limit the expression of his power as much as he chooses. Your **mind** and mine can unite in shining your ego away, releasing the strength of God into everything you think and do. Do not settle for anything less than this release, and refuse to accept anything but this release as your goal. Watch your **mind** carefully for any beliefs that hinder your **mind's** accomplishment, and step away from them.

Ch. 5. Sec. 5.

Whatever you accept into your **mind** has reality for you. It is your acceptance of it that makes it real. If you enthrone the ego in your **mind**, your allowing the ego to enter, making the ego your reality. This is because the **mind** is capable of creating reality or making illusions.

The Holy Spirit and the ego are the only choices open to you. God created one, the choice for the Holy Spirit, and so you cannot eradicate It. You made the other, the choice for the ego, and so you can eradicate it.

Ch. 7. Sec. 6.

The **mind** that accepts attack cannot love. That is because the **mind** believes attack can destroy love, and therefore does not understand what love is. If the **mind** does not understand what love is, the **mind** that attacks cannot perceive itself as loving. The **mind** that attacks, loses the awareness of being, and induces feelings of confusion. Your thinking has done this because of its power, but your thinking can also save you from this because the **mind's** power is not of your making. Your ability to direct your thinking as you choose is part of the **mind's** power. If you do not believe you can direct your thinking you have denied the power of your thinking, and thus rendered your thinking powerless in your belief.

Ch. 8. Sec. 7.

The **mind** cannot be made physical, but the **mind** can be made manifest through the physical if the **mind** uses the body to go beyond itself. By reaching out to the body, the **mind** extends itself.

The removal of blocks in the **mind** is the only way to guarantee help and healing. Help and healing are the normal expressions of a **mind** that is working through the body, but not in the body.

Ch. 10. Sec. Intro.

Every response you make to everything you perceive is up to you, because your **mind** determines your perception of everything that happens to you.

Ch. 10. Sec. 4.

Oneness cannot be divided. If you perceive other gods your **mind** is split, and you will not be able to limit the split, because the split is the sign that you have removed part of your **mind** from God's Will. This means the split **mind** is out of control. To be out of control is to be out of reason, and then the **mind** does become unreasonable. By defining the **mind** wrongly, you perceive the **mind** as functioning wrongly.

Ch. 14. Sec. 8.

Let your **mind** wander not through darkened corridors, away from light's center. You may choose to lead yourself astray, but the Holy Spirit will surely lead you to where God and Her Daughter await your recognition. God and Her Daughter are joined in giving you the gift of oneness, before which all separation vanishes. Unite with what you are.

Where God is, there are you. Such is the truth. Everything God created knows its Creator.

Discussion notes: Practical Truth • Practical Action • Heartfelt Thought

---

Topic 4

Christ

Christ: The divine Identity that is everywhere and within all creation. The shared experience of God's Spirit. The Self that God placed within all by the extension of the Spirit. Christ is the author of true vision within everyone (the higher Self) and our shared identity of oneness with everything. Jesus fully embodied the Christ and serves as a model for transcending the ego's influence through awakening into Christ consciousness. Note that the Holy Spirit is the mediator between the Christ Mind and our ego mind.

Christ vision: Spiritual sight. Seeing beyond the body and the ego by way of divine Spirit. Interpreting others' behavior as either an act of love or a calling out for love. Seeing both as no reason for defense or attack and every reason for extending love. The ability to mentally see beyond all worldly interference to the light of holiness in everything.

Ch. 9. Sec. 1.

Do not try to look beyond yourself for truth, for truth can only be within you. Say, therefore:

> ***Christ** is in me, and where **Christ** is, God must be, for **Christ** is part of God.*

Ch. 11. Sec. 5.

Every brother you meet becomes a witness for **Christ** or for the ego, depending on what you perceive in him. Everyone convinces you of what you want to perceive, and of the reality of the kingdom you have chosen for your vigilance. Everything you perceive is a witness to the thought system you want to be true. Every brother has the power to release you, if you choose to be free. You cannot accept false witness of him unless you have evoked false witnesses against him. If he speaks not of **Christ** to you, you spoke not of **Christ** to him. You hear but your own voice, and if **Christ** speaks through you, you will hear the **Christ**.

Ch. 11. Sec. 6.

Let the **Christ** in you interpret for you, and do not try to limit what you see by narrow little beliefs that are unworthy of God's Daughter.

Ch. 12. Sec. 6.

Correction is for all who cannot see. To open the eyes of the blind is the Holy Spirit's mission, for He knows that all who cannot see have not lost their vision, but merely sleep. He would awaken the blind from the sleep of forgetting to the remembering of God. **Christ's** eyes are open, and **Christ** will look upon whatever you see with love if you accept **Christ's** vision as your vision. The Holy Spirit keeps the vision of **Christ** for every Son of God who sleeps. In His sight, the Son of God is perfect, and He longs to share **Christ's** vision with you.

Yet you must learn the cost of sleeping, and refuse to pay it.

Ch. 12. Sec. 7.

Through the eyes of **Christ**, only the real world exists and only the real world can be seen. As you decide so will you see. And all that you see is witness to your decision.

Ch. 13. Sec. 5.

Do not seek vision through your eyes, for you made your way of seeing that you might see in darkness, and in this you are deceived. Beyond this darkness, and yet still within you, is the vision of **Christ**, Who looks on all in light. Your "vision" comes from fear, as **Christ's** vision comes from love. And **Christ** sees for you, as your witness to the real world. **Christ** is the Holy Spirit's manifestation, looking always on the real world, and calling forth its witnesses and drawing the real world to you. **Christ** loves what She sees within you.

You have but two emotions, one you made, which is fear, and one was given you by God, which is love. Each is a way of seeing, and different worlds arise from fear and love's different sights. See through the vision of love that is given you by God.

Beyond your darkest dreams **Christ** sees God's guiltless Daughter within you, shining in perfect radiance that is undimmed by your dreams. And this perfect radiance you will see as you look with **Christ**, for **Christ's** vision is the gift of love to you.

Ch. 13. Sec. 7.

*The Holy Spirit leads me unto **Christ**, and where else would I go?*

*What need have I but to awake in **Christ**?*

Then follow Holy Spirit in joy, with faith that He will lead you safely through all dangers to your peace of mind this world may set before you. Kneel not before altars to sacrifice, and seek not what you will surely lose. Content yourself with what you will surely keep, and be not restless, for you undertake a quiet journey to the peace of God, where God would have you be in quietness.

Ch. 22. Sec. 4.

The Love of **Christ** will light your faces, and shine from your faces into a darkened world that needs the light.

Think of the loveliness that you will see, who walk with the **Christ**! And think how beautiful will each of you look to the other! How happy you will be to be together, after such a long and lonely journey where you walked alone. The gates of Heaven, open now for you, and now you will open to the sorrowful. And all who look upon the **Christ** in you will rejoice. How beautiful the sight you saw beyond the veil, which you will bring to light the tired eyes of those as weary now as once you were. How thankful will they be to see you come among them, offering **Christ's** forgiveness to dispel their faith in sin.

Those who would let illusions be lifted from their minds are this world's saviors, walking the world with their Redeemer, and carrying **Christ's** message of hope and freedom and release from suffering to everyone who needs a miracle to save them.

Ch. 24. Sec. 5.

The **Christ** in you is very still.

Where could your peace arise, but from forgiveness? The **Christ** in you looks only on the truth, and sees no condemnation that could need forgiveness. The **Christ** is at peace because She sees no sin. Identify with the **Christ**. She is your eyes, your ears, your hands, your feet. How gentle are the sights the **Christ** sees, the sounds She hears.

Ch. 25 Sec. Intro.

The **Christ** in you inhabits not a body. Yet **Christ** is in you. And thus it must be that you are not within a body. What is within you cannot be outside you. And it is certain that you cannot be apart from what is at the very center of your life. What gives you life cannot be housed in death. **Christ** is within a frame of Holiness whose only purpose is that He may be made manifest to those who know Him not, that the **Christ** may call to them to come to Him and see Him where they thought their bodies were. Then will their bodies melt away, that they may frame the **Christ's** Holiness in them.

Ch. 26. Sec. 9.

Look with loving eyes on your sister who carries **Christ** within her, that you may behold her glory and rejoice that Heaven is not separate from you.

Ch. 30. Sec. 8.

The **Christ** in your sister is perfect. Is it this **Christ** that you would look upon? Then let there be no dreams about your sister that you would prefer to seeing the **Christ**. And you will see the **Christ** in your sister because you let Her come to you. And when **Christ** has appeared to you, you will be certain you are like the **Christ**, for She is the changeless in your sister and in you.

You look upon this changeless **Christ** when you decide there is not one appearance you would hold in place of what your sister really is. Let no temptation to prefer a dream allow uncertainty to enter here. Be not made guilty and afraid when you are tempted by a dream of what your sister is. But do not give a dream power to replace the changeless **Christ** in your sister in your sight of her. There is no false appearance but will fade, if you request a miracle instead. There is no pain from which your sister is not free, if you would have her be but what she is. Why should you fear to see the **Christ** in your sister? You but behold yourself in what you see. As your sister is healed are you made free of guilt, for her appearance is your own appearance to you.

Ch. 31. Sec. 8.

You always choose between your weakness and the strength of **Christ** in you. And what you choose is what you think is real. Simply by never using weakness to direct your actions, you have given weakness no power. And the light of **Christ** in you is given charge of everything you do. For you have brought your weakness unto **Christ**, and **Christ** has given you strength instead of weakness.

Trials are but lessons that you failed to learn presented once again, so where you made a faulty choice before, you now can make a better one, and thus escape all pain that what you chose before has brought to you. In every difficulty, all distress, and each perplexity

Christ calls to you and gently says, "My brother, choose again." **Christ** would not leave one source of pain unhealed, nor any image left to veil the truth. **Christ** would not leave you comfortless, alone in dreams of hell, but would release your mind from everything that hides **Christ's** face from you. **Christ's** Holiness is yours because **Christ** is the only power that is real in you. **Christ's** strength is yours because **Christ** is the Self that God created as God's only Son.

Discussion notes: Practical Truth • Practical Action • Heartfelt Thought

---

TOPIC 5

ANTI-CHRIST

anti-Christ: A symbol for the ego. The belief in a power that can oppose the omnipotence of God and deny the reality of our Christ within. An idol.

Ch. 29. Sec. 8.

An idol is a false impression, or a false belief; some form of **anti-Christ**, that constitutes a gap between the Christ and what you see. An idol is a wish, made tangible and given form, and thus an idol is perceived as real and seen outside the mind. Yet an idol is still a thought. All forms of **anti-Christ** oppose the Christ. And fall before Christ's face like a dark veil that seems to shut you off from the Christ, alone in darkness. Yet the light is there. A cloud does not put out the sun. No more a veil can banish what the veil seems to separate, nor darken by one speck of the light itself.

This world of idols is a veil across the face of Christ, because this world's purpose is to separate your sister from yourself. A dark and fearful purpose, yet it is only a thought without the power to change one blade of grass from something living to a sign of death.

What is an idol? Nothing! An idol must be believed before it seems to come to life, and given a power that an idol may be feared.

An idol is established by belief, and when the belief is withdrawn the idol "dies." This belief in idols is the **anti-Christ**; the strange idea there is a power outside omnipotence, a place beyond the infinite, a time transcending the eternal. Here, the world of idols has been set by the idea this power and place and time are given form, and shape the world where the impossible has happened. Here, in the world of idols the deathless come to die, the all-encompassing come to suffer loss, the timeless come to be made the slaves of time. Here, the world of idols does the changeless change; the peace of God, forever given to all living things, give way to chaos. And the Daughter of God, as perfect, sinless and as loving as her Mother, goes there to hate a little while; to suffer pain and finally to die.

Nothing and nowhere must an idol be, while God is everything and everywhere.

Discussion notes: Practical Truth • Practical Action • Heartfelt Thought

TOPIC 6

HOLY SPIRIT

Holy Spirit: The communication link to God that is within everyone. The voice for God; the divine teacher. Our internal Guide. Our higher Self. The Holy Spirit is the mediator between the Christ Mind and our ego mind.

Ch. 5. Sec. 1.

The **Holy Spirit** is referred to as the Healer, the Comforter and the Guide.

The **Holy Spirit** is the Christ Mind, which is aware of the knowledge that lies beyond perception. The Voice of the **Holy Spirit** is the Call to Atonement, or the restoration of the integrity of the mind.

The **Holy Spirit** is the Mind of the Atonement. The **Holy Spirit** represents a state of mind close enough to One-mindedness that transfer to it is at last possible.

Ch. 5. Sec. 2.

The Voice of the **Holy Spirit** does not command, because It is incapable of arrogance. The Voice of the **Holy Spirit** does not demand, because It does not seek control. The Voice of the **Holy Spirit** does not overcome, because It does not attack. The Voice of the **Holy Spirit** merely reminds. The Voice of the **Holy Spirit** is compelling only because of what It reminds you of. The Voice of the **Holy Spirit** brings to your mind the other way, remaining quiet even in the midst of the turmoil you may make.

Ch. 5. Sec. 3.

The **Holy Spirit** is God's Answer to the ego. The **Holy Spirit** has the task of undoing what the ego has made.

The **Holy Spirit** is the Mediator between the interpretations of the ego and the knowledge of the Spirit. The **Holy Spirit** can therefore perform the function of reinterpreting what the ego makes, not by destruction but by understanding. Understanding is light, but you yourself do not know this light. It is therefore the task of the **Holy Spirit** to reinterpret what the ego makes on behalf of God.

Peace is the ego's greatest enemy because, according to the ego's interpretation of reality, war is the guarantee of the ego's survival. The ego becomes strong in strife. If you believe there is strife you will react viciously, because the idea of danger has entered your mind. The idea itself is an appeal to the ego. The **Holy Spirit** is as vigilant as the ego to the call of danger, opposing the call of danger with the **Holy Spirit's** strength, just as the ego welcomes the call of danger. The **Holy Spirit** counters the ego's call to war by welcoming peace.

Ch. 5. Sec. 3. (cont.)

You have not made truth, but truth can still set you free. Look as the **Holy Spirit** looks, and understand as the **Holy Spirit** understands. The **Holy Spirit** is in communion with God always, and She is part of you. The **Holy Spirit** is your Guide to salvation, because She holds the remembrance of things past and things to come, and brings them to the present. The **Holy Spirit** holds this gladness gently in your mind, asking only that you increase this gladness in God's Name by sharing gladness to increase God's joy in you.

Ch. 6. Sec. 5.c.

The **Holy Spirit** sorts out the true from the false in your mind, and teaches you to judge every thought you allow to enter your mind with the light of what God put there. Whatever is in accord with this light that God put there in your mind, the **Holy Spirit** retains, to strengthen the Kingdom in you. What is partly in accord with the Kingdom in you, the **Holy Spirit** accepts and purifies. Remember, however, that what the **Holy Spirit** rejects the ego accepts. This is because the **Holy Spirit** and the ego are in fundamental disagreement about everything, being in fundamental disagreement about what you are. The ego's beliefs on this crucial issue about what you are varies, and that is why the ego promotes different moods. The **Holy Spirit** never varies on this point, and so the one mood He engenders is joy. The **Holy Spirit** protects joy by rejecting everything that does not foster joy, and so He alone can keep you wholly joyous.

Ch. 7. Sec. 10.

The **Holy Spirit** will direct you only so as to avoid pain. Surely no one would object to this goal if one recognized it. The problem is not if what the **Holy Spirit** says is true, but whether you want to listen to what She says. The **Holy Spirit's** main function is to teach you to tell pain and joy apart.

The **Holy Spirit** always sides with you and with your strength. The **Holy Spirit** never asks for sacrifice, but the ego always does. The **Holy Spirit's** Voice will teach you how to distinguish between pain and joy, and will lead you out of the confusion you have made.

Ch. 11. Sec. 2.

The **Holy Spirit** cannot speak to an unwelcoming host, because He will not be heard. The Eternal Guest remains, but the **Holy Spirit's** Voice grows faint in alien company. The **Holy Spirit** needs your protection, only because your care is a sign that you want Him. Think like the **Holy Spirit** ever so slightly, and the little spark becomes a blazing light that fills your mind so that He becomes your only Guest. Whenever you ask the ego to enter, you lessen the **Holy Spirit's** welcome. Whatever journey you choose to take, the **Holy Spirit** will go with you, waiting.

Your willingness need not be perfect, because the **Holy Spirit's** willingness is. If you will merely offer the **Holy Spirit** a little place, He will lighten it so much that you will gladly let it be increased. And by this increase of your willingness, you will begin to remember creation.

Would you be hostage to the ego or host to God? You will accept whom you invite. You are free to determine who shall be your guest, and how long that guest shall remain with you.

Ch. 14. Sec. 7.

The **Holy Spirit** asks of you but this; bring to Her every secret you have locked away from Her. Open every door to the **Holy Spirit**, and bid Her enter the darkness and lighten the darkness away. At your request the **Holy Spirit** enters gladly. The **Holy Spirit** brings the light to darkness if you make the darkness open to Her. But what you hide the **Holy Spirit** cannot look upon.

The vision of Christ is not for the **Holy Spirit** alone, but for the Christ within you. Bring, therefore, all your dark and secret thoughts to the **Holy Spirit**, and look upon them with Her. The **Holy Spirit** holds the light, and the ego holds the darkness. The light and the darkness cannot coexist when Both of You, the **Holy Spirit** and the Christ within you, together look on the light and the darkness. The **Holy Spirit's** judgment must prevail, and She will give Her judgment to you as you join your perception to Hers.

Discussion notes: Practical Truth • Practical Action • Heartfelt Thought

TOPIC 7

SON/DAUGHTER OF GOD

Son/Daughter of God: Our true identity is that we are all a son or daughter of God. Mankind is not separate from the universal Self who encompasses all beings. We are God's extension and continuation of love and grace. Everyone is a part of God's creation, at one with God and each other. We are all the incarnation of God; otherwise we would not exist. God is the true identity of everything.

Sonship: This is a singular term that means the collective Oneness. All that God created, us and everything, is in an eternal relationship with the Divine. The inclusive Oneness of all that is.

God: The eternal Energy. The infinite Source. Energy and Source encompasses everything. This Energy/Source (God) is expansion, extension, evolution, connection, force, order, flow, unity, rebirth and Love. Words help us connect with God's life-giving Essence, but words are unable to express the true reality of God and Creation.

Ch. 8. Sec. 6.

Listen to the story of the prodigal son, and learn what God's treasure is and what your treasure is: This son of a loving father left his home and thought he had squandered everything for nothing of any value, although he had not understood its worthlessness at the time. The son was ashamed to return to his father, because the son thought he had hurt his father. Yet when the son came home, the father welcomed him with joy, because the son himself was his father's treasure. His father wanted nothing else.

God wants only **His Son** because **His Son** is His only treasure.

Ch. 9. Sec. 6.

If your sisters are part of you, will you accept them? Only your sisters can teach you what you are, for your learning is the result of what you taught them. What you call upon in your sisters you call upon in yourself. And as you call upon acceptance in your sisters, acceptance becomes real to you. **God has but one Daughter**, knowing **God's Daughters all as One**. Everyone God created is part of you and shares Her glory with you. God's glory belongs to Her, but Her glory is equally yours. You cannot, then, be less glorious than God is.

Ch. 10. Sec. 5.

You do not realize how much you have denied yourself, and how much God, in His Love, would not have it so. Yet God would not interfere with you, because God would not know **His Son** if **His Son** were not free. To interfere with you would be to attack Himself, and God is not insane. When you deny God, you are insane. Would you have God share your insanity? God will never cease to love **His Son**, and **God's Son** will never cease to love Him. That unceasing love was the condition of **God's Son's** creation, fixed forever in the Mind of God. To know that love is sanity and to deny that love is insanity. God gave Himself to you in your creation, and His gifts are eternal.

Do not deny yourself the joy that was created for you for the misery you have made for yourself. God has given you the means for undoing what you have made. Listen, and you will learn how to remember *what you are*.

Ch. 11. Sec. 1.

If you believe you are absent from God, you will believe that God is absent from you. There is no end to **God and Her Daughter**, for we are the universe. God is not incomplete, and God is not childless. Because God did not will to be alone, She created a Daughter like Herself. The universe of love does not stop because you do not see love, nor have your closed eyes lost the ability to see love. Look upon the glory of God's creation, and you will learn what God has kept for you.

God has given you a place in Her mind that is yours forever.

God is your heritage, because God's one gift is Herself. Give, then, without limit and without end, to learn how much God has given you. Your ability to accept God depends on your willingness to give as She gives.

Ch. 11. Sec. 4.

Blessed is the **Son of God** whose radiance is of his Father, and whose glory he wills to share as his Father shares glory with him. There is no condemnation in the Son, for there is no condemnation in the Father. Sharing the perfect Love of the Father the Son must share what belongs to Him, for otherwise he will not know the Father or the Son. Peace be unto you who rest in God, and in whom the whole **Sonship** rests.

Ch. 29. Sec. 6.

Swear not to die, you holy **Daughter of God**! The Daughter of Life cannot be killed. The **Daughter of God** is immortal as her Mother. What the **Daughter of God** is cannot be changed. The **Daughter of God** is the only thing in all the universe that must be one. What seems eternal now all will have an end. The stars will disappear, and night and day will be no more. All things that come and go, the tides, the seasons and the lives of all; all things that change with time and bloom and fade will not return. Where time has set an end is not where the eternal is. **God's Daughter** can never change. **God's Daughter** will be as she was and as **God's Daughter** is, for time did not appoint her destiny, nor set the hour of the her birth and death. Forgiveness will not change **God's Daughter**, who is already guiltless.

Ch. 21. Sec. 7.

No one believes the **Son of God** is powerless. And so those who see themselves as helpless must believe that they are not the **Son of God**.

Discussion notes: Practical Truth • Practical Action • Heartfelt Thought

---

PART TWO

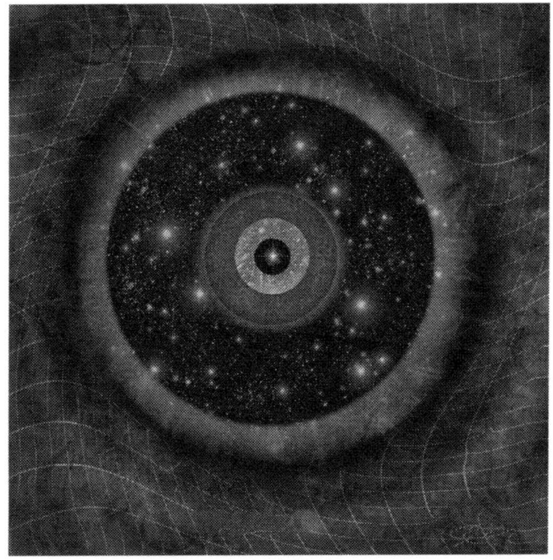

www.jgmgraphicart.com

Topics

8. HELL
9. DEVIL
10. HEAVEN
11. (THE) KINGDOM
12. EARTH
13. REAL WORLD
14. PRISON
15. ALTAR

Note: All chapter and section notations for the passages are referencing a previously published book titled *A Course in Miracles Abridged Edition.*

TOPIC 8

HELL

hell: A state of mind in which we seem to be separate, vulnerable, deficient, unfulfilled, and mistreated. A feeling that someone or something is trying to control or harm us, and we have to fight or flee to be safe. The pursuit of the egoistic thought system that leads us to selfish and destructive behaviors rooted in fear and guilt causing pain and suffering in us and others.

Ch. 15. Sec. 1.

The belief in **hell** is inescapable to those who identify with the ego. Their nightmares and their fears are all associated with **hell**. The ego teaches that **hell** is in the future, for this is what all the ego's teaching is directed to. **Hell** is the ego's goal.

The Holy Spirit teaches thus: There is no **hell**. **Hell** is only what the ego has made of the present. The belief in **hell** is what prevents you from understanding the present, because you are afraid that the present will lead you to **hell**. The Holy Spirit leads as steadily to Heaven as the ego drives to **hell**. For the Holy Spirit, Who knows only the present, uses the present to undo the fear by which the ego would make the present useless. There is no escape from fear in the ego's use of time, which is past and future. For time, according to the ego's teaching, is nothing but a teaching device for compounding guilt until guilt becomes all-encompassing, demanding vengeance forever.

Ch. 31. Sec. 8.

There is no place for **hell** within a world whose loveliness can yet be so intense and so inclusive that this lovely world is but a step from there to Heaven. To your tired eyes I bring a vision of a different world, so new and clean and fresh you will forget the pain and sorrow that you saw before. Yet this is a vision which you must share with everyone you see, for otherwise you will not behold this vision of a different world. To give this gift is how to make this vision of a different world yours. And God ordained, in loving kindness, that lovely world be for you.

Let us be glad that we can walk the world, and find so many chances to perceive another situation where God's gift can once again be recognized as ours! And thus will all the vestiges of **hell**, the secret sins and hidden hates be gone. And all the loveliness which the vestiges of **hell** concealed appear like lawns of Heaven to our sight, to lift us high above the thorny roads we traveled on before the Christ appeared. And in this choice for the Christ is everyone made free.

Discussion notes: Practical Truth • Practical Action • Heartfelt Thought

---

TOPIC 9

DEVIL

devil: An egoic projection that shifts the blame for destructive calamity and suffering onto an imagined powerful external entity, making it the responsible source. This fear-based assertion enlarges the feeling of being separate from our Creator, thereby causing anxiety and victim-minded thinking. Humans can be powerfully influential and industrious beings, and this power can be responsible for catastrophic harm or incredible healing. The results are usually labeled good or evil, love or hate.

Ch. 3. Sec. 7.

The "**devil**" is a frightening concept because the "**devil**" seems to be extremely powerful and extremely active. The "**devil**" is perceived as a force in combat with God, battling God for possession of God's creations. The "**devil**" deceives by lies, and builds kingdoms in which everything is in direct opposition to God. Yet the "**devil**" attracts men rather than repels men, and men are willing to "sell" the "**devil**" their souls in return for gifts of no real worth. This makes absolutely no sense.

All beliefs are real to the believer. The mind can make the belief in separation very real and very fearful, and this belief in separation is the "**devil**."

The "**devil**" is powerful, active, destructive and clearly in opposition to God, because the belief in separation literally denies God's Fatherhood. Look at your life and see what the "**devil**" has made. But realize that this making will surely dissolve in the light of truth, because the belief in separation's foundation is a lie. Your creation by God is the only Foundation that cannot be shaken, because the light is in it. Your starting point is truth, and you must return to your Beginning. Much has been seen since then, but nothing has really happened. Your Self is still in peace, even though your mind is in conflict. You have not yet gone back far enough, and that is why you become so fearful. As you approach the Beginning, you feel the fear of the destruction of your own thought system upon you as if this destruction were the fear of death. There is no death, but there is a belief in death.

Be glad! The light will shine from the true Foundation of life, and your own thought system will stand corrected.

Discussion notes: Practical Truth • Practical Action • Heartfelt Thought

____

____

____

____

TOPIC 10

HEAVEN

Heaven: A state of mind in which we see the world as a place of union, peace, joy, and serenity, without the veil of fear. An awareness of love; an experience of peace. Heaven can be experienced in this world of time through the conduit of unified relationships, which is accomplished through the extending and receiving of love and acceptance. Everyone's eternal home becomes known at time's end.

Ch. 12. Sec. 6.

Heaven is your home, and being in God, **Heaven** must also be in you.

Ch. 13. Sec. 11.

God wills you be in **Heaven**, and nothing can keep you from being in **Heaven**, or **Heaven** from you. Your wildest mis-perceptions, your weird imaginings, your blackest nightmares all mean nothing. They will not prevail against the peace God wills for you. The Holy Spirit will restore your sanity because insanity is not the Will of God.

God willed you **Heaven**, and will always *will* you **Heaven**, and nothing else. The Holy Spirit knows only of God's Will. There is no chance that **Heaven** will not be yours, for God is sure, and what God *wills* is as sure as God is.

Ch. 15. Sec. 1.

Time is inconceivable without change, yet holiness does not change. Learn from this holy instant more than merely that hell does not exist. In this redeeming instant lies **Heaven**. And **Heaven** will not change. Change is an illusion, taught by those who cannot see themselves as guiltless. There is no change in **Heaven** because there is no change in God. In the holy instant, in which you see yourself as bright with freedom, you will remember God. For remembering God is to remember freedom.

How long is an instant? As long as it takes to re-establish perfect sanity, perfect peace and perfect love for everyone, for God and for yourself. An instant is as long as it takes to remember immortality, and your immortal creations who share immortality with you. An instant is as long as it takes to exchange hell for **Heaven**. An instant is long enough to transcend all of the ego's making, and ascend unto your Father.

Ch. 15. Sec. 3.

I asked you earlier, "Would you be hostage to the ego or host to God?" Let this question be asked you by the Holy Spirit every time you make a decision. For every decision you make does answer this question of hostage or host, and invites sorrow or joy accordingly. Every decision you make is for **Heaven** or for hell, and brings you the awareness of what you decided for.

Ch. 16. Sec. 5.

This world is the opposite of **Heaven**, being made to be **Heaven's** opposite, and everything here in this world takes a direction exactly opposite of what is true. In **Heaven**, where the meaning of love is known, love is the same as union. Here, in this world where the illusion of love is accepted in love's place, love is perceived as separation and exclusion.

To everyone, **Heaven** is completion. There can be no disagreement on this, because both the ego and the Holy Spirit accept that **Heaven** is completion. The ego and the Holy Spirit are, however, in complete disagreement on what completion is, and how completion is accomplished. The Holy Spirit knows that completion lies first in union, and then in the extension of union. To the ego completion lies in triumph, and in the extension of the "victory", even to the final triumph over God. In this triumph over God, the ego sees the ultimate freedom of the self, for nothing would remain to interfere with the ego. This triumph over God is the ego's idea of **Heaven**.

Ch. 18. Sec. 6.

There is nothing outside you. That is what you must ultimately learn, for leaning that there is nothing outside you is that realization the Kingdom of **Heaven** is restored to you. For God created only this, and God did not depart from you nor leave you separate from Himself. The Kingdom of **Heaven** is the dwelling place of the Son of God, who left not his Father and dwells not apart from Him. **Heaven** is not a place. **Heaven** is merely an awareness of perfect Oneness, and the knowledge that there is nothing else; nothing outside this perfect Oneness, and nothing else within.

Ch. 23. Sec. 2.

No one wants madness, nor does anyone cling to his madness if he sees that this is what madness is. What protects madness is the belief that madness is true. It is the function of insanity to take the place of truth. Insanity must be seen as truth to be believed.

There is no life outside of **Heaven**. Where God created life, there life must be. In any state apart from **Heaven** life is illusion. Outside of **Heaven**, only the conflict of illusion stands; senseless, impossible and beyond all reason, and yet perceived as an eternal barrier to **Heaven**. Illusions are but forms of chaos. Illusions content is never true.

Ch. 25. Sec.4.

In you is all of **Heaven**. Every leaf that falls is given life in you. Each bird that ever sang will sing again in you. And every flower that ever bloomed has saved its perfume and its loveliness for you. What aim can supersede the Will of God and of Her Daughter, that **Heaven** be restored to her for whom **Heaven** was created as her only home? How better could your own mistakes be brought to truth than by your willingness to bring the light of **Heaven** with you, as you walk beyond the world of darkness into light?

Ch. 25. Sec. 7.

What is dependable except God's Love? And where does sanity abide except in God? The One Who speaks for God can show you this Love. It is God's Will that you remember that you abide in God's Love, and so emerge from deepest mourning into perfect joy. Accept the function that has been assigned to you in God's Own plan to show God's Son that hell and **Heaven** are different, not the same.

Ch. 26. Sec. 3.

Salvation stops just short of **Heaven**, for only perception needs salvation. **Heaven** was never lost, and so cannot be saved. Yet who can make a choice between the wish for **Heaven** and the wish for hell unless he recognizes they are not the same?

Ch. 26. Sec. 4.

What is **Heaven** but a song of gratitude and love and praise by everything created to the Source of its creation?

Here the Daughter of God Herself comes to receive each gift that brings her nearer to her home. Not one is lost, and none is cherished more than any other. Each gift reminds her of her Mother's Love as surely as the rest. What but a miracle could change her mind, so that she understands that love cannot be feared? What other miracle is there but this miracle that love cannot be feared? And what else need there be but the gift of love to make the space between you disappear?

Where sin once was perceived will rise a world that will become an altar to the truth, and you will join the lights of **Heaven** there, and sing their song of gratitude and praise. And each one joins the singing at the altar to truth that was raised within the tiny spot that sin proclaimed to be its own. And what was tiny then has soared into a magnitude of song in which the universe has joined with but a single voice.

This tiny spot of sin that stands between you and your sister still is holding back the happy opening of **Heaven's** gate. How little is the hindrance of sin that withholds the wealth of **Heaven** from you. And how great will be the joy in **Heaven** when you join the mighty chorus to the Love of God!

Ch. 29. Sec. 5.

There is a place in you where this whole world has been forgotten; where no memory of sin and of illusion lingers still. There is a place in you which time has left, and echoes of eternity are heard. There is a resting place so still no sound except a hymn to **Heaven** rises up to gladden God the Father and the Son. And where God the Father and the Son are is **Heaven** and is peace.

The changelessness of **Heaven** is in you, so deep within that nothing in this world but passes by, unnoticed and unseen. The still infinity of endless peace surrounds you gently in **Heaven's** soft embrace, so strong and quiet, tranquil in the might of its Creator, nothing can intrude upon the sacred Son of God within.

Here is the role the Holy Spirit gives to you who wait upon the Son of God, and would behold him waken and glad. He is a part of you and you of him, because he is his Father's Son, and not for any purpose you may see in him. Nothing is asked of you but to accept the changeless and eternal that abide in him, for your Identity is there. The peace in you can but be found in him. And every thought of love you offer your brother but brings you nearer to your wakening to peace eternal and to endless joy.

Discussion notes: Practical Truth • Practical Action • Heartfelt Thought

Topic 11

(The) Kingdom

(the) Kingdom: The reality of oneness. Truth without the illusions of sin and guilt. God's Kingdom is love.

Ch. 6. Sec. 4.

Remember that the Holy Spirit is the Answer, not the question.

When God created you, God made you part of Her. That is why attack within the **Kingdom** is impossible. You made the ego without love, and so the ego does not love you. You could not remain within the **Kingdom** without love, and since the **Kingdom** is love, you believe that without love you are without the **Kingdom**. This enables the ego to regard itself as separate and outside its maker, thus speaking for the part of your mind that believes you are separate and outside the Mind of God. Then the ego raises the question that it can never answer. That question, "What are you?"

Hear, then, the one answer of the Holy Spirit to all the questions the ego raises: You are a child of God, a priceless part of Her **Kingdom**, which She created as part of Her. Nothing else exists and only this is real. You have chosen a sleep in which you have had bad dreams, but the sleep is not real and God calls you to awake.

Ch. 6. Sec. 5.

You have believed that you are without the **Kingdom**, and have therefore excluded yourself from the **Kingdom** in your belief.

As long as belief in God and His **Kingdom** is assailed by any doubts in your mind, God's perfect accomplishment is not apparent to you. This is why you must be vigilant on God's behalf. The ego speaks against God's creation, and therefore engenders doubt.

Ch. 6. Sec. 5. (cont.)

Truth is without illusions and therefore within the **Kingdom**. Everything outside the **Kingdom** is illusion. By making another kingdom that you valued more, which is the kingdom of illusions, you did not keep only the **Kingdom** of God in your mind, and thus placed part of your mind outside the **Kingdom**. What you made has imprisoned your will, and given you a sick mind that must be healed. Your vigilance against this sickness of doubt is the way to heal the sick mind. Once your mind is healed it radiates health, and thereby teaches healing. This establishes you as a teacher who teaches like me.

*Be vigilant only for God and Her **Kingdom**.*

Ch. 7. Sec. 2.

Sickness and separation are not of God, but the **Kingdom** is of God. If you obscure the **Kingdom**, you are perceiving what is not of God.

Ch. 7. Sec. 3.

God's meaning waits in the **Kingdom**, because that is where God placed it. God's meaning does not wait in time. God's meaning merely rests in the **Kingdom** because it belongs there, as you do. How can you who are God's meaning perceive yourself as absent from God's **Kingdom**? You can see yourself as separated from your meaning only by experiencing yourself as unreal. This is why the ego is insane; the ego teaches that you are not what you are.

God has lit your mind Himself, and keeps your mind lit by His light because His light is what your mind is.

Discussion notes: Practical Truth • Practical Action • Heartfelt Thought

____

____

____

____

TOPIC 12

EARTH

earth: The physical place where our mind and body interact with things through the experience of feelings, thoughts, and actions. The earth can be a place where love resides and tragedy seems to reign, a place of beauty or decay, a place of wonder or disaster—all of which is dependent upon our interpretation.

Ch. 12. Sec. 7.

You cannot see the Holy Spirit, but you can see His manifestations. And unless you do, you will not realize the Holy Spirit is there. Miracles are the Holy Spirit's witnesses, and speak for His presence. Do the Holy Spirit's work, for you share in His function. As your function in Heaven is creation, so your function on **earth** is healing. God shares His function with you in Heaven, and the Holy Spirit shares His function with you on **earth**.

Ch. 14. Sec. 4.

Ask not to be forgiven, for this has already been accomplished. Ask, rather, to learn how to forgive, and to restore what always was to your unforgiving mind. Atonement, which is accepting that we are all one, becomes real and visible to those who use it. On **earth** this is your only function, and you must learn that healing is all you want to learn.

The Holy Spirit, Who remembers what you are, merely teaches you how to remove the blocks that stand between you and what you know.

Ch. 14. Sec. 9.

In this world you can become a spotless mirror, in which the Holiness of your Creator shines forth from you to all around you. You can reflect Heaven here. Yet no reflections of the images of other gods must dim the mirror that would hold God's reflection in it. **Earth** can reflect Heaven or hell; God or the ego. You need but leave the mirror clean and clear of all the images of hidden darkness you have drawn upon it. God will shine upon the mirror of Herself.

Reflections are seen in light. In darkness reflections are obscure, and their meaning seems to lie only in shifting interpretations, rather than in themselves. The reflection of God needs no interpretation. The reflection of God is clear.

Ch. 20. Sec. 4.

To each who walks this **earth** in seeming solitude is a savior given, whose special function here is to release your sister, and so to free herself by being the savior for another. In the world of separation each is appointed separately, though they are all the same. Yet those who know that they are all the same need not salvation. And each one finds her savior when she is ready to look upon the face of Christ, and see her sister sinless.

Ch. 21. Sec. 4.

The Holy Spirit's purpose was accepted by the part of your mind the ego knows not of. And yet this part, with which you now identify, is not afraid to look upon itself. This part of your mind knows no sin. How, otherwise, could this part of your mind have been willing to see the Holy Spirit's purpose as your mind's purpose?

And now the ego is afraid. Yet what the ego hears in terror, the other part of your mind hears as the sweetest music; the song the other part longed to hear since first the ego came into your mind. The song of freedom, which sings the praises of another world, brings to the mind hope of peace. For the other part remembers Heaven, and now the mind sees that Heaven has come to **earth** at last, from which the ego's rule has kept Heaven out so long.

Ch. 24. Sec. 7.

The test of everything on **earth** is simply this; "What is everything on **earth** for?" The answer to this question makes whatever it is to be what it is for you. Everything on **earth** has no meaning of itself, yet you can give reality to everything, according to the purpose that you serve, truth or illusion.

Ch. 29. Sec. 3.

Make way for love, which you did not create, but which you can extend. On **earth** this extension means to forgive your brother, so that the darkness may be lifted from your mind. When light has come to your brother through your forgiveness, he will not forget you, his savior, leaving you unsaved. For it was in your face that he saw the light that he would keep beside himself, as he walks through darkness to the everlasting light with you.

Ch. 30. Sec. 2.

God turns to you to ask the world be saved, for by your own salvation is the world healed. And no one walks upon the **earth** but must depend on your decision, that your sister learn death has no power over her, because your sister shares your freedom as she shares your will. It is your will to heal your sister, and because you have decided with her, she is healed.

Discussion notes: Practical Truth • Practical Action • Heartfelt Thought

___

___

___

___

TOPIC 13

(THE) REAL WORLD

real world: A state of mind in which the egoic world is freed from projections of guilt and separation, accomplished through the miracles of changed perception. This does not change the physical world; rather, it changes the way we see the world. We see the world of love, happiness, and joy through the Christ vision.

Ch. 11. Sec. 7.

You have made many illusionary ideas that you have placed between yourself and your Creator, and these beliefs are the world as you perceive it. To believe that you can perceive the **real world** is to believe that you can know yourself.

Ch. 11. Sec. 8.

You believe in a world that takes, because you believe that you can get by taking. And by that perception you have lost sight of the **real world**. You are afraid of the world as you see it, but the **real world** is still yours for the asking. Do not deny the **real world** to yourself, for it can only free you. Nothing of God will enslave Her Daughter whom She created free and whose freedom is protected by Her Being. Blessed are you who are willing to ask the truth of God without fear, for only thus can you learn that God's answer is the release from fear.

Would you not exchange your fears for truth, if the exchange is yours for the asking? For if God is not deceived in you, you can be deceived only in yourself. Yet you can learn the truth about yourself from the Holy Spirit. When you perceive yourself without deceit, you will accept the **real world** in place of the false one you have made. And then your Mother will lean down to you and take the last step for you, by raising you unto Herself.

Ch. 12. Sec. 8.

The **real world** was given you by God in loving exchange for the world you made and the world you see. Only take the **real world** from the hand of Christ and look upon it. The **real world's** reality will make everything else invisible, for beholding the **real world** is total perception. And as you look upon the **real world** you will remember that it was always so. Nothingness will become invisible, for you will at last have seen truly. Redeemed perception is easily translated into knowledge, for only perception is capable of error. Being corrected perception gives place to knowledge, which is forever the only reality.

Ch. 13. Sec. 7.

Sit quietly and look upon the world you see, and tell yourself:

"The **real world** is not like this. The **real world** has no buildings and there are no streets where people walk alone and separate. There are no stores where people buy an endless list of things they do not need. The **real world** is not lit with artificial light, and night comes not upon it. There is no day that brightens and grows dim. In the **real world** there is no loss. Nothing is there but shines, and shines forever."

The world you see must be denied, for sight of the world you see is costing you a different kind of vision, the vision of Christ. You cannot see both worlds, for each of them involves a different kind of seeing, and depends on what you cherish. The sight of one is possible because you have denied the other. Both worlds are not true, yet either one will seem as real to you as the amount to which you hold that world dear.

You do not really want the world you see, for the world you see has disappointed you since time began. The homes you built have never sheltered you. The roads you made have led you nowhere, and no city that you built has withstood the crumbling assault of time. Nothing you made but has the mark of death upon it. Hold your world not dear, for it is old and tired and ready to return to dust even as you made it. This aching world has not the power to touch the living world at all.

Christ is still there. Christ's Being does not depend upon your recognition. Christ lives within you in the quiet present, and waits for you to leave the past behind and enter into the world Christ holds out to you in love.

Ch. 17. Sec. 2.

The **real world**, in its loveliness, you will learn to reach. Fantasies are all undone, and no one and nothing remain still bound by fantasies, and by your own forgiveness you are free to see. The stars will disappear in light, and the sun that opened up the world to beauty will vanish.

Perception will be meaningless when perception has been perfected, for everything that has been used for learning will have no function.

The **real world** is attained simply by the complete forgiveness of the old; the world you see without forgiveness.

Ch. 18. Sec. 9.

This world of light, this circle of brightness is the **real world**, where guilt meets with forgiveness. Here the world outside is seen anew, without the shadow of guilt upon it. Here is the new perception, where everything is bright and shining with innocence, washed in the waters of forgiveness, and cleansed of every evil thought you laid upon the outside world. Here in the **real world** there is no attack upon the Son of God, and you are welcome. Here in the **real world** is your innocence, waiting to clothe you and protect you, and make you ready for the journey inward.

Ch. 25. Sec. 7.

The Holy Spirit has the power to change the whole foundation of the world you see to something else; a basis not insane, and on which a sane perception can be based, another **real world** perceived. In this **real world** nothing attests to death and cruelty; to separation and to differences. For here in the **real world** is everything perceived as one, and no one loses that each one may gain.

Ch. 30. Sec. 5.

The **real world** is the state of mind in which the only purpose of the world is seen to be forgiveness. Fear is not the **real world's** goal, for the escape from guilt becomes the **real world's** aim. The value of forgiveness is perceived and takes the place of idols, which are sought no longer, for their "gifts" are not held dear. No rules are idly set, and no demands are made of anyone or anything to twist and fit into the dream of fear. Instead, there is a wish to understand all things created as they really are. And in the **real world** it is recognized that all things must be first forgiven, and then understood.

Here, in the dream of fear, is thought that understanding is acquired by attack. There, in the **real world**, it is clear that by attack is understanding lost. The folly of pursuing guilt as goal is fully recognized. And idols are not wanted there in the **real world**, for guilt is understood as the sole cause of pain in any form. No one is tempted by guilts vain appeal, for suffering and death have been perceived as things not wanted and not striven for. The possibility of freedom has been grasped and welcomed, and the means by which freedom can be gained can now be understood. The world becomes a place of hope, because the world's only purpose is to be a place where hope of happiness can be fulfilled.

How light and easy is the step across the narrow boundaries of the world of fear when you have recognized Whose hand you hold! Within your hand is everything you need to walk with perfect confidence away from fear forever, and to go straight on, and quickly reach the gate of Heaven itself. For the Christ, Whose hand you hold, was waiting but for you to join Him. Now that you have come, would the Christ delay in showing you the way that Christ must walk with you?

Give up the world of the ego! You never wanted it. What "happiness" have you sought here in the world of the ego that did not bring you pain? Joy has no cost. Joy is your sacred right, and in Christ you do not pay for joy.

Discussion notes: Practical Truth • Practical Action • Heartfelt Thought

___

___

___

___

TOPIC 14

PRISON

Ch. 18. Sec. 6.

This thing you call the body, you made to serve your guilt and stands between you and other minds. You see yourself locked in a separate **prison**, removed and unreachable, incapable of reaching out as being reached. You hate this **prison** you have made.

The place you set aside to house your hate, the body, is not a **prison**, but an illusion of yourself.

The body is outside you, and but seems to surround you, shutting you off from others and keeping you apart from them. The body is not there. There is no barrier between God and Her Daughter. You cannot put a barrier around yourself, because God placed none between Herself and you.

You are surrounded only by God. What limits can there be on you whom She encompasses?

Ch. 20. Sec. 3.

Prisoners bound with heavy chains for years, starved and emaciated, weak and exhausted, and with eyes so long cast down in darkness they remember not the light, do not leap up in joy the instant they are made free. It takes a while for the **prisoners** to understand what freedom is. You groped but feebly in the dust and found your brother's hand, uncertain whether to let your brother's hand go or to take hold on life so long forgotten. Strengthen your hold and raise your eyes unto your strong companion, in whom the meaning of your freedom lies. Your brother seemed to be crucified beside you. And yet his holiness remained untouched and perfect, and with him beside you, you shall this day enter with him to Paradise, and know the peace of God.

Here in the peace of God there is only holiness and joining without limit. For what is Heaven but union, direct and perfect, and without the veil of fear upon it? Here are we one, looking with perfect gentleness upon each other and on ourselves. Here all thoughts of any separation between us become impossible. You who were **prisoners** in separation are now made free in Paradise.

Ch. 31. Sec. 3.

The mind that thinks it is a sin has but one purpose; that the body be the source of sin, to keep the mind in the **prison** house of the body that the mind chose. The mind guards and holds itself at bay, a sleeping **prisoner** to the snarling dogs of hate and evil, sickness and attack; of pain and age, of grief and suffering. Here in the mind's **prison** house are the thoughts of sacrifice preserved, for here guilt rules, and orders that the world be like itself; a place where nothing can find mercy, nor survive the ravages of fear except in murder and in death. For here in the mind's **prison** house are you made sin, and sin cannot abide the joyous and the free, for the joyous and free are enemies which sin must kill. In death is sin preserved, and those who think that they are sin must die for what they think they are.

Let us be glad that you will see what you believe, and that the mind has been given you to change what you believe. Open your mind to change, and there will be no ancient penalty exacted from you or anyone. For God has said there is no sacrifice that can be asked; there is no sacrifice that can be made.

Discussion notes: Practical Truth • Practical Action • Heartfelt Thought

---

TOPIC 15

ALTAR

altar: The place within our consciousness that chooses what we are devoted to, where one chooses between God and the ego, between truth and illusion, between love and fear.

Ch. 11. Sec. 4.

Christ is at God's **altar**, waiting to welcome Her Daughter. But come wholly without condemnation, for otherwise you will believe that the door is barred and you cannot enter. The door to God's **altar** is not barred, and it is impossible that you cannot enter the place where God would have you be. But love yourself with the Love of Christ, for so does your Mother love you. You can refuse to enter, but you cannot bar the door that Christ holds open. "Come unto Christ who holds the door open for you, for while I live the door cannot be shut, and I live forever."

At God's **altar** Christ waits for the restoration of Herself in you. God knows Her Daughter as wholly blameless as Herself, and God is approached through the appreciation of Her Daughter. Christ waits for your acceptance of Her as yourself, and of Christ's Wholeness as yours. For Christ is the Daughter of God, Who lives in Her Creator and shines with Her glory. Christ is the extension of the love and the loveliness of God, as perfect as Her Creator and at peace with Her.

Ch. 12. Sec. 3.

If you will recognize that all the attack you perceive is in your own mind and nowhere else, you will at last have placed its source, and where attack begins it must end. For in this same place, which is in your mind, also lies salvation. The **altar** of God where Christ abideth is there also. Bring your perceptions of the world to this **altar**, for God's **altar** is the **altar** to truth. There you will see your vision changed, and there you will learn to see truly. From this place, where God and His Son dwell in peace and where you are welcome, you will look out in peace and behold the world truly. Yet to find the place, you must relinquish your investment in this world as you project it, allowing the Holy Spirit to extend the real world to you from the **altar** of God.

Discussion notes: Practical Truth • Practical Action • Heartfelt Thought

PART THREE

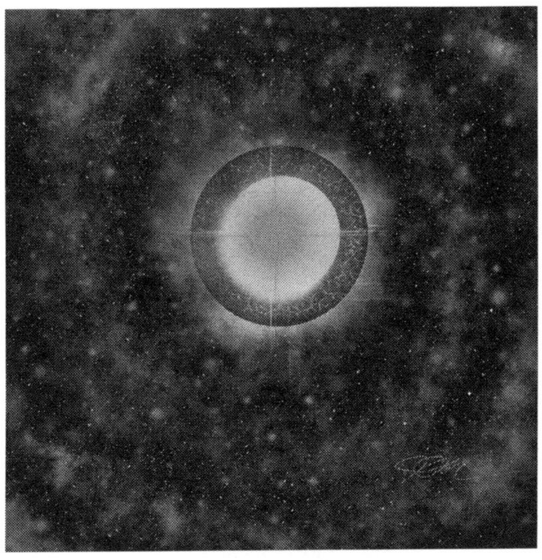

www.jgmgraphicart.com

Topics

16. **DREAM**
17. **HALLUCINATION**
18. **DEATH**
19. **REASON**
20. **AWAKEN**
21. **REALITY**
22. **HOLY INSTANT**
23. **HOLY RELATIONSHIP**

Note: All chapter and section notations for the passages are referencing a previously published book titled *A Course in Miracles Abridged Edition.*

TOPIC 16

DREAM

dream: The mind experiencing egoistic perceptions in the physical world, creating illusions and deceptions. Dreams of guilt and fear can be exchanged for peace and joy through awakening into higher perceptions of love and forgiveness by the gift of transformative miracles revealed to us by Spirit. Miracles are the means to heal fearful dreams.

Ch. 10. Sec. 1.

You are at home in God, **dreaming** of exile but perfectly capable of awakening to true reality. You recognize from your own experience that what you see in **dreams** you think is real, while you are asleep. Yet the instant you waken you realize that everything that seemed to happen in the **dream** did not happen at all.

Ch. 17. Sec. 1.

The betrayal of the Son of God lies only in illusions, and all his "sins" are but his own imagining. God's Son's true reality is forever sinless. God's Son need not be forgiven but awakened. In God's Son's **dreams**, he has betrayed himself, his brothers, and his God. Yet what is done in **dreams** has not been really done. It is impossible to convince the **dreamer** that this betrayal is so, for **dreams** are what **dreams** are because of their illusion of reality. Only in waking is the full release from **dreams**, for only then does it become perfectly apparent that the **dreams** had no effect upon reality at all, and the **dream** did not change true reality.

Ch. 18. Sec. 2.

Dreams are the best example you could have of how perception can be utilized to substitute illusions in the place of truth. **Dreams** are a way of looking at the world, and changing the world to suit the ego better.

And while you see the world as you would have it be, you do not doubt that it is real. Yet here is a world, clearly within your mind, that seems to be outside your mind.

The Holy Spirit accepts your **dreams** and uses them as means for waking. You would have used your **dreams** to remain asleep. I said before that the first change, before **dreams** disappear, is that your **dreams** of fear are changed to happy **dreams**.

Undoing guilt in everyone will be a happy **dream**, and one which you will share with all who come within your sight. Through the undoing of guilt, the blessing the Holy Spirit has laid upon the happy dream will be extended.

Heaven is sure. This is no **dream**. Heaven's coming means that you have chosen truth.

Ch. 27. Sec. 7.

You are the **dreamer** of the world of **dreams**. Nothing more fearful than an idle **dream** has terrified God's Daughter, and made her think that she has lost her innocence, denied her Mother, and made war upon herself.

Accept the **dream** the Holy Spirit gave instead of your dream. It is not difficult to change a **dream** once the **dreamer** has been recognized. Rest in the Holy Spirit, and allow Her gentle **dreams** to take the place of those you **dreamed** in terror and in fear of death. The Holy Spirit brings forgiving **dreams**, in which the choice is not who is the murderer and who shall be the victim. In the **dreams** She brings there is no murder and there is no death. The **dream** of guilt is fading from your sight, although your eyes are closed. A smile has come to lighten up your sleeping face. The sleep is peaceful now, for these are happy **dreams**.

Dream softly of your sinless sister, who unites with you in holy innocence. And from this **dream** of your sinless sister, the Lord of Heaven will Herself awaken Her beloved Daughter. **Dream** of your sister's kindnesses instead of dwelling in your **dreams** on her mistakes. Select your sister's thoughtfulness to **dream** about instead of counting up the hurts she gave. Forgive your sister's illusions, and give thanks to her for all the helpfulness she gave. And do not brush aside your sister's many gifts because she is not perfect in your **dreams**.

Ch. 28. Sec. 2.

If you are the **dreamer**, you perceive this much at least: that you have caused the **dream**, and can accept another **dream** as well. But for this change in *content* of the **dream**, it must be realized that it is you who **dreamed** the **dreaming** that you do not like. The **dream** is but an effect that you have caused.

In forgiving **dreams** is no one asked to be the victim and the sufferer. These are the happy **dreams** the miracle exchanges for your own **dreams**. The **dreamer** of a **dream** is not awake, but does not know he sleeps.

The miracle establishes you **dream** a **dream**, and that the **dreams** content is not true. This is a crucial step in dealing with illusions. No one is afraid of illusions when he perceives he made the illusions up. The fear was held in place because he did not see that he was author of the **dream**, and not a figure in the **dream**.

The miracles, which change perceptions, demonstrates what the Holy Spirit would have you learn, and shows you the miracle's effects are what you want. In the Holy Spirit's forgiving **dreams** are the effects of your dream undone, and hated enemies now perceived as friends with merciful intent. The enemies' hostility is seen as causeless now, because they did not make your **dream**. And you can accept the role of maker of their hate, because you see that their hate has no effects. Now are you freed from this much of the **dream**; the world is neutral, and the bodies that still seem to move about as separate things need not be feared.

This world is full of miracles. Miracles stand in shining silence next to every **dream** of pain and suffering, of sin and guilt. Miracles are the **dream's** alternative, the choice to be the **dreamer**, rather than deny your active role in making up the **dream**. The body is released because the mind acknowledges "this is not done to me, but I am doing this." And thus the mind is free to make another choice instead.

Ch. 28. Sec. 4.

There is a way of finding certainty right here and now. Refuse to be a part of fearful **dreams** whatever form they take, for you will lose identity in **dreams**. You find yourself by not accepting fearful **dreams** as causing you and giving you effects. You stand apart from the fearful **dream**, but not apart from a sister who **dreams** them. Thus you separate the **dreamer** from the **dream**, join in one with your sister, and let the **dream** go. The **dream** is but illusion in the mind. And with the mind you would unite, but never with the **dream**. It is the **dream** you fear, and not the mind. You see the **dream** and the mind as the same, because you think that you are but a **dream**.

Like you, your sister thinks she is a **dream**. Think, rather, of your sister as a mind in which illusions still persist. Your sister's body and her **dreams** but seem to make a little gap, where your dreams have joined with hers.

The Holy Spirit is in both your minds, and She is One, because there is no gap that separates God's Oneness from Itself. The gap between your bodies matters not, for what is joined in God is always One.

Ch. 29. Sec. 5.

Forgiving **dreams** are the means to step aside from **dreaming** of a world outside yourself. And leading finally beyond all **dreams**, unto the peace of everlasting life.

Ch. 29. Sec. 9.

Forgiving **dreams** remind you that you live in safety and have not attacked yourself. Forgiving **dreams** become a sign that you have made a new beginning, and not another attempt to worship more idols and to keep attacking. Forgiving **dreams** are kind to everyone who figures in the **dream**. And so forgiving **dreams** bring the **dreamer** full release from **dreams** of fear.

Discussion notes: Practical Truth • Practical Action • Heartfelt Thought

---

TOPIC 17

HALLUCINATION

hallucination: An unfounded or mistaken impression or notion of reality. A perception of something with no reality. A delusion.

Ch. 8. Sec. 1.

The distractions of the ego may seem to interfere with your learning, but the ego has no power to distract you unless you give the ego the power to do so. The ego's voice is a **hallucination**. You cannot expect the ego to say "I am not real." Yet you are not asked to dispel your **hallucinations** alone. You are merely asked to evaluate your **hallucinations** in terms of their results to you, on the basis of loss of peace.

Ch. 20. Sec. 8.

Hallucinations disappear when they are recognized for what they are. This recognition of **hallucinations** is the healing and the remedy. Believe **hallucinations** not and they are gone. And all you need to do is recognize that you did this. Once you accept this simple fact and take unto yourself the power you gave them, you are released from them. One thing is sure; **hallucinations** serve a purpose, and when that purpose is no longer held they disappear. Therefore, the question never is whether you want **hallucinations**, but always, do you want the purpose that they serve?

For what you see is merely how you elect to meet your goal's purpose. **Hallucinations** serve to meet the goal of madness. **Hallucinations** are the means by which the outside world, projected from within, seems to witness to **hallucination's** reality. It still is true that nothing is without. Yet upon nothing are all projections made. For within is the projection that gives the "nothing" all the meaning that the **hallucination** holds.

What has no meaning cannot be perceived. And meaning always looks within to find itself, and then looks out. All meaning that you give the world outside must thus reflect the sight you saw within. Vision is the means by which the Holy Spirit translates your nightmares into happy dreams; your wild **hallucinations** that show you all the fearful outcomes of imagined sin into the calm and reassuring sights with which the Holy Spirit would replace them. These gentle sights and sounds are looked on happily, and heard with joy. The happy dreams are the Holy Spirit's substitutes for all the terrifying sights and screaming sounds the ego's purpose brought to your horrified awareness. The happy dreams step away from sin, reminding you that it is not reality which frightens you, and that the errors which you made can be corrected.

Discussion notes: Practical Truth • Practical Action • Heartfelt Thought

Topic 18

DEATH

death: (1) The expiration of the physical form called a body. (2) The biological proof of the earthly concept that we are not eternal, allegedly confirming our separation from the undying God. In this viewpoint, we are not eternal because we can die and God cannot.

Ch. 6. Sec. 5.a.

When your body and your ego and your dreams are gone, you will know that you will last forever. Perhaps you think this is accomplished through **death**, but nothing is accomplished through **death**, because **death** is nothing. Everything is accomplished through life, and life is of the mind and in the mind. The body neither lives nor dies, because the body cannot contain you who are life.

Ch. 12. Sec. 7.

The ego is not a traitor to God, to Whom treachery is impossible. But the ego is a traitor to you who believe that you have been treacherous to your Father. That is why the undoing of guilt is an essential part of the Holy Spirit's teaching. For as long as you feel guilty you are listening to the voice of the ego, which tells you that you have been treacherous to God and therefore deserve **death**. You will think that **death** comes from God and not from the ego because, by confusing yourself with the ego, you believe that you want **death**. And from what you want God does not save you.

When you are tempted to yield to the desire for **death**, remember that I did not die. You will realize that this is true when you look within and see the Christ. Would I have overcome **death** for myself alone? And would eternal life have been given me of the Father unless the Father had also given eternal life to you?

When you learn to make the Christ manifest, you will never see **death**. For you will have looked upon the deathless in yourself, and you will see only the eternal as you look out upon a world that cannot die.

Ch. 19. Sec. 4.

From the ego came sin and guilt and **death**, in opposition to life and innocence, and to the Will of God Herself.

The arrogance of sin, the pride of guilt, the sepulcher of separation, all are part of your unrecognized dedication to **death**.

The body can but serve your purpose to follow the truth of the Holy Spirit. As you look on the body, so will the body seem to be. **Death**, were **death** true, would be the final and complete disruption of communication, which is the ego's goal.

Ch. 19. Sec. 4. (cont.)

When anything seems to you to be a source of fear, when any situation strikes you with terror and makes your body tremble and the cold sweat of fear comes over your body, remember it is always for one reason; the ego has perceived your body as a symbol of fear, a sign of sin and **death**.

Discussion notes: Practical Truth • Practical Action • Heartfelt Thought

---

TOPIC 19

REASON

Ch. 21. Sec. 6.

The home of madness, the belief that we are the body, cannot be the home of **reason**. Yet it is easy to leave the home of madness if you "see" **reason**. You do not leave insanity by going somewhere else. You leave insanity simply by accepting **reason** where madness was. Madness and **reason** see the same things, but it is certain that they look upon the same things differently.

Reason, like love, would reassure you, and seeks not to frighten you. The power to heal the Daughter of God is given you because your sister must be one with you. **Reason** is given you to understand that this oneness is so. For **reason** leads steadily away from madness toward the goal of truth. That you and your sister are joined is your salvation; the gift of Heaven, not the gift of fear.

Reason assures you Heaven's joining is what you want, and all you want. Listen to the Holy Spirit Who speaks with **reason**, and brings your **reason** into line with Hers. Be willing to let **reason** be the means by which She would direct you how to leave insanity behind. Hide not behind insanity in order to escape from **reason**. What madness would conceal the Holy Spirit still holds out for everyone to look upon with gladness.

Ch. 22. Sec. 3.

The introduction of **reason** into the ego's thought system is the beginning of its undoing, for **reason** and the ego are contradictory.

Reason sees through errors, telling you what you thought was real is not. **Reason** can see the difference between sin and mistakes, because **reason** wants correction. Therefore, **reason** tells you what you thought was uncorrectable can be corrected, and thus what you thought was uncorrectable must have been an error, not a sin. The ego's opposition to correction leads to the ego's fixed belief in sin and disregard of errors. The ego looks on nothing that can be corrected. Thus does the ego damn, and **reason** save.

Reason is not salvation in itself, but **reason** makes way for peace and brings you to a state of mind in which salvation can be given to you. "Sin" is a block, set like a heavy gate, locked and without a key, across the road to peace. No one who looks on sin without the help of **reason** would try to pass sin's locked gate. The body's eyes behold sin as solid granite, so thick it would be madness to attempt to pass sin's locked gate. Yet **reason** sees through sin easily, because sin is an error. The form the error takes cannot conceal sin's emptiness from **reason's** eyes.

Mistakes, regardless of their form, can be corrected. Sin is but error in a special form that the ego venerates. The ego would preserve all errors and make them sins. For here is the ego's own stability, the ego's heavy anchor in the shifting world it made; the rock of sin on which the ego's church is built, and where the ego's worshipers are bound to bodies, believing the body's freedom is their own.

The body's eyes see only form. The body's eyes cannot see beyond what they were made to see. And the body's eyes were made to look on error and not see past the form. The body's eyes is indeed a strange perception, for they can see only illusions, unable to look beyond the granite block of sin, and stopping at the outside form of nothing. Yet how can sight that stops at nothingness, as if nothingness were a solid wall, see truly? The body's sight is held back by form, having been made to guarantee that nothing else but form will be perceived.

These bodily eyes, made not to truly see, will never see. See how the body's eyes rest on externals and cannot go beyond. Watch how the body's eyes stop at nothingness, unable to go beyond the form to see the true meaning. Nothing is so blinding as perception of form. For sight of form means understanding has been obscured.

Let your awareness of your brother not be blocked by your perception of his sins and of his body. What is there in your brother that you would attack except what you associate with his body, which you believe can sin? Beyond your brother's errors is his holiness and your salvation.

Reason sees a holy relationship as what the holy relationship is; a common state of mind, where you both give errors gladly to correction, that you both may happily be healed as one.

Discussion notes: Practical Truth • Practical Action • Heartfelt Thought

TOPIC 20

AWAKEN AND WAKE

awaken: To raise one's consciousness. A moment of awareness of true reality that was previously unrealized. The continuance of such realizations helps us recognize higher consciousness, which brings clarity, well-being, and harmony.

Ch. 2. Sec. 5.

Corrective learning always begins with the **awakening** of spirit, and the turning away from the belief in physical sight. This turning away often entails fear, because you are afraid of what your spiritual sight will show you.

What the physical eye sees is not corrective, nor can error be corrected by any device that can be seen physically. As long as you only believe in what your physical sight tells you, your attempts at correction of spirit will be misdirected.

Ch. 3. Sec. 2.

Nothing can prevail against a Daughter of God who commends her spirit into the Hands of her Mother. By doing this the mind **awakens** from its sleep and remembers its Creator. All sense of separation disappears. Because the truly innocent's hearts are pure, the innocent defend true perception instead of defending themselves against it.

Ch. 4. Sec. 4.

I do not attack your ego. I do work with your higher mind, the home of the Holy Spirit, whether you are asleep or **awake**, just as your ego does with your lower mind, which is the home of the ego. I am your vigilance in your higher mind, because you are too confused to recognize your own hope to **awake**. I am not mistaken. Your mind will elect to join with mine, and together we are invincible.

Ch. 5. Sec. 2.

Rest does not come from sleeping but from **waking**. The Holy Spirit is the Call to **awaken** and be glad. The world of time is very tired, and our task is the joyous one of **waking** the mind to the Call for God. Hear only this Call for God through the Holy Spirit within you, and teach your brothers to listen for the Call, as I am teaching you.

As we share this goal to hear the call for God, we increase this goal's power to attract the whole Sonship, and to bring it back into the oneness in which the Sonship was created. Remember that "yoke" means "join together," and "burden" means "message". Let us restate "My yoke is easy and my burden light" in this way; "Let us join together, for my message is light".

Ch. 6. Sec. 5.

Like any good teacher, the Holy Spirit knows more than you do now, but She teaches only to make you equal with Her. Giving God's joy is an ongoing process, not in time but in eternity. So God thought, "My children sleep and must be **awakened**".

How can you **wake** children in a more kindly way than by a gentle Voice that will not frighten them, but will merely remind the sleeping children that the night is over and the light has come? You simply reassure the sleeping children that they are safe now. Then you train the children to recognize the difference between sleeping and **waking**, so the children will understand they need not be afraid of dreams. And so when bad dreams come, the children will call on the light to dispel the bad dreams.

A wise teacher does not emphasize what you must avoid to escape from harm, but what you need to learn to have joy.

Children do confuse fantasy and reality, and they are frightened because they do not recognize the difference. The Holy Spirit makes no distinction among dreams. She merely shines the dreams away. The Holy Spirit's light is always the Call to **awaken**, whatever you have been dreaming. Nothing lasting lies in dreams, and the Holy Spirit, shining with the light from God Herself, speaks only for what lasts forever.

Ch. 9. Sec. 6.

You are not yet **awake**, but you can learn how to **awaken**. Very simply, the Holy Spirit teaches you to **awaken** others. As you see others **waken** you will learn what **waking** means, and because you have chosen to **wake** others, their gratitude and their appreciation of what you have given them will teach you the value of being **awake**.

Ch. 13. Sec. 11.

Can God's Son lose himself in dreams, when God has placed within God's Son the glad Call to **waken** and be glad? God's Son cannot separate himself from what is in him. God's Son's sleep will not withstand the Call to **wake**. The mission of redemption will be fulfilled as surely as the creation will remain unchanged throughout eternity. You do not have to know that Heaven is yours to make it so. Heaven is yours.

Discussion notes: Practical Truth • Practical Action • Heartfelt Thought

___

___

___

___

TOPIC 21

REALITY

Ch. 4. Sec. 1.

The ego tries to exploit all situations into forms of praise for itself in order to overcome its doubts. The ego will remain doubtful as long as you believe in the ego's existence. You who made the ego cannot trust it, because in your right mind you realize the ego is not real. The only sane solution is not to try to change **reality**, which is indeed a fearful attempt, but to accept **reality** as **reality** is. You are part of the **reality**, which stands unchanged beyond the reach of your ego but within easy reach of spirit. When you are afraid, be still and know that God is real, and you are His beloved Son in whom He is well pleased. Do not let your ego dispute this **reality**, because the ego cannot know what is as far beyond the ego's reach as you are.

Ch. 9. Sec. 1.

Reality cannot "threaten" anything except illusions, since true **reality** can only uphold truth. The very fact that the Will of God, which is what you are, is perceived as fearful, demonstrates that you are afraid of what you are. It is not, then, the Will of God of which you are afraid, but your will.

Your will is not the ego's will, and that is why the ego is against you. What seems to be the fear of God is really the fear of your own split **reality**.

If you do not know what your **reality** is, why would you be so sure that it is fearful? You have set up this strange situation so that it is impossible to escape from this situation without a Guide Who does know what your **reality** is. The purpose of this Guide is merely to remind you of what you want. The Holy Spirit is merely making every possible effort, within the limits you impose on Her, to re-establish your own will in your awareness.

You have imprisoned your will beyond your own awareness, where your will remains, but cannot help you. When I said that the Holy Spirit's function is to sort out the true from the false in your mind, I meant that She has the power to look into what you have hidden and recognize the Will of God there. Her recognition of this Will can make it real to you because She is in your mind, and therefore She is your **reality**. If, then, the Holy Spirit's perception of your mind brings your mind's **reality** to you, She is helping you to remember what you are. The only source of fear in this process is what you think you will lose.

Ch. 11. Sec. 8.

Children perceive frightening ghosts and monsters and dragons, and they are terrified. Yet if these children ask someone they trust for the meaning of what they perceive, and are willing to let their own frightening interpretations go in favor of true **reality**, their fear goes with them. When a child is helped to translate his "ghost" into a curtain, his "monster" into a shadow, and his "dragon" into a dream the child is no longer afraid, and laughs happily at his own fear.

You, my child, are afraid of your brothers and of your Father and of yourself. But you are merely deceived in them. Ask what their **reality** is from the Teacher of **reality**, which is the Holy Spirit, and hearing Him answer, you too will laugh at your fears and replace them with peace. For fear lies not in **reality**, but in the minds of children who do not understand **reality**. It is only their lack of understanding that frightens children, and when the children learn to perceive truly, they are not afraid. And because of this the children will ask for truth again when they are frightened. It is not the **reality** of your brothers or your Father or yourself that frightens you, it is your mis-perception of them.

Ch. 12. Sec. 1.

There is but one Teacher of true **reality**, Who understands what true **reality** is. The Holy Spirit does not change Her Mind about **reality** because true **reality** does not change. Although your interpretations of **reality** are meaningless in your divided mind, The Holy Spirit's interpretations of **reality** remain consistently true. The Holy Spirit gives Her interpretations to you because they are for you. Do not attempt to "help" a sister in your way, for you cannot help yourself. But hear a sister's call for the help of God, and you will recognize your own need for the Mother.

Ch. 21. Sec. 5.

Reality needs no cooperation from you to be itself. But your awareness of **reality** needs your help, because **reality** is your choice.

Listen to what the ego says, and see what the ego directs you to see, and it is sure that you will see yourself as tiny, vulnerable and afraid.

Discussion notes: Practical Truth • Practical Action • Heartfelt Thought

Topic 22

HOLY INSTANT

holy instant: (1) Any instant when we still our minds and become centered and present. In this stillness, we have no sense of fear, and nothing stands in the way of our connection to God's acceptance. (2) An opportunity to receive guidance and identify with what we are. (3) The moment in which we experience a feeling of peace, joy, and love. A release from the past and future and an alignment with unity and oneness. The holy instant is a device that can be used to teach and share love's meaning. Ultimately, our goal is to make every instant a holy instant.

Ch. 15. Sec. 4.

The **holy instant** is this instant and every instant. The one instant you want the **holy instant** to be, *it* is. The one instant you would not have the **holy instant** be, *it* is lost to you. You must decide when the **holy instant** is. Delay *it* not. For beyond the past and future, where you will not find the **holy instant**, it stands in shimmering readiness for your acceptance. Yet, you cannot bring the **holy instant** into glad awareness while you do not want *it*, for the **holy instant** holds the whole release from littleness.

Your practice must therefore rest upon your willingness to let all littleness go. The instant in which magnitude dawns upon you is but as far away as your desire for it. As long as you do not desire magnitude and cherish littleness instead, by so much is the **holy instant** far from you. By so much as you want magnitude will you bring the **holy instant** nearer. Think not that you can find salvation in your own way and have littleness. Give over every plan you have made for your salvation in exchange for God's plan.

Be humble before God, and yet great in God. And value no plan of the ego before the plan of God.

Make the **holy instant** yours at once, for the release from littleness in the mind of the host of God depends on willingness, and not on time.

Ch. 15. Sec. 10.

The **holy instant** is truly the time of Christ. For in this liberating instant no guilt is laid upon the Son of God, and his unlimited power is thus restored to the Son of God. Learn now that sacrifice of any kind is nothing but a limitation imposed on giving. And by this limitation on giving, you have limited acceptance of the gift of liberation I offer you.

The time of Christ is the time appointed for the gift of freedom, offered to everyone. And by your acceptance of the gift of freedom, you offer freedom to everyone.

Ch. 17. Sec. 5.

To give thanks to one another is to appreciate the **holy instant**, and thus enable the **holy instant's** results to be accepted and shared.

As you begin to recognize and accept the thankful gifts you have so freely given to your sister, you will also accept the effects of the **holy instant** and use them to correct all your mistakes and free you from the results of your mistakes. And learning this freedom, you will have also learned how to release all the Daughtership, and offer this release in gladness and thanksgiving to the Holy Spirit, Who gave you your release, and Who would extend this freedom through you.

Ch. 17. Sec. 8.

The **holy instant** is nothing more than a special case, or an extreme example, of what every situation is meant to be. The **holy instant** is the shining example, the clear and unequivocal demonstration of the meaning of every relationship and every situation, seen as a whole. Where faith has accepted every aspect of the situation, and faithlessness has not forced any exclusion on it. The **holy instant** is a situation of perfect peace, simply because you have let the **holy instant** be what the **holy instant** is.

Ch. 18. Sec. 5.

It is no dream to love your sister as yourself. Nor is your holy relationship a dream.

When you feel the holiness of your relationship is threatened by anything, stop instantly and offer the Holy Spirit your willingness, in spite of fear, to let the Holy Spirit exchange this instant of fear for the **holy instant** that you would rather have. Forget not that your relationship is one with your sister, and so it must be that whatever threatens the peace of one is an equal threat to the other.

Whoever is saner at the time the threat is perceived should remember how deep is her indebtedness to the other and how much gratitude is due her. Let her remember this, and say:

> *I desire this **holy instant** for myself, that I may share it with my sister, whom I love. It is not possible that I can have this **holy instant** without my sister, or her without me. Yet it is wholly possible for us to share the **holy instant** now.*

And so I choose this instant as the one to offer to the Holy Spirit, that Her blessing may descend on us, and keep us both in peace.

Ch. 20. Sec. 6.

The **holy instant** is of greater value now. You have learned you really want but one true relationship, which is the holy relationship. This is no time for sadness. Perhaps you fear your brother a little yet; perhaps a shadow of the fear of God remains with you. Yet what is the shadow of fear to those who have been given one true relationship beyond the body?

Discussion notes: Practical Truth • Practical Action • Heartfelt Thought

TOPIC 23

HOLY RELATIONSHIP

holy relationship: A relationship of forgiveness and truth. The process of personal growth through the Christ vision, where one's perceptions change the experience of separation into an embrace of the oneness of everyone we meet and everything we see.

Ch. 17. Sec. 5.

The **holy relationship** is the expression of the holy instant while living in this world. And as the *unholy* **relationship** is a continuing hymn of hate in praise of its maker the ego, so is the **holy relationship** a happy song of praise to the Redeemer of relationships.

The **holy relationship** is a major step toward the perception of the real world. The **holy relationship** is the old *unholy* **relationship** transformed and seen anew. The **holy relationship** represents the reversal of the *unholy* relationship. Be comforted in this reversal; the only difficult phase is in the beginning. For in the beginning, the goal of the relationship is abruptly shifted to the exact opposite of what the relationship was. This shift in purpose is the first result of offering the relationship to the Holy Spirit, to use for His purposes.

At once the Holy Spirit's goal replaces yours. This is accomplished very rapidly, but this change in goals makes the relationship seem disturbed, disjunctive and even quite distressing. The reason is quite clear. For the old troubled relationship as it was, is out of line with the relationship's new goal of offering it the Holy Spirit, and clearly unsuited to the new holy purpose that had been accepted for the old relationship. In the relationship's unholy condition, your own goal was all that seemed to give relationship meaning. Now the previous way seems to make no sense. Many relationships have been broken off at this point, and the pursuit of your old goal re-established in another relationship. But once an *unholy* relationship has accepted the goal of holiness, the *unholy* relationship can never again be what it was.

Ch. 20. Sec. 5.

In this world, God's Daughter comes closest to herself in a **holy relationship**. There, in a **holy relationship**, she begins to find the certainty her Mother has in Her Daughter.

Peace to your **holy relationship**, which has the power to hold the unity of the Daughter of God together. You give to one another for everyone, and in your gift is everyone made glad.

Ch. 21. Sec. 3.

The Holy Spirit sees perception as a means to teach you that the vision of a **holy relationship** is all you want to see. .

Ch. 22. Sec. 1.

Christ comes to what is like Himself; the same, not different. For Christ is always drawn unto Himself. And what draws you together draws Christ to you. Here in the **holy relationship** are Christ's sweetness and Christ's gentle innocence protected from attack. And here in the **holy relationship** can Christ return in confidence, for faith in one another is always faith in Christ. You are indeed correct in looking on each other as Christ's chosen home. And who is drawn to Christ is drawn to God as surely as Both are drawn to every **holy relationship**, the home prepared for Christ and God, as earth is turned to Heaven.

Ch. 22. Sec. Intro.

Who has need for sin? Only the lonely and alone, who see their sisters different from themselves have need of sin. For an *unholy* relationship is based on differences, where each one thinks the other has what she has not. Both come together, each to complete herself and rob the other. Both stay until they think that there is nothing left to steal, and then move on. And so both in an *unholy* relationship wander through a world of strangers, unlike themselves, living with their bodies, perhaps under a common roof that shelters neither; in the same room and yet a world apart.

A **holy relationship** starts from a different premise. Each one has looked within themselves and seen no lack. Accepting her completion, she would extend her completion by joining with another, whole as herself. She sees no difference between these selves, for differences are only of the body. Therefore, she looks on nothing she would take from the other.

Think what a **holy relationship** can teach! Here in the **holy relationship** is belief in differences undone. Here in the **holy relationship** is the faith in differences shifted to sameness.

Ch. 22. Sec. 4.

To all who share the Love of God, the grace is given to the givers of what they have received. And so all who share the Love of God learn that God's grace is theirs forever. This veil you lift together opens the way to truth to more than you.

How easy is it to offer this miracle of God's love and grace to everyone! For by receiving this miracle of love and grace, you learned this miracle was not given you alone but to all. Such is the function of a **holy relationship**; to receive together and give as you received. Standing before the veil, it still seems difficult to receive and give together. But hold out your joined hands and touch this heavy-seeming block, and you will learn how easily your fingers slip through the veil's nothingness. This veil is no solid wall. And only an illusion stands between you and the holy Self you share.

Ch. 22. Sec. 6.

A **holy relationship**, lovely in its innocence, mighty in strength, and blazing with a light far brighter than the sun that lights the sky you see, is chosen of your Father as a means for His Own plan.

Child of peace, the light has come to you. The light you bring you do not recognize, and yet you will remember this light. Who can deny himself the vision of sinlessness that he brings to others? And who would fail to recognize a gift of light he let be laid in Heaven through himself? The gentle service that you give the Holy Spirit is service to yourself. You who are now His means must love all that He Loves. And what you bring is your remembrance of everything that is eternal. No trace of anything in time can long remain in minds that serve the timeless. And no illusion can disturb the peace of a relationship that has become the means of peace.

When you have looked upon your brother with complete forgiveness, from which no error is excluded and nothing kept hidden, what mistake can there be anywhere you cannot overlook? What form of suffering could block your sight, preventing you from seeing past the suffering? And what illusion could be there you will not recognize as a mistake; a shadow through which you walk completely undismayed?

Discussion notes: Practical Truth • Practical Action • Heartfelt Thought

PART FOUR

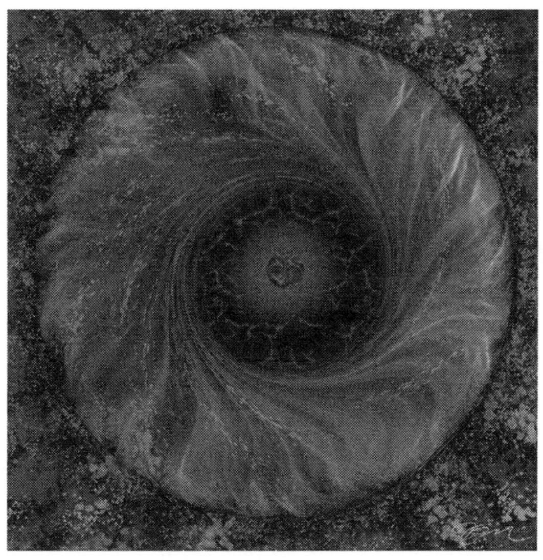

www.jgmgraphicart.com

Topics

Note: All chapter and section notations for the passages are referencing a previously published book titled *A Course in Miracles Abridged Edition.*

TOPIC 24

ILLUSION

illusion: Something that deceives by producing a false or misleading impression of reality. Beliefs that are not true.

Ch. 7. Sec. 7.

Illusions are investments. **Illusions** will last as long as you value them. Values are relative, but values are powerful because values are mental judgments. The only way to dispel **illusions** is to withdraw all investment from them, and **illusions** will have no life for you because you will have put **illusions** out of your mind. While you include **illusions** in your mind, you are giving life to them.

Ch. 11. Sec. 5.

No one can escape from **illusions** unless one looks at them, for not looking at **illusions** is the way they are protected. There is no need to shrink from **illusions**, for they cannot be dangerous. We are ready to look more closely at the ego's thought system because together we have the lamp that will dispel that thought system, and since you realize you do not want it, you must be ready to escape from **illusions**.

Ch. 16. Sec. 3.

What you accept into your mind does not really change your mind. **Illusions** are but beliefs in what is not there. And the seeming conflict between truth and **illusion** can only be resolved by separating yourself from the **illusion** and not from truth.

Ch. 16. Sec. 4.

You have come close to truth, and only the **illusion** of fear stands between you and the bridge that leads you into truth.

Across the bridge is your completion. Fear not to cross the bridge to the abode of peace and perfect holiness. Only there is the completion of God and of His Son established forever.

Every **illusion** you accept into your mind, by judging the **illusion** to be attainable, removes your own sense of completion, and thus denies the Wholeness of your Father. Every fantasy, be it of love or hate, deprives you of knowledge, for fantasies are the veil behind which truth is hidden. To lift the veil that seems so dark and heavy, it is only needful to value truth beyond all fantasy, and to be entirely unwilling to settle for **illusion** in place of truth.

The Holy Spirit is the Bridge to God, made from your willingness to unite with God and created by God's joy in union with you. The journey that seemed endless is almost complete, for what is endless is very near. You have almost recognized the journey's end. Turn firmly away from all **illusions** now, and let nothing stand in the way of truth.

Ch. 16. Sec. 5.

Salvation lies in the simple fact that **illusions** are not fearful because **illusions** are not true. **Illusions** but seem to be fearful to the extent to which you fail to recognize **illusions** for what they are; and you will fail to do this recognition to the extent to which you want **illusions** to be true. And to the same extent you are denying truth, and so you are failing to make the simple choice between truth and **illusion**; God and fantasy.

Ch. 22. Sec. 2.

Truth is the opposite of **illusions** because truth offers joy. What else but joy could be the opposite of misery? To leave one kind of misery and seek another is hardly an escape. To change one **illusion** for another is to make no change. The search for joy in misery is senseless, for how could joy be found in misery? All that is possible in the dark world of misery is to select some aspects out of misery, see the aspects as different, and define the difference as joy. Yet to perceive a difference where none exists will surely fail to make a difference.

Illusions carry only guilt and suffering, sickness and death, to their believers. The form in which **illusions** are accepted is irrelevant. No form of misery in reason's eyes can be confused with joy. Joy is eternal. Reason will tell you that the only way to escape from misery is to recognize misery and go the other way.

Ch. 23. Sec. 1.

Illusions have no place where love abides, love protects you from everything that is not true. You dwell in peace as limitless as its Creator, and everything is given those who would remember the Creator.

Discussion notes: Practical Truth • Practical Action • Heartfelt Thought

TOPIC 25

ERROR

error: A mistake, wrong-thinking, mis-perception, or mis-creation by the mind. Only the mind is capable of errors, but errors are expressed through the body. Errors may be perceived as sin, however, errors are corrected through forgiveness and choosing to let go of the story held in our mind.

Ch. 1. Sec. 1.

Miracles honor you because you are lovable. Miracles dispel illusions about yourself and perceive the light in you. Miracles thus atone for your **errors** by freeing you from your nightmares. By releasing your mind from the imprisonment of your illusions, miracles restore your sanity.

Ch. 1. Sec. 3.

"Recognize your **errors** and choose to abandon them. "

Error cannot really threaten truth, for truth can always withstand **error**. Only the **error**, not truth, is actually vulnerable. You are free to establish your kingdom where you see fit, but the right choice is inevitable if you remember this:

Spirit is in a state of grace forever.
Your reality is only spirit.
Therefore you are in a state of grace forever.

Ch. 2. Sec. 4.

Only the mind is capable of **error**. The body can act wrongly only when the body is responding to mis-thought of the mind.

Ch. 3. Sec. 2.

The way to correct distortions is to withdraw your faith in them and invest your faith only in what is true. Truth overcomes all **error**, and those who live in **error** and emptiness can never find lasting solace. If you perceive truly you are canceling out mis-perceptions in yourself and in others simultaneously. Because you see others as they are, you offer others your acceptance of their truth so they can accept the truth for themselves. This is the healing that the miracle induces.

Ch. 9. Sec. 3.

To the ego it is kind and right and good to point out the **errors** in others and "correct" them. This makes perfect sense to the ego, which is unaware of what **errors** are and what correction is. **Errors** are of the ego, and correction of **errors** lies in the relinquishment of the ego. When you correct a sister, you are telling her that she is wrong. Your sister is still right, because she is a Daughter of God. Your sister's ego is always wrong, no matter what the ego says or does.

If you point out the **errors** of your sister's ego you must be seeing her through your ego, because the Holy Spirit does not perceive her **errors**. The ego makes no sense, and the Holy Spirit does not attempt to understand anything that arises from the ego. The Holy Spirit does not judge the ego, knowing that nothing the ego makes means anything.

When you react at all to **errors**, you are not listening to the Holy Spirit.

When a sister behaves insanely, you can heal her only by perceiving the sanity in her. If you perceive your sister's **errors** and accept them, you are accepting your **errors**. If you want to give your **errors** over to the Holy Spirit, you must also do this with your sisters. Your sister is as right as you are, and if you think she is wrong you are condemning yourself.

It is not up to you to change your sister, but merely to accept her as she is. Your sisters' **errors** do not come from the truth that is in her, and can have no effect at all on the truth in you. To perceive **errors** in anyone, and to react to perceived **errors** as if they were real, is to make them real to you. You will not escape paying the price for these mis-perceptions, not because you are being punished for it, but because you are following the wrong guide, the ego, and will therefore lose your way.

Your sister's perceived **errors** are not of her, any more than your **errors** are of you. Accept your sister's **errors** as real, and you have attacked yourself.

The Holy Spirit in you forgives all things in you and in your sister. Your sister's **errors** are forgiven with yours. Any attempt you make to correct a sister means that you believe correction by you is possible, and this attempt can only be the arrogance of the ego. Correction is of God, Who does not know of arrogance.

Ch. 12. Sec. 1.

Understand that you do not respond to anything directly, but rather to your interpretation of it. Your interpretation thus becomes the justification for the response. That is why analyzing the motives of others is hazardous to you. If you decide that someone is really trying to attack you or desert you or enslave you, you will respond as if your brother had actually done so, by having made his **error** real to you.

To interpret **error** wrongly is to give **error** power, and having done this you will overlook truth.

Discussion notes: Practical Truth • Practical Action • Heartfelt Thought

____

____

____

____

TOPIC 26

SIN (ERROR)

sin: The belief (perception) that an action or thought is wicked, immoral, or selfish. The label that is assigned to an action or thought that is believed to go against God's laws or goodness. Some religions claim they know what is sinful and project those beliefs onto everyone. They believe sin is punishable and irreversible unless a sacrifice is made. This belief can create feelings of guilt and separation from God. If we think God demands punishment or sacrifice for sin, this belief can cause confusion about the nature of unconditional love. The ego's goal is to convince us that sin has a permanent effect unless a price is paid. The good news is that there is no sin but rather errors, mistakes, wrong decisions, or hurtful actions. These, therefore, can be forgiven and healed; although some may feel harder to forgive than others. Note that errors, mistakes, wrong decisions, or hurtful actions can cause pain, chaos, and destruction here on earth.

Ch. 19. Sec. 2.

The Son of God can be mistaken; he can deceive himself; he can even turn the power of his mind against himself. But he cannot **sin**. There is nothing he can do that would really change his true reality in any way, nor make him really guilty. To make guilty is what **sin** would do, for such is **sin's** purpose. For the wages of **sin** is death, and yet how can the immortal die?

To the ego, this belief in **sin** is no mistake. For this belief in **sin** is the ego's reality; this is the ego's "truth" from which escape seems to be impossible.

Would you not rather believe that **sin** be nothing more than a mistake, entirely correctable, and so easily escaped from that its whole correction is like walking through a mist into the sun? For that is all correction is. Perhaps you would be tempted to agree with the ego that it is far better to be **sinful** than mistaken. Yet think carefully before you allow yourself to make this choice between **sin** and mistake. Approach the choice not lightly, for choice of **sin** or mistake is the choice of hell or Heaven.

Ch. 19. Sec. 3.

Errors, which are mistakes and not **sins**, are quickly recognized and quickly given to correction, to be healed, not hidden. You will be healed of **sin** and all **sin's** ravages the instant that you give **sin** no power over your sister. And you will help each other overcome mistakes by joyously releasing each other from the belief in **sin**.

Look upon your Redeemer, the Christ, and behold what the Redeemer would show you in your sister, and let not **sin** arise again to blind your eyes. For **sin** would keep you separate from your sister, but your Redeemer would have you look upon her as yourself. Your holy relationship with your sister is now a temple of healing; a place where all the weary ones can come and rest. Here is the rest that waits for all, after the journey. And the journey's end is brought nearer to all by your holy relationship.

Ch. 20. Sec. 6.

The body is the ego's idol; the belief in **sin** made flesh and then projected outward. This belief in **sin** produces what seems to be a wall of flesh around the mind, keeping the mind prisoner in a tiny spot of space and time, beholden unto death, and given but an instant in which to sigh and grieve and die in honor of its master, which is the belief in **sin**.

And here in the world of flesh, he is more dead than living. Yet it is also here in the world of flesh he makes his choice again between idolatry and love. Here in the world of flesh it is given him to choose to spend this instant paying tribute to the body, or let himself be given freedom from the body. Here in the world of flesh he can accept the holy instant. And here in the world of flesh he can learn relationships are his salvation, and not his doom.

Ch. 21. Sec. 4.

The Holy Spirit will never teach you that you are **sinful**. Errors the Holy Spirit will correct, and the Holy Spirit's correction makes no one fearful. You are indeed afraid to look within and see the **sin** you think is there inside you.

Loudly the ego tells you not to look inward, for if you do your eyes will light on **sin**, and God will strike you blind. You believe **sin** is within you, and so you do not look within.

What if you looked within and saw no **sin**?

Ch. 21. Sec. 7.

Could he, who believes in **sin**, admit that no one made him powerless but himself?

Forget not that the choice of **sin** or truth, helplessness or power, is the choice of whether to attack or heal. For healing comes of power, and attack of helplessness. Whom you attack you cannot want to heal. And whom you would have healed must be the one you chose to be protected from attack. And what is this decision, between whether to attack or to heal, but the choice of whether to see your brother through the body's eyes, or let him be revealed to you through Christ's vision?

Ch. 23. Sec. 1.

You who are beloved of God the Mother are no illusion, being as true and holy as Herself. The stillness of your certainty of your Mother and of yourself is home to Both of You, Who dwell as One and not apart. Open the door of the Mother's most holy home, and let forgiveness sweep away all trace of the belief in **sin** that keeps God homeless to you. You are not a stranger in the house of God.

Ch. 25. Sec. 5.

The state of **sinlessness** is merely this:

The whole desire to attack is gone, and so there is no reason to perceive the Daughter of God as other than she is. The need for guilt is gone because guilt has no purpose, and guilt is meaningless without the goal of **sin**. Attack and **sin** are bound as one illusion, each the cause and aim and justifier of the other. Attack and **sin** are each meaningless alone, but seems to draw a meaning from the other. Attack and **sin** each depend upon the other for whatever sense attack or **sin** seems to have. And no one could believe in one unless one believes the other were true, for attack and **sin** each attests the other must be true.

Discussion notes: Practical Truth • Practical Action • Heartfelt Thought

TOPIC 27

JUDGMENT

judgment: The mental process of deciding and selecting what to accept or reject. When wrongly used, judgment promotes a world of separation and specialness. The correct use of this process is to judge the ego's voice as insane and replace it with the sanity of Spirit.

Ch. 2. Sec. 8.

The Last **Judgment** is one of the most threatening ideas in your thinking. This is because you do not understand the meaning of the Last **Judgment**. **Judgment** is not an attribute of God.

The Last **Judgment** is a final healing rather than a meting out of punishment, however much you may think that punishment is deserved. Punishment is a concept totally opposed to right-mindedness, and the aim of the Last **Judgment** is to restore right-mindedness to you. The Last **Judgment** might be called a process of right evaluation. This process of right evaluation simply means that everyone will finally come to understand what is worthy and what is not. After this right evaluation is in your thinking, the ability to choose can be directed rationally. Until this distinction is made, however, the vacillations between free and imprisoned *will* cannot but continue.

The first step toward freedom involves a sorting out of the false from the true. Everyone will ultimately look upon their own creations and choose to preserve only what is good, just as God Herself looked upon what She had created and knew that it was good. At this point, the mind can begin to look with love on the mind's own creations because of their worthiness. At the same time the mind will inevitably disown its mis-creations which, without the power of belief, the mind's mis-creations will no longer exist.

The term "Last **Judgment**" is frightening not only because **judgment** has been projected onto God, but also because of the association of "last" with death. If the meaning of the Last **Judgment** is objectively examined, it is quite apparent that the Last **Judgment** is really the doorway to life. No one who lives in fear is really alive. Your own last **judgment** cannot be directed toward yourself, because you are not your own creation. You can, however, apply **judgment** meaningfully and at any time to everything you have made, and retain in your memory only what is creative and good. This is what your right-mindedness can dictate. The purpose of time is solely to "give you time" to achieve this **judgment**. The Last **Judgment** is your own perfect **judgment** of your own perfect creations. When everything you retain is lovable, there is no reason for fear to remain with you.

Ch. 3. Sec. 5.

Perception is impossible without a belief in "more" and "less." At every level perception involves selectivity. Perception is a continual process of accepting and rejecting, organizing and reorganizing, shifting and changing. Evaluation is an essential part of perception, because **judgments** are necessary in order to select.

Ch. 3. Sec. 6.

Judgment is symbolic because beyond perception there is no **judgment**. When the Bible says "**Judge** not that ye be not **judged**," the Bible means that if you **judge** the reality of others you will be unable to avoid **judging** your own reality.

The choice to **judge** rather than to know is the cause of the loss of peace. **Judgment** is the process on which perception rests. I have discussed this before in terms of the selectivity of perception, pointing out that evaluation is perception's obvious prerequisite. **Judgment** always involves rejection. **Judgment** never emphasizes only the positive aspects of what is **judged**, whether in you or in others.

You have no idea of the tremendous release and deep peace that comes from meeting yourself and your brothers totally without **judgment**. When you recognize what you are and what your brothers are, you will realize that **judging** them in any way is without meaning.

Ch. 4. Sec. 4.

Judgment, like any other defense, can be used to attack or protect; to hurt or to heal. The ego should be brought to **judgment** and found wanting there. Without your own allegiance, protection and love, the ego cannot exist. Let the ego be **judged** truly and you will withdraw allegiance, protection and love from the ego.

Ch. 6. Sec. 5.

The Holy Spirit does not teach you to **judge** others, because She does not want you to teach error and learn to **judge** others yourself. The Holy Spirit would hardly be consistent if She allowed you to strengthen what you must learn to avoid. In the mind of the thinker, then, the Holy Spirit is **judgmental**, but only in order to unify the mind so the mind of the thinker can perceive without **judgment**. The Holy Spirit's **judgment** enables your mind to teach without **judgment**, and therefore to learn to be without **judgment**. Therefore, the Holy Spirit's lesson is:

Be vigilant only for God and Her Kingdom.

Ch. 15. Sec. 5.

The holy instant is the Holy Spirit's most useful learning device for teaching you love's meaning. For the holy instant's purpose is to suspend **judgment** entirely. **Judgment** always rests on the past, for past experience is the basis on which you **judge**. **Judgment** becomes impossible without the past, for without the past you do not understand anything. You would make no attempt to **judge**, because without the past, it would be quite apparent to you that you do not understand what anything means. You are afraid to forget past experiences because you believe that without the ego, all would be chaos. Yet I assure you that without the ego, all would be love.

Discussion notes: Practical Truth • Practical Action • Heartfelt Thought

____

____

____

____

TOPIC 28

MISTAKE

Ch. 15. Sec. 10.

It is in your power to make the time of Christ be now. It is possible to make the time of Christ be now all at once because there is but one shift in perception that is necessary, for you made but one **mistake**. The one **mistake** seems like many, but it is all the same **mistake**. For though the ego takes many forms, the **mistake** is always the same idea. "What is not love is always fear, and nothing else."

Ch. 19. Sec. 3.

The Holy Spirit cannot punish sin. **Mistakes** She recognizes, and would correct all **mistakes** as God entrusted Her to do. But sin She knows not, nor can She recognize **mistakes** that cannot be corrected. For a **mistake** that cannot be corrected is meaningless to Her. **Mistakes** are for correction, and **mistakes** call for nothing else. What calls for punishment must call for nothing. Every **mistake** must be a call for love. What, then, is sin? What could sin be but a **mistake** you would keep hidden; a call for help that you would keep unheard and thus unanswered?

In time, the Holy Spirit clearly sees the Daughter of God can make **mistakes**. On this you share Her vision. Yet you do not share Her recognition of the difference between time and eternity. And when correction is completed, time is eternity.

Discussion notes: Practical Truth • Practical Action • Heartfelt Thought

TOPIC 29

SACRIFICE

sacrifice: (1) A belief that someone must lose if another is to gain. (2) A perception that we must pay a price to receive God's love. The ego, not God, needs or demands a sacrifice.

Ch. 3. Sec. 1.

God does not believe in retribution. God's Mind does not create that way. God does not hold your "evil" deeds against you.

Sacrifice arises solely from fear, and frightened people can be vicious. **Sacrificing** in any way is a violation. Good teachers never terrorize their students. To terrorize is to attack, and this attacking results in rejection of what the teacher offers. The result is learning failure.

The lion and the lamb lying down together symbolize that strength and innocence are not in conflict, but naturally live in peace. "Blessed are the pure in heart for they shall see God" is another way of saying the same thing. A pure mind knows the truth and this is its strength. A pure mind does not confuse destruction with innocence because a pure mind associates innocence with strength, not with weakness.

Ch. 7. Sec. 7.

The gifts you offer to the ego are always experienced as **sacrifices**, but the gifts you offer to the Kingdom are gifts to you. The gifts you offer to the Kingdom will always be treasured by God because they belong to Her beloved Daughters, who belong to Her. All power and glory are yours because the Kingdom is God's.

Ch. 15. Sec. 10.

Your confusion of **sacrifice** and love is so profound that you cannot conceive of love without **sacrifice**. And it is this confusion that you must look upon; **sacrifice** is attack, not love. If you would accept but this one idea, that **sacrifice** is attack and not love, your fear of love would vanish. Guilt cannot last when the idea of **sacrifice** has been removed. For if there is **sacrifice**, someone must pay and someone must get. And the only question that remains is how much is the price of **sacrifice**, and for getting what.

As a host to the ego, you believe that you can give all your guilt away whenever you want, and thereby purchase peace. And the payment for peace does not seem to be your payment. While it is obvious that the ego does demand payment but the ego never seems to be demanding payment of you. The ego will never let you perceive this idea that the ego is actually demanding payment of you, since this recognition would make the ego homeless. For when this recognition dawns clearly, you will not be deceived by any fearful form the ego takes to protect itself from your sight. Each fearful form will be recognized as but a cover for the one idea that hides behind all the forms of fear; that love demands **sacrifice**, and love is therefore inseparable from attack and fear. And that guilt is the price of love, which must be paid by fear.

For the ego would have you believe that total love would demand total **sacrifice**.

Ch. 21. Sec. 3.

Those who believe in sin must think the Holy Spirit asks for **sacrifice**, for this is how they think their purpose is accomplished. Brother, the Holy Spirit knows that **sacrifice** brings nothing. The Holy Spirit makes no bargains. And if you seek to limit Him, you will hate Him because you are afraid. The gift He has given you is more than anything that stands this side of Heaven.

Your faith in **sacrifice** has given **sacrifice** great power in your sight; except you do not realize you cannot see love because of your faith in **sacrifice**. The intention of **sacrifice** is in the mind, which tries to use the body to carry out the means for sin in which the mind believes. Thus, is the joining of mind and body an inescapable belief of those who value sin. And so is **sacrifice** invariably a means for limitation, and thus for hate.

In the light of true vision, the body is looked upon quite differently. You can have faith in the body to serve the Holy Spirit's goal, and give the body power to serve as means to help the blind to see. But in their seeing the blind must look past the body, as do you.

Ch. 26. Sec. 1.

Sacrifice is the symbol of the central theme that somebody must lose. **Sacrifice's** focus on the body is apparent, for **sacrifice** is always an attempt to limit loss. To see a sister in another body, separate from yours, is the expression of a wish to see a little part of her and **sacrifice** the rest. Look at the world through the eyes of separation, and you will see nothing attached to anything beyond itself. All seeming entities can come a little nearer, or go a little farther off, but cannot join. The world you see is based on "**sacrifice**" of oneness. This world of **sacrifice** is a picture of complete disunity and total lack of joining.

The little that the body fences off becomes the little self, preserved through **sacrifice** of all the rest of oneness. In this perception of yourself as a body, the body's loss would be a **sacrifice** indeed. And for this little separate body to belong to you, you have placed limits on everything outside, just as limits are placed on everything you think is yours inside the body.

The body can be made to **sacrifice**. And while you see your sister as a body, apart from you and separate, you are demanding **sacrifice** of her and you. What greater **sacrifice** could be demanded than that God's Daughter perceive herself without her Mother? And her Mother be without Her Daughter? Yet every **sacrifice** demands that the Mother and Her Daughter be separate and without the other.

Without your special function, which is to share in oneness, this world has no meaning for you. Yet, this body minded world can become a treasure house, as rich and limitless as Heaven itself. No instant passes here in this world in which your sister's holiness cannot be seen.

You can lose sight of oneness, but you can not make **sacrifice** a true reality. Hear, then, the song your sister sings of oneness to you and let the world recede. See the oneness and rejoice with your sister.

Ch. 29. Sec. 1.

It is not love that asks a **sacrifice**. But fear demands the **sacrifice** of love, for in love's presence fear cannot abide. For hate to be maintained, love must be feared.

Discussion notes: Practical Truth • Practical Action • Heartfelt Thought

___

___

___

___

TOPIC 30

SALVATION

salvation: (1) Correction to the thoughts of separation and judgment through love and the acceptance of everyone we meet and everything we see. To recognize we are neither above nor below anyone and that we all journey together. (2) The undoing of the belief in sin and guilt. A change of mind through the power of perceptual miracles. The awakening of the mind so we can experience love and forgiveness instead of fear and guilt.

Ch. 4. Sec. 6.

Salvation is a collaborative venture. **Salvation** cannot be undertaken successfully by those who disengage themselves from the Daughtership, because they are disengaging themselves from the Christ. God will come to you as you give God to your sisters. The function of love is one.

Ch. 8. Sec. 3.

When you meet anyone, remember any meeting is a holy encounter. As you see your brother you will see yourself. As you treat your brother you will treat yourself. As you think of your brother you will think of yourself. Never forget this, for in your brother you will find yourself or lose yourself. Whenever two Sons of God meet, they are given another chance at **salvation**. Do not leave anyone without giving **salvation** to him and receiving **salvation** yourself. For I am always there with you, in remembrance of you.

Ch. 12. Sec. 1.

Only appreciation is an appropriate response to your sister. Gratitude is due your sister for both her loving thoughts and her appeals for help, for both are capable of bringing love into your awareness if you perceive her love and appeals truly. And all your sense of strain comes from your attempts not to do just this. How simple, then, is God's plan for **salvation**.

Ch. 12. Sec. 3.

The question is always twofold; first, what is to be saved? And second, how can it be saved?

Whenever you become angry with a brother, for whatever reason, you are believing that the ego is to be saved, and to be saved by attack. If a brother attacks, you are agreeing with this belief; and if you attack, you are reinforcing that the ego can be saved by attack. Remember that those who attack are poor in spirit.

Salvation is for the mind, and **salvation** is attained through peace that arises out of love. The mind is the only thing that can be saved and the only way to save the mind is through love. Any response other than love, arises from a confusion about the "what" and the "how" **salvation** is obtained. Never lose sight of this, that **salvation** is found in love, and never allow yourself to believe, even for an instant, that there is another answer than love.

Ch. 14. Sec. 3.

The Holy Spirit knows that all **salvation** is escape from guilt. You have no other "enemy", and against this strange distortion of the purity of the Son of God, the Holy Spirit is your Friend. He is the strong protector of the innocence that sets you free.

Let the Holy Spirit, therefore, be the only guide that you would follow to **salvation**. He knows the way, and leads you gladly on your way to guiltlessness. Without His guidance, you will think you know the way alone, and you will decide against your peace as surely as you decided before, that **salvation** lay in you alone. **Salvation** is of Him to Whom God gave it for you. Forget the Holy Spirit not and He will make every decision for you, for your **salvation** and for the peace of God in you.

Ch. 18. Sec. 4.

Salvation is easy just because **salvation** asks nothing you cannot give right now.

Ch. 25. Sec. 7.

Salvation is rebirth of the idea no one can lose for anyone to gain. And everyone must gain, if anyone would be a gainer. Here is sanity restored. And on this single rock of truth, that no one can lose for anyone to gain, can faith in God's eternal saneness rest in perfect confidence and perfect peace. Reason is satisfied, for all insane beliefs can be corrected here. And sin must be impossible, if this belief in loss and gain is true. This is the rock on which **salvation** rests, the vantage point from which the Holy Spirit gives meaning and direction to the plan in which your special function has a part.

No one can suffer for the Will of God to be fulfilled. **Salvation** is God's Will because you share it. Not for you alone, but for the Self that is the Daughter of God. The Self cannot lose **salvation**, for if she could the loss would be her Mother's, and in God the Mother, no loss is possible. And this sane because it is the truth.

Ch. 31. Sec. 6.

Salvation is undoing. If you choose to see the body, you behold a world of separation, unrelated things, and happenings that make no sense at all. This one body appears and disappears in death; that one body is doomed to suffering and loss. And no one is exactly as she was an instant previous, nor will she be the same as she is now an instant hence. Who could have trust where so much change is seen, for who is worthy if she be but dust?

Salvation is undoing of all this belief that we are a body.

Salvation does not ask that you behold the spirit and perceive the body not. **Salvation** merely asks that this should be your choice. For you can see the body without help, but do not understand how to behold a world apart from the body. It is your world of bodies **salvation** will undo, and let you see another world your eyes could never find.

Discussion notes: Practical Truth • Practical Action • Heartfelt Thought

---

TOPIC 31

ATONEMENT

Atonement: Rectifying the false belief that we are separate from God and from all of God's creations by accepting that we are all one with God. Release from the guilt of separation through forgiveness of ourselves, others, and everything we resist. Acceptance that we are all joined and not separate. Healing the thoughts of separation returns the mind to wholeness. At-one-ment.

Ch. 5. Sec. 4.

Atonement, which is to heal the belief in separation, is the way out of fear. The Holy Spirit will help you reinterpret everything that you perceive as fearful, and teach you that only what is loving is true. Truth is yours because truth is part of you, just as you are part of God because God created you.

The Holy Spirit **atones** in all of us by undoing the fear of separation, and thus lifts the burden you have placed in your mind. By following the Holy Spirit, you are led back to God where you belong, and how can you find the way except by taking your brother with you? You must learn to see your brothers as they are, and understand your brothers belong to God as you do. How could you treat your brother better than by rendering unto God the things that are God's?

I place the peace of God in your heart and in your hands, to hold and share. The heart is pure to hold the peace of God, and the hands are strong to give it. We cannot lose. The Thoughts of God are with you.

Ch. 13. Sec. 9.

Atonement brings a re-evaluation of everything you cherish, for **Atonement** is the means by which the Holy Spirit can separate the false and the true, to correct errors, which you have accepted into your mind without distinction. You do not believe the Daughter of God is guiltless because you see the past, and see her not now as she truly is, which is guiltless. When you condemn a sister you are saying, "I who was guilty choose to remain so. "You have denied a sister's freedom, and by so doing you have denied the witness unto your freedom. You could as easily have freed your sister from the past, and lifted from her mind the cloud of guilt that binds her to guilt. And in your sister's freedom would have been your own freedom.

Lay not your guilt upon your sister.

Ch. 14. Sec.4.

When you accept a brother's guiltlessness you will see the **Atonement** in your brother. For by proclaiming the guiltlessness in your brother you make guiltlessness yours, and you will see what you sought. Your brother's guiltlessness is your **Atonement**. Grant guiltlessness to your brother, and you will see the truth of what you have acknowledged.

Ask not to be forgiven, for this has already been accomplished. Ask, rather, to learn how to forgive, and to restore what always was to your unforgiving mind. **Atonement** becomes real and visible to those who use **Atonement** to learn how to forgive.

Ch. 16. Sec. 7.

Remember that you always choose between truth and illusion; between the real **Atonement** that would heal, and the ego's "atonement" that would separate and that would destroy. The power of God and all Her Love, without limit, will support you as you seek only your place in the plan of **Atonement,** which is acceptance through forgiveness to heal separation, arising from Her Love. Be an ally of God and not the ego in seeking how **Atonement** can come to you. God's help suffices, for Her Messenger understands how to restore the Kingdom to you, and to place all your investment in salvation in your relationship with Her.

Discussion notes: Practical Truth • Practical Action • Heartfelt Thought

PART FIVE

www.jgmgraphicart.com

Topics

Note: All chapter and section notations for the passages are referencing a previously published book titled *A Course in Miracles Abridged Edition.*

Topic 32

AUTHORITY PROBLEM

authority problem: Our attempt to create a self-image without including our divinity as a source to express our true Self. This belief in our egoic authority can cause us to project our deficiencies onto another person, which creates guilt and fear. We have power of free will, and God does not control how we use it.

Ch. 3. Sec. 7.

Every system of thought must have a starting point. It is a mistake to believe that a thought system based on lies is weak. Nothing made by a child of God is without power. It is essential to realize that a child of God is not without power, because otherwise you will be unable to escape from the prison you have made.

You cannot resolve the **authority problem** by depreciating the power of your mind.

Be glad! The light will shine from the true Foundation of life, and your own egoic thought system will stand corrected. Your Kingdom is not of this world because the Kingdom was given you from beyond this world. Only in this world is the idea of an **authority problem** meaningful. This world is not left by death but by truth, and truth can be known by all those for whom the Kingdom was created, and for whom the Kingdom waits.

Discussion notes: Practical Truth • Practical Action • Heartfelt Thought

TOPIC 33

BEHAVIOR (THE GOLDEN RULE)

behavior: The way in which one acts or conducts oneself, especially toward others.

Ch. 1. Sec. 3.

You respond to what you perceive, and as you perceive so shall you **behave**. **The Golden Rule** asks you to do unto others as you would have them do unto you. This means that the perception of both you and others must be accurate. **The Golden Rule** is the rule for appropriate **behavior**. You cannot **behave** appropriately unless you perceive correctly. Since you and your neighbor are equal members of one family, as you perceive both you and your neighbor, so you will do to both. You should look outward from the perception of your own holiness to the holiness of others.

Discussion notes: Practical Truth • Practical Action • Heartfelt Thought

TOPIC 34

ATTACK

attack: The expression of anger toward others. An attempt to justify our own guilt by projecting it unto others.

Ch. 3. Sec. 3.

If you **attack** "error" in another, you will hurt yourself. You cannot know your brother when you **attack** him. **Attack** is always made upon a stranger. You are making your brother a stranger by mis-perceiving him, and so you cannot know him. It is because you have made your brother a stranger that you are afraid of him. Perceive your brother correctly so that you can know him.

Ch. 8. Sec. 7.

When **attack,** in any form, enters your mind you are equating yourself with a body, since this is the ego's interpretation of the body. You do not have to **attack** physically to accept this interpretation that you are a body. You are accepting this interpretation simply by the belief that **attack** can get you something you want. If you did not believe this, the idea of **attack** would have no appeal for you. When you equate yourself with a body you will always experience depression. When a child of God thinks of herself in this way she is belittling herself, and seeing her sisters as similarly belittled. Since she can find herself only in her sister, she has cut herself off from salvation.

If you use the body for **attack**, it is harmful to you. If you use the body only to reach the minds of those who believe they are bodies, and teach them through the body that this is not so, you will understand the power of the mind that is in you. If you use the body for teaching others that they are not a body, you cannot use the body for **attack**. In the service of uniting, the body becomes a beautiful lesson in communion.

Communication ends separation. **Attack** promotes separation. The body is beautiful or ugly, peaceful or savage, helpful or harmful, according to the use to which the body is put. Misuse the body and you will misunderstand the body.

When you look upon a sister as a physical entity, her power and glory are "lost" to you, and so are yours. You have **attacked** her, but you must have **attacked** yourself first. Do not see your sister this way. Do not allow your sister to belittle herself in your mind, but give her freedom from her belief in littleness, and thus escape from yours. As part of you, your sister is holy. As part of Christ, you are holy.

Ch. 10. Sec. 2.

When you **attack**, you are denying yourself. You are specifically teaching yourself that you are not *what you are*. Your denial of reality precludes the acceptance of God's gift, because you have accepted something else in place of God's gift. If you understand that this denial of *what you are* is always an **attack** on truth, and truth is God, you will realize why denial of *what you are* is always fearful. If you further recognize that you are part of God, you will understand why it is that you always **attack** yourself first.

If you realized the complete havoc this denial of *what you are* makes of your peace of mind you could not make such an insane decision. You make the denial that you are a part of God only because you still believe it can get you something you want.

Ch. 10. Sec. 3.

When you think you are **attacking** yourself, it is a sure sign that you hate what you think you are. And this **attack** on yourself, and only this **attack** on what you are, can be **attacked** by you. What you think you are can be very hateful, and what this strange image makes you do can be very destructive.

Love cannot suffer, because love cannot **attack**. The remembrance of love therefore brings invulnerability with love.

Ch. 12. Sec. 3.

If you will recognize that all the **attack** you perceive is in your own mind and nowhere else, you will at last have placed the source of **attack**, and where the **attack** begins it must end. For in this same mind also lies salvation.

Ch. 12. Sec. 5.

Only love is strong because love is undivided. The strong do not **attack** because they see no need to do so. Before the idea of **attack** can enter your mind, you must have perceived yourself as weak. Because you **attacked** yourself and believed that the **attack** was effective, you behold yourself as weakened. No longer perceiving yourself and your brothers as equal, and regarding yourself as weaker, you attempt to "equalize" the situation you made. You use **attack** to do so because you believe that their **attack** was successful in weakening you.

That is why the recognition of your own invulnerability is so important to the restoration of your sanity. For if you accept your invulnerability, you are recognizing that **attack** has no effect. Once you realize this invulnerability you will no longer see any sense in **attack**, for **attack** does not work and cannot protect you.

The Holy Spirit's Love is your strength.

Ch. 23. Sec. 2.

Can an **attack** in any form be love? What form of condemnation is a blessing? Be not deceived when madness takes a form you think is lovely. What is intent on your destruction is not your friend.

Attack in any form has placed your foot upon the twisted stairway that leads away from Heaven. Yet any instant it is possible to have all this undone. How can you know whether you chose the stairs to Heaven or the way to hell? Quite easily. How do you feel? Is peace in your awareness? Are you certain which way you go? If not, you walk alone. Ask, then, your Friend to join with you, and give you certainty of where you go.

Ch. 24. Sec. 1.

Would it be possible for you to hate your sister if you were like her? Could you **attack** your sister if you realized you journey with her, to a goal that is the same? Would you not help your sister reach the same goal in every way you could, if her attainment of it were perceived as yours?

Discussion notes: Practical Truth • Practical Action • Heartfelt Thought

____

____

____

____

TOPIC 35

CHARITY

charity: Generosity and helpfulness, especially toward the needy, suffering, or disfavored. Aid given to those in need. Benevolent goodwill toward or love of humanity, lenient judgment of others, forbearance.

Ch. 2. Sec. 5.

Like all aspects of the belief in space and time, healing is temporary. However, as long as time persists, healing is needed as a means of protection. This is because healing rests on **charity**, and **charity** is a way of perceiving the perfection of another even if you cannot perceive the perfection in yourself. Most of the loftier concepts of which you are capable now are time-dependent. **Charity** is really a weaker reflection of a much more powerful love-encompassment that is far beyond any form of **charity** you can conceive of as yet. **Charity** is essential to right-mindedness in the limited sense in which right-mindedness can now be attained.

Charity is a way of looking at another as if she had already gone far beyond her actual accomplishments in time. Since her own thinking is faulty, she cannot see the Atonement for herself, or she would have no need of **charity**. The **charity** that is accorded her is both an acknowledgment that she needs help, and a recognition that she will accept help. Both of these perceptions of the need and acceptance of help, clearly imply their dependence on time, making it apparent that **charity** still lies within the limitations of this world.

Practical Truth • Practical Action • Heartfelt Thought

TOPIC 36

DEPRESSION

depression: Feelings of despondency and dejection. A state of feeling sad, lonely, guilty, or hopeless. Note that the passages below are not refuting mental health issues, but rather expressing a general concept for depression.

Ch. 4. Sec. 4.

When you are sad, know this need not be. **Depression** comes from a sense of being deprived of something you want and do not have. Remember that you are deprived of nothing except by your own decisions, and then decide otherwise.

When you are anxious, realize that anxiety comes from the capriciousness of the ego, and know this need not be. You can be as vigilant against the ego's dictates as vigilant for them.

Watch your mind for the temptations of the ego, and do not be deceived by it. The ego offers you nothing. When you have given up this voluntary dis-spiriting, you will see how your mind can focus and rise above fatigue and heal.

Ch. 8. Sec. 7.

There is nothing so frustrating to a learner as a curriculum they cannot learn. The leaner's sense of adequacy suffers, and becomes **depressed**. Being faced with an impossible learning situation of inadequacy is the most **depressing** thing in the world. In fact, this inadequacy is ultimately why the world itself is **depressing**. The Holy Spirit's curriculum is never **depressing**, because it is a curriculum of joy. Whenever the reaction to learning is **depression**, this reaction is because the true goal of the curriculum has been lost sight of.

Ch. 8. Sec. 7. (cont.)

The opposite of joy is **depression**. When your learning promotes **depression** instead of joy, you cannot be listening to God's joyous Teacher, the Holy Spirit, and learning the Holy Spirit's lessons.

Whenever you see another as limited to or by the body, you are imposing this limitation on yourself. Are you willing to accept this limitation of the body, when your whole purpose for learning should be to escape from limitations?

Ch. 9. Sec. 1.

Any attempt to deny what *is* must be fearful, and if the attempt is strong to deny what *is*, it will induce panic. Willing against reality, though impossible, can be made into a very persistent goal even though you do not want it. But consider the result of this strange decision to will against reality. You are devoting your mind to what you do not want.

You cannot distort reality and know what reality is. And if you do distort reality you will experience anxiety, **depression** and ultimately panic, because you are trying to make yourself unreal. When you feel anxiety, **depression**, and panic, do not try to look beyond yourself for truth, for truth can only be within you. Say, therefore:

> *Christ is in me, and where Christ is, God must be, for Christ is part of God.*

Ch. 10. Sec. 5.

The rituals of the god of sickness are strange and very demanding. Joy is never permitted, for **depression** is the sign of allegiance to the god of sickness. **Depression** means that you have forsworn God.

Ch. 10. Sec. 5. (cont.)

Depression is isolation, and so **depression** could not have been created. Daughter of God, you have not sinned, but you have been much mistaken. Yet this mistake can be corrected and God will help you, knowing that you could not sin against God.

Ch. 29. Sec. 4.

Depression or assault must be the theme of every dream, for **depression** and assault are made of fear. The thin disguise of pleasure and of joy, in which **depression** and assault may be wrapped, but slightly veils the heavy lump of fear that is their core. And it is this fear the miracle perceives, and not the wrappings in which the fear is bound.

Discussion notes: Practical Truth • Practical Action • Heartfelt Thought

---

TOPIC 37

RESPONSIBILITY

Ch. 2. Sec. 6.

You may believe that you are **responsible** for what you do, but not for what you think. The truth is that you are **responsible** for what you think, because it is only at this level of thought that you can exercise choice. What you do comes from what you think. You cannot separate yourself from the truth by "giving" autonomy to behavior. Whenever you are afraid, the fear is a sure sign that you have allowed your mind to mis-create.

You do not need guidance except at the mind level. Correction belongs only at the level where change is possible. Change does not mean anything at the symptom level, where change cannot work.

The correction of fear is your **responsibility**. When you ask for release from fear, you are implying that fear is not your **responsibility**. You should ask, instead, for help in the conditions that have brought the fear about. At the mind level you can help correct fear. You are much too tolerant of mind wandering, and are passively condoning your mind's mis-creations.

Ch. 6. Sec. Intro.

The relationship of anger to attack is obvious, but the relationship of anger to fear is not always so apparent. Anger always involves projection of separation, which must ultimately be accepted as one's own **responsibility**, rather than being blamed on others. Anger cannot occur unless you believe that you have been attacked, that your attack is justified in return, and that you are in no way **responsible** for it.

Ch. 7. Sec. 8.

Do not be afraid of the ego. The ego depends on your mind, and as you made the ego by believing in it, so you can dispel the ego by withdrawing belief from it. Do not project the **responsibility** for your belief in the ego onto anyone else, or you will preserve the belief in the ego. When you are willing to accept sole **responsibility** for the ego's existence you will have laid aside all anger and all attack, because anger and attack come from an attempt to project **responsibility** for your own errors. But having accepted the errors as yours, do not keep them. Give the errors over quickly to the Holy Spirit to be undone completely, so that all the errors effects will vanish from your mind.

Ch. 8. Sec. 3.

"Know thyself." There is nothing else to seek. Everyone is looking for herself and for the power and glory she thinks she has lost. Whenever you are with anyone, you have another opportunity to find power and glory. Your power and glory are in your sisters because their power and glory are yours. The ego tries to find power and glory in yourself alone, because the ego does not know where to look. The Holy Spirit teaches you that if you look only at yourself you cannot find yourself, because that is not what you are.

Whenever you are with a sister, you are learning what you are because you are teaching what you are to your sister. Your sister will respond either with pain or with joy, depending on which teacher, the ego or the Holy Spirit, you are following. Your sister will be imprisoned or released according to your decision, and so will you. Never forget your **responsibility** to your sister, because the decision of which teacher you follow is your **responsibility** to yourself. Give your sister her place in the Kingdom and you will have given yourself your place in the Kingdom.

Ch. 10. Sec. Intro.

Nothing beyond yourself can make you fearful or loving, because nothing is beyond you. Time and eternity are both in your mind, and time and eternity will conflict until you perceive time solely as a means to regain eternity. You cannot do this as long as you believe that anything happening to you is caused by factors outside yourself. You must learn that time is solely at your disposal, and that nothing in the world can take this **responsibility** from you.

Ch. 18. Sec. 7.

You still have too much faith in the body as a source of strength. What plans do you make that do not involve the body's comfort or protection or enjoyment in some way? This makes the body an end and not a means in your interpretation, and this always means you still find sin attractive. No one accepts Atonement for himself who still accepts sin as his goal. You have thus not met your one **responsibility**, which is the acceptance of our sinlessness.

It is extremely difficult to reach Atonement by fighting against sin.

Ch. 25. Sec. 9.

The little problems that you keep and hide become your secret sins, because you did not choose to let them be removed for you. And so your secret sins gather dust and grow, until they cover everything that you perceive. And bitterness, with vengeance justified and mercy lost, condemns you as unworthy of forgiveness. The unforgiven have no mercy to bestow upon another. That is why your sole **responsibility** must be to take forgiveness for yourself.

Discussion notes: Practical Truth • Practical Action • Heartfelt Thought

---

Topic 38

TWO VOICES

two voices: The ego's voice and the Spirit's voice.

Ch. 5. Sec. 2.

The Holy Spirit is the spirit of joy. The Holy Spirit is God's Answer to the separation.

When the ego was made, God placed in the mind the Call to joy. This Call to joy is so strong that the ego always dissolves at Its sound. That is why you must choose to hear one of **two voices** within you. One, the call of the ego, you made yourself, and that one is not of God. But the other, the Call to joy, is given you by God, Who asks you only to listen to It. The Holy Spirit, the spirit of joy, is in you in a very literal sense.

You are the Kingdom of Heaven, but you have let the belief in darkness enter your mind and so you need a new light. The Holy Spirit is the radiance that you must let banish the idea of darkness.

The choice for the Holy Spirit is the choice for God.

Ch. 5. Sec. 2. (cont.)

The Holy Spirit is your Guide in choosing. The Holy Spirit is in the part of your mind that always speaks for the right choice, because the Holy Spirit speaks for God. The Holy Spirit is your remaining communication with God, which you can interrupt but cannot destroy. The Holy Spirit is the way in which God's Will is done on earth as it is in heaven. Both heaven and earth are in you, because the call of both voices is in your mind. The Voice for God comes from your own altars to God. These altars are not things; they are devotions. Yet you have other devotions now. Your divided devotion has given you the **two voices**, and you must choose at which altar you want to serve. The decision is very simple. The decision is made on the basis of which call is worth more to you.

The Holy Spirit is the Call to awaken and be glad. Our task is the joyous one of waking the mind to the Call for God. Hear only the Call for God through the Holy Spirit within you, and teach others to listen as I am teaching you.

Ch. 7. Sec. 5.

As you can hear **two voices**, so you can see in two ways. One way shows you an image, or an idol that you may worship out of fear, but will never love. The other shows you only truth, which you will love because you will understand truth. Understanding is appreciation, because what you understand you can identify with, and by making what you understand part of you, you have accepted what you understand with love. That is how God created you; in understanding, in appreciation, and in love. The whole glory and perfect joy that is the Kingdom lies in you to give.

Discussion notes: Practical Truth • Practical Action • Heartfelt Thought

Topic 39

LEARN AND TEACH

learn and teach: The process of examining the thoughts about what we believe we are–for the purpose of undoing the sense of separation from God and others. It is sorting out truth from illusion to help us rise to higher perceptions; an awakening in us that is expressed into this world.

Ch. 2. Sec. 2.

Learning is temporary. The ability to **learn** has no value when change is no longer necessary. The eternally creative have nothing to **learn**. You can **learn** to improve your perceptions, and can become a better and better **learner**. This will bring you into closer and closer accord with the Daughtership, but the Daughtership itself is a perfect creation and perfection is not a matter of degree. Only while there is a belief in differences is **learning** meaningful.

Ch. 4. Sec. 1.

A good **teacher** must believe in the ideas he **teaches**, but he must meet another condition; he must believe in the students to whom he offers the ideas.

Many stand guard over their ideas because they want to protect their thought systems as they are, and **learning** means change. Change is always fearful to the separated, because they cannot conceive of change as a move towards healing the separation.

Ch. 7. Sec. 4.

The Holy Spirit must work through you, to **teach** you, The Holy Spirit is in you. This is an intermediary step toward the knowledge that you are in God because you are part of God.

The ego does not want to **teach** everyone all it has **learned**, because that would defeat the ego's purpose. The Holy Spirit **teaches** you to use what the ego has made, and to **teach** the opposite of what the ego has "**learned**". All you need do is make the effort to **learn**, for the Holy Spirit has a unified goal for the effort.

All abilities should therefore be given over to the Holy Spirit, Who understands how to use them properly. The Holy Spirit uses all abilities only for healing, because the Holy

Spirit knows you only as whole. By healing you **learn** of wholeness, and by **learning** of wholeness you **learn** to remember God.

The ego always seeks to divide and separate. The Holy Spirit always seeks to unify and heal.

Ch. 8. Sec. 1.

You cannot **learn** simultaneously from two **teachers** who are in total disagreement about everything. Their joint curriculum presents an impossible **learning** task. The two **teachers** are **teaching** you entirely different things in entirely different ways, which might be possible except that both are **teaching** you about yourself. Your true reality is unaffected by both **teachers**, but if you listen to both, your mind will be split about what your reality is.

Ch. 8. Sec. 2.

Only one **Teacher**, the Holy Spirit, knows what your reality is. **Learning** to remove the obstacles to that knowledge of what your reality is, is the purpose of the Holy Spirit. The ego does not know what it is trying to **teach**. The ego is trying to **teach** you what you are without knowing what you are. The ego is expert only in confusion.

Learning is joyful if **learning** leads you along your natural path, and facilitates the development of what you have.

Ch. 16. Sec. 3.

As you **learn** the joy of **teaching**, your gratitude to your Self, Who **teaches** you what your Self is, will grow and help you honor the Self in you. And you will **learn** the Self's power and strength and purity, and love the Self within as God does. God's Kingdom has no limits and no end, and there is nothing in God that is not perfect and eternal. All this is you, and nothing outside of this is you.

Discussion notes: Practical Truth • Practical Action • Heartfelt Thought

____

____

____

____

PART SIX

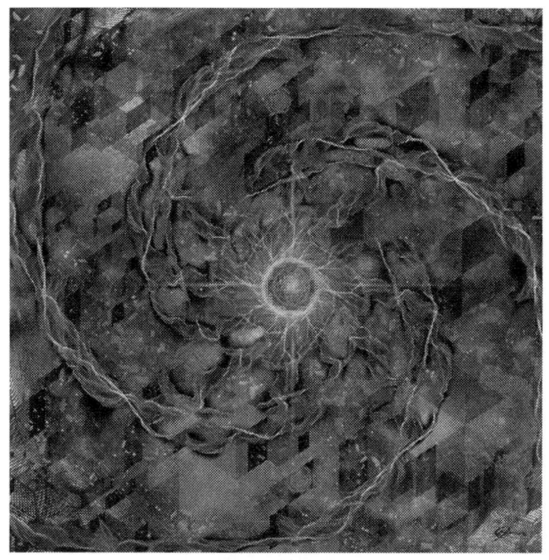

www.jgmgraphicart.com

Topics

Note: All chapter and section notations for the passages are referencing a previously published book titled *A Course in Miracles Abridged Edition.*

TOPIC 40

IDOL

idol: The allegiance to an external thing, body, place, substance, possession, relationship, idea, or achievement that we believe holds our escape from pain and the answer to pleasure. A belief that those effects will bring us to completion as a substitution for what the divine has to offer.

Ch. 29. Sec. 7.

Seek not outside yourself. Heaven cannot be found where Heaven is not. Each **idol** that you worship when God calls will never answer in God's place. There is no other answer you can substitute for God's answer, and find the happiness God's answer brings.

Seek not outside yourself. For all your pain comes simply from a futile search for what you want, insisting what you want must be found. What if what you want is not there outside of you? Do you prefer that you be right or happy? Be you glad that you are told where happiness abides, which is within you, and seek no longer elsewhere.

No one who comes to outside **idols** but must still have hope, some lingering illusion, or some dream that there is something outside of yourself that will bring happiness and peace to you. If everything is in you this cannot be so. This seeking outside of yourself is the purpose you bestow upon the body; that the body seeks for what you lack, and give you what would make yourself complete. And thus you wander aimlessly about, in search of something that you cannot find, believing that you are what you are not.

All **idols** of this world were made to keep the truth within from being known to you, and to maintain allegiance to the dream that you must find what is outside yourself to be complete and happy. It is vain to worship **idols** in the hope of peace. God dwells within you, the Christ, and your completion lies in God. No **idol** takes God's place. Look not to **idols**. Do not seek outside yourself.

Let us forget the purpose of the world the past has given it. For otherwise, the future will be like the past, and but a series of depressing dreams, in which all **idols** fail you, one by one, and you see death and disappointment everywhere.

You choose your dreams, for they are what you wish for, perceived as if the dream had been given you. Your **idols** do what you would have them do, and your **idols** have the power you ascribe to them. And you pursue your **idols** vainly in the dream, because you want the **idol's** power as your own.

An **idol** cannot take the place of God. Let the Holy Spirit remind you of God's Love for you, and do not seek to drown His Voice in chants of deep despair to **idols** of yourself. Seek not outside your Father for your hope. For hope of happiness is not despair.

Ch. 29. Sec. 8.

What is an **idol**? Do you think you know? For **idols** are unrecognized as such, and never seen for what the **idols** really are. The **idol's** purpose is obscure, and **idols** are feared and worshiped. Be the **idol** a body or a thing, a place, a situation or a circumstance, an object owned or wanted, or a right demanded or achieved, the **idol** is the same.

Let not the **idol's** form deceive you. **Idols** are but substitutes for your reality. In some way, you believe the **idols** will complete your little self, for safety in a world perceived as dangerous, with forces massed against your confidence and peace of mind. The **idols** seem to have the power to supply your lacks, and add the value that you do not have.

Each worshipper of **idols** harbors hope her special deities will give her more than others possess. It must be more. It does not really matter more of what; more beauty, more intelligence, more wealth, or even more affliction and more pain. But more of something, is an **idol** for. And when one **idol** fails another **idol** takes its place, with hope of finding more of something else. Be not deceived by forms the "something" takes.

If Heaven is within, why would you seek for **idols** that would make Heaven less? God gave you all there is. And to be sure you could not lose all God gave you, did God also give the same to every living thing as well. And thus is every living thing a part of you, as of God, Herself.

Ch. 30. Sec. 3.

It is not form you seek. What form can be a substitute for God the Father's Love? What form can take the place of all the love in the Divinity of God the Son? What **idol** can make two of what is one? You do not want an **idol**. An **idol** will not bestow on you the gift you seek. When you decide upon the form of what you want, you lose the understanding of the form's purpose. So you see your will within the **idol**, thus reducing your will to a specific form. Yet this could never be your will, because what shares in all creation cannot be content with small ideas and little things.

Behind the search for every **idol** lies the yearning for completion. Wholeness has no form because wholeness is unlimited. To seek a special person or a thing to add to you to make yourself complete, can only mean that you believe some form is missing. And by finding this missing form, you will achieve completion in a form you like. This is the purpose of an **idol**; that you will not look beyond the **idol** to find the source of the belief that you are incomplete.

It never is the **idol** that you want. But the completion you think the **idol** offers you, you want indeed. Your will to be complete is but God's Will. God knows not form. Creation gives no separate person and no separate thing the power to complete the Son of God. What **idol** can be called upon to give the Son of God what he already has, which is wholeness and completion?

Beyond all **idols** is the Thought God holds of you. Completely unaffected by the turmoil and the terror of the world, the dreams of birth and death that here are dreamed, the myriad of forms that fear can take; quite undisturbed, the Thought God holds of you remains exactly as it always was. Surrounded by a stillness so complete no sound of battle comes remotely near; the Thought God Holds of you rests in certainty and perfect peace.

Ch. 30. Sec. 4.

All **idols** are the false ideas you made to fill the gap you think arose between yourself and what is true.

Appearances deceive because they are appearances, and not reality. Dwell not on appearances in any form. Appearances but obscure reality, and appearances bring fear because they hide the truth.

Appearances can but deceive the mind that wants to be deceived. And you can make a simple choice that will forever place you far beyond deception. You need not concern yourself with how this simple choice will be done, for this you cannot understand. But you will understand that mighty changes have been quickly brought about, when you decide one very simple thing; you do not want whatever you believe an **idol** gives. For thus the Daughter of God declares that she is free of **idols**. And thus is God's Daughter free.

Discussion notes: Practical Truth • Practical Action • Heartfelt Thought

TOPIC 41

GAP

gap: The illusionary space between ourselves and God and ourselves and others that is brought about by the belief that we are separate and incomplete.

Ch. 28. Sec. 7.

God asks for nothing, and Her Daughter need ask for nothing. For there is no lack in God's Daughter. An empty space, a little **gap**, would be a lack. And it is only there in a **gap** of lack that she could want for something she has not. A space where God is not, a **gap** between the Mother and the Daughter is not the Will of Either, Who have promised to be One. God's promise is a promise to Herself, and there is no one who could be untrue to what She wills as part of what She is. The promise that there is no **gap** between Herself and what She is cannot be false. What *will* can come between what must be One, and in Whose Wholeness, there can be no **gap**?

The beautiful relationship you have with all your sisters is a part of you because this beautiful relationship is a part of God Herself.

Ch. 29. Sec. 1.

There is no time, no place, no state where God is absent. There is nothing to be feared. There is no way in which a **gap** could be conceived of in the Wholeness that is God. The compromise the least and littlest **gap** would represent in God's eternal Love is quite impossible. For a **gap** in God's Love would mean God's Love could harbor just a hint of hate, God's gentleness could sometimes turn to attack, and God's eternal patience sometimes fail. All this you believe when you perceive a **gap** between your brother and yourself.

Here, in this **gap** that you perceive, is the fear of God most plainly seen. For love can seem treacherous to those who fear, since fear and hate can never be apart. No one who hates but is afraid of love, and therefore must be afraid of God. He, who is afraid of God, fears to love and loves to hate, and so he thinks that love is fearful; hate is love. This is the consequence the little **gap** brings to those who cherish it.

The **gap** between you and your brother is not one of space between two separate bodies. And this **gap** but seems to be dividing off your separate minds.

The body could not separate your mind from your brother's unless you wanted the body to be a cause of separation and of distance seen between you and him. Thus do you endow the body with a power that lies not within itself but rather belongs to your mind. And herein lies the body's power over you. For now you think that the body determines when your brother and you meet, and you think that the body limits your ability to make communion with your brother's mind.

There is a shock that comes to those who learn their savior, who is your brother, is their enemy no more. There is a wariness that is aroused by learning that the body is not real. And there are overtones of seeming fear around the happy message, "God is Love."

Yet all that happens when the **gap** of fear is gone is peace eternal. Nothing more than eternal peace, and nothing less. Without the fear of God, what could induce you to abandon God? What toys or trinkets in the **gap** of fear could serve to hold you back an instant from God's Love? Would you allow the body to say "no" to Heaven's calling, were you not afraid to find a loss of self in finding God?

Discussion notes: Practical Truth • Practical Action • Heartfelt Thought

TOPIC 42

FREEDOM

Ch. 8. Sec. 2.

The ego tries to teach that you want to oppose God's Will. The Holy Spirit leads you steadily along the path of **freedom**, teaching you how to disregard or look beyond everything that would hold you back.

We have said that the Holy Spirit teaches you the difference between pain and joy. That is the same as saying the Holy Spirit teaches you the difference between imprisonment and **freedom**. You cannot make this distinction without the Holy Spirit because you have taught yourself that imprisonment is **freedom**.

The Holy Spirit's teaching takes only one direction and has only one goal. The Holy Spirit's direction is **freedom**, and His goal is God. When you have learned that your will is God's, you could no more will to be without God than God could will to be without you. This is **freedom** and this is joy.

Ch. 8. Sec. 4.

Freedom cannot be learned by tyranny of any kind, and the perfect equality of all God's Daughters cannot be recognized through the dominion of one mind over another. God's Daughters are equal in will, all being the Will of their Mother.

Freedom is the only gift you can offer to God's Daughters, being an acknowledgment of what they are and what God is. **Freedom** is creation, because **freedom** is love. Whom you seek to imprison you do not love. Therefore, when you seek to imprison anyone, including yourself, you do not love her and you cannot identify with her. When you imprison yourself, you are losing sight of your true identification with the Mother.

Your identification is with the Mother and with the Daughter. If you are part of One you must be part of the Other, because the Mother and the Daughter are One.

Ch. 23. Sec. Intro.

Nothing around you is but part of you. Look on everything around you lovingly, and see the light of Heaven in everything. So will you come to understand all that is given you is lovingness. In kind forgiveness will the world sparkle and shine, and everything you once thought sinful now will be reinterpreted as part of Heaven. How beautiful it is to walk, clean and redeemed and happy, through a world in bitter need of the redemption that your innocence bestows upon the world! What can you value more than this redemption? For here in the world in which you walk is your salvation and your **freedom**.

Discussion notes: Practical Truth • Practical Action • Heartfelt Thought

---

TOPIC 43

WAR

war: A state of hostility, conflict, or antagonism. A struggle or competition between opposing forces.

Ch. 8. Sec. 1.

Every response to the ego is a call to **war**, and **war** does deprive you of peace. Yet in this **war** there is no opponent. This **war** of the ego is the reinterpretation of reality that you must make to secure peace. Those whom you perceive as opponents are part of your peace, which you are giving up peace by attacking them.

Ch. 13. Sec. 11.

Forgetfulness and sleep and even death become the ego's best advice for dealing with the perceived and harsh intrusion of guilt on peace. Yet no one sees himself in conflict and ravaged by a cruel **war** unless he believes that both opponents in the **war** are real. Believing this he must escape, for such a **war** would surely end his peace of mind, and so destroy him. Yet if he could but realize the **war** is between real and unreal powers, he could look upon himself and see his freedom. No one finds himself ravaged and torn in endless battles if he himself perceives these endless battles to be unreal and wholly without meaning.

Ch. 23. Sec. Intro.

No one is strong who has an enemy, and no one can attack unless he thinks he has one. Belief in enemies is therefore the belief in weakness, and what is weak is not the Will of God.

How strange indeed becomes this **war** against yourself!

Walk you in glory, with your head held high, and fear no evil. The innocent are safe because they share their innocence. Nothing the innocent see is harmful, for their awareness of the truth releases everything from the illusion of harmfulness. And what seemed harmful now stands shining in their innocence, released from sin and fear and happily returned to love. The innocent share the strength of love because they looked on innocence. And every error disappeared because the innocent saw it not.

Ch. 23. Sec. 1.

The memory of God comes to the quiet mind. It cannot come where there is conflict, for a mind at **war** against itself remembers not eternal gentleness. The means of **war** are not the means of peace, and what the warlike would remember is not love. **War** is impossible unless belief in victory is cherished. Conflict within you must imply that you believe the ego has the power to be victorious. Why else would you identify with the ego? Surely you realize the ego is at war with God.

Do you not realize a **war** against yourself would be a **war** on God? Is victory conceivable? And if victory were, is this a victory that you would want? The death of God, if it were possible, would be your death. Is this a victory? The ego always marches to defeat, because the ego thinks that triumph over the Daughter of God is possible. And God thinks otherwise. This is no **war**; only the mad belief the Will of God can be attacked and overthrown. You may identify with this mad belief, but never will this belief that you can overthrow God be more than madness. And fear will reign in madness, and will seem to have replaced love there. This is the conflict's purpose. And to those who think that the mad idea is possible, the means also seem real.

Sister, the **war** against yourself is almost over. The journey's end is at the place of peace. God loves you perfectly, completely and eternally.

War is the condition in which fear is born, and grows and seeks to dominate. Peace is the state where love abides, and seeks to share itself. Conflict and peace are opposites. Where one abides the other cannot be; where either goes the other disappears. Far beyond this senseless **war** of conflict, the memory of God shines, ready to be remembered when you side with peace.

Ch. 23. Sec. 4.

Do not remain in conflict, for there is no **war** without attack. The fear of God is fear of life, and not of death. Yet God remains the only place of safety. In God there is no attack, and no illusion in any form stalks Heaven. What is not loving must be an attack. Every illusion is an assault on truth, and every assault on truth does violence to the idea of love.

Discussion notes: Practical Truth • Practical Action • Heartfelt Thought

TOPIC 44

ALONE

Ch. 11. Sec. 1.

To be **alone** is to be separated from infinity, but how can this be if infinity has no end? No one can be beyond the limitless, because what has no limits must be everywhere. There are no beginnings and no endings in God, whose universe is Herself. Can you exclude yourself from the universe, or from God Who is the universe? Do you really believe that part of God can be missing or lost to Her?

What holds for God holds for you.

Ch. 15. Sec. 5.

The past is the ego's chief learning device, for it is in the past that you learned to define your own needs and acquired methods for meeting your needs on your own separate terms. Separation is the source of guilt, and to appeal to separation for salvation is to believe you are **alone**. To be **alone** is to be guilty. For to experience yourself as **alone** is to deny the Oneness of the Father and His Son, and thus to attack true reality.

Ch. 31. Sec. 2.

Together is your joint inheritance remembered and accepted by you both. **Alone** your inheritance is denied to both of you. Is it not clear that while you still insist on leading or on following, you think you walk **alone**, with no one by your side? This is the road to nowhere, for the light cannot be given while you walk **alone**, and so you cannot see which way you go. And thus, because you choose to walk **alone**, there is confusion, and a sense of endless doubting as you stagger back and forward in the darkness and **alone**. Yet these are but appearances of what the journey is, and how the journey must be made. For next to you is One Who holds the light before you, so that every step is made in certainty and sureness of the road. A blindfold can indeed obscure your sight, but the blindfold cannot make the way itself grow dark. And the Holy Spirit Who travels with you has the light.

Discussion notes: Practical Truth • Practical Action • Heartfelt Thought

TOPIC 45

PAIN AND PLEASURE

Ch. 27. Sec. 6.

Pain demonstrates the body must be real. **Pain** is a loud, obscuring voice whose shrieks would silence what the Holy Spirit says, and keep the Holy Spirit's words from your awareness. **Pain** compels attention, drawing attention away from the Holy Spirit and focusing attention upon itself. **Pain's** purpose is the same as **pleasure**, for they both are means to make the body real.

Sin's attention shifts from **pain** to **pleasure**, and again to **pain**. For either **pain** or **pleasure's** witness is the same, and carries but one message: "You are here, within this body, and you can be hurt. You can have **pleasure**, too, but only at the cost of **pain**."

Discussion notes: Practical Truth • Practical Action • Heartfelt Thought

TOPIC 46

PRAISE GOD

Ch. 4. Sec. 7.

The Bible repeatedly states that you should **praise God**. This hardly means that you should tell God how wonderful God is. God has no ego with which to accept such **praise**, and has no perception with which to judge such **praise**. But unless you take your part in the creation, God's joy is not complete because your joy is incomplete.

God is praised whenever any mind learns to be wholly helpful. The truly helpful are invulnerable, because they are not protecting their egos and so nothing can hurt them. Their helpfulness is their **praise of God**, and God will return their **praise of Him** because they are like Him, and they can rejoice together. The truly helpful are God's miracle workers, whom God directs until we are all united in the joy of the Kingdom.

Ch. 13. Sec. 10.

Alone we are all lowly, but together we shine with brightness so intense that none of us alone can even think of our brightness. Before the glorious radiance of the Kingdom, guilt melts away and is transformed into kindness, guilt will never more be what guilt was. Every reaction you experience will be so purified that your reactions are fitting as a hymn of **praise** unto your Mother. See only **praise of God** in what She has created, for God will never cease Her **praise** of you. United in this **praise** we stand before the gates of Heaven where we will surely enter in our sinlessness. God loves you.

Discussion notes: Practical Truth • Practical Action • Heartfelt Thought

TOPIC 47

WILLINGNESS

willingness: The quality or state of being prepared to do something; readiness.

Ch. 8. Sec. 8.

No one can doubt the ego's skill in building up false cases. Nor can anyone doubt your **willingness** to listen to the false cases until you choose not to accept anything except truth. When you lay the ego aside, the ego will be gone. The Holy Spirit's Voice is as loud as your **willingness** to listen. It cannot be louder without violating your freedom of choice, which the Holy Spirit seeks to restore, never to undermine.

Ch. 16. Sec. 6.

The Holy Spirit needs only your **willingness** to share Her perspective and give it to you completely. And your **willingness** need not be complete because Her **willingness** is perfect. It is the Holy Spirit's task to atone for your unwillingness by Her perfect faith, and it is Her faith you share with Her there. Out of your recognition of your unwillingness for your release, the Holy Spirit's perfect **willingness** is given you. Call upon the Holy Spirit, for Heaven is at Her Call. And let Her call on Heaven for you.

Ch. 18. Sec. 4.

The holy instant is the result of your determination to be holy. The holy instant is the answer. The desire and the **willingness** to let the holy instant come precedes its coming. You prepare your mind for the holy instant only to the extent of recognizing that you want it above all else. It is not necessary that you do more; indeed, it is necessary that you realize that you cannot do more. Do not attempt to give the Holy Spirit what He does not ask, or you will add the ego to Him and confuse the two. The Holy Spirit asks but little. It is He who adds the greatness and the might. The Holy Spirit joins with you to make the holy instant far greater than you can understand. It is your realization that you need do so little that enables the Holy Spirit to give so much.

Trust not your good intentions. They are not enough. Come to the holy instance not in arrogance, assuming that you must achieve a state of holiness that the holy instant's coming brings with itself. The miracle of the holy instant lies in your **willingness** to let the holy instant be what it is. And in your **willingness** for this lies also your acceptance of yourself as you were meant to be.

Humility will never ask that you remain content with littleness. Your difficulty with the holy instant arises from your fixed conviction that you are not worthy of it. And what is this unworthiness but the determination to be as you would make yourself?

The holy instant does not come from your **willingness** alone. It is always the result of your small **willingness** combined with the unlimited power of God's Will. You have been wrong in thinking that it is needful to prepare yourself for God. It is impossible to make arrogant preparations for holiness, and not believe that it is up to you to establish the conditions for peace. God has established the conditions. The conditions do not wait upon your **willingness** for what the conditions for peace are. Your **willingness** is needed only to make it possible to teach you what the conditions for peace are.

You merely ask the question. The answer is given. Seek not to answer, but merely to receive the answer as it is given. In preparing for the holy instant, do not attempt to make yourself holy to be ready to receive holiness. That is but to confuse your role with God's. Atonement cannot come to those who think that they must first atone, but only to those who offer the Atonement, nothing more than simple **willingness** to make way for it. Purification is of God alone, and therefore for you. Rather than seek to prepare yourself for God, try to think thus:

I who am host to God am worthy of Him.
God Who established His dwelling place in me created it as He would have it be.
It is not needful that I make it ready for God,
but only that I do not interfere with His plan to restore to me my own awareness of my readiness, which is eternal.
I need add nothing to God's plan.
But to receive it, I must be willing not to substitute my own in place of it.

Discussion notes: Practical Truth • Practical Action • Heartfelt Thought

___

___

___

PART SEVEN

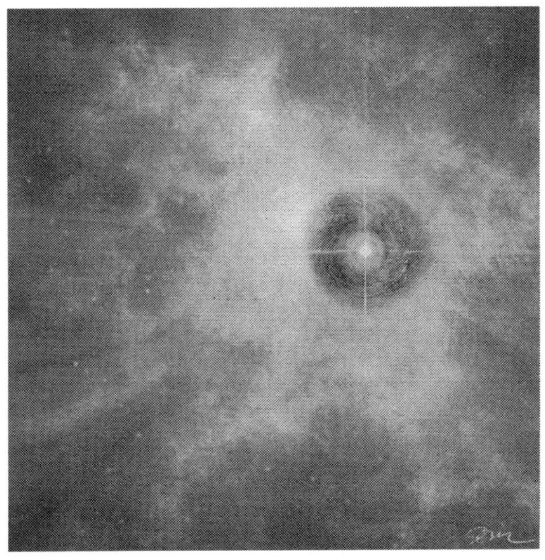

www.jgmgraphicart.com

Topics

Note: All chapter and section notations for the passages are referencing a previously published book titled *A Course in Miracles Abridged Edition.*

TOPIC 48

CONCEPT OF THE SELF

self: A concept constructed from the beliefs one holds about oneself and the perceptions one construes from the reactions of others. We are all saviors of the world by the acceptance and forgiveness of everyone and everything through the Christ vision.

Ch. 31. Sec. 5.

A **concept of the self** is made by you. It bears no likeness to your Self at all. Your concept of the self is an idol, made to take the place of your reality as Son of God. The **concept of the self** the world would teach, is not the thing that it appears to be.

Concepts are learned. They are not natural. Apart from learning, concepts do not exist. Concepts are not given, so they must be made. Now must the Holy Spirit find a way to help you see this **concept of the self** must be undone, if any peace of mind is to be given you.

The **concept of the self** has always been the great preoccupation of the world. And everyone believes that he must find the answer to the riddle of himself. Salvation can be seen as nothing more than the escape from concepts. Salvation does not concern itself with content of the mind, but with the simple statement that the mind thinks. And what can think has choice, and can be shown that different thoughts have different consequence. So the mind can learn that everything it thinks reflects the deep confusion that the mind feels about how it was made and what the mind is. And vaguely does the **concept of the self** appear to answer what the mind does not know.

Seek not your Self in symbols. There can be no concept that can stand for what you really are.

You will make many **concepts of the self** as learning goes along. Each concept will show the changes in your own relationships, as your perception of yourself is changed. There will be some confusion every time there is a shift, but be you thankful that the learning of the world is loosening its grasp upon your mind. And be you sure and happy in the confidence that the world's grasp will go at last, and leave your mind at peace. The role of the accuser will appear in many places and in many forms. And each will seem to be accusing you. Yet have no fear your peace of mind will not be undone.

There will come a time when images have all gone by, and you will see what you really are. It is to this unsealed and open mind that truth returns, unhindered and unbound. Where **concepts of the self** have been laid aside is truth revealed exactly as truth is.

Ch. 31. Sec. 7.

You cannot give yourself your innocence, for you are too confused about yourself. But should one sister dawn upon your sight as wholly worthy of forgiveness, then your **concept of yourself** is wholly changed. No longer do you choose that you should be the sign of evil and of guilt in your sister. And as you give your trust to what is good in this sister, you give your trust to the good in you.

By focusing upon the good in her, the body grows decreasingly persistent in your sight, and will at length be seen as little more than just a shadow circling round the good. And this will be your **concept of yourself**, when you have reached the world beyond the sight your eyes alone can offer you to see. For you will not interpret what you see without the Aid that God has given you. And in God's sight there is another world.

Have faith in your sister who walks with you, so that your fearful **concept of yourself** may change. Look upon the good in your sister. Hold out your hand, that you may have the gift of kind forgiveness which you offer one whose need for forgiveness is just the same as yours. And let the cruel **concept of yourself** be changed to one that brings the peace of God.

The cruel **concept of the self** stands like a shield, a silent barricade before the truth, and hides the truth from your sight. All things you see are images, because you look on all things as through a barrier that dims your sight and warps your vision, so that you behold nothing with clarity. The light is kept from everything you see. At most, you glimpse a shadow of what lies beyond. At least, you merely look on darkness, and perceive the terrified imaginings that come from guilty thoughts and concepts born of fear. And what you see is hell, for fear is hell. All light that is given you is for release; the sight, the vision and the inner Guide all lead you out of hell with those you love beside you, and the universe with them.

Behold your role as savior within the universe! To every part of true creation has the Lord of Love and life entrusted all salvation from the misery of hell. And to each one has God allowed the grace to be a savior to the holy ones especially entrusted to each other's care.

And this role as a savior is learned when first you look upon one sister as you look upon yourself, and sees the mirror of yourself in her. Thus, is the cruel **concept of yourself** laid aside, for nothing stands between your sight and what you look upon, to judge what you behold. And in this single vision do you see the face of Christ, and understand that you look on everyone as you behold this one sister. For there is light where darkness was before, and now the veil is lifted from your sight.

Discussion notes: Practical Truth • Practical Action • Heartfelt Thought

___

___

___

___

TOPIC 49

HEALING AND SICKNESS

heal: To correct the perception that we are separate from God and others. The mending of the mind's belief that the self is comprised only of a body that suffers. Healing is releasing the fearful illusion that we are vulnerable and can be victims of the world. Our body experiences physical sickness, but our true identity is in our spirit, not our body. Healing occurs when we let go of the attachment to the body and embrace the unity with God and others.

sickness: (1) The part of the mind that believes in separation and prevents us from recognizing the oneness of all creation. (2) The expression of fear and vulnerability that may be displaced onto the body.

Ch. 2. Sec. 5.

You can do much on behalf of your own **healing** and that of others, if in a situation calling for help, you think of it this way:

I am here only to be truly helpful.

I am here to represent Him Who sent me.

I do not have to worry about what to say or what to do, because He Who sent me will direct me.

I am content to be wherever He wishes, knowing He goes there with me.

*I will be **healed** as I let Him teach me to **heal**.*

Ch. 5. Sec. Intro.

To **heal** is to make happy. The light that belongs to you is the light of joy.

It is impossible for a child of God to love her neighbor except as herself. That is why the **healer's** prayer is:

Let me know this sister as I know myself.

Ch. 7. Sec. 4.

Healing is a way of forgetting the sense of danger the ego has induced in you, by not recognizing the ego's existence in your brother. This strengthens the Holy Spirit in both of you, because by not recognizing the ego's existence in your brother is a refusal to acknowledge fear. Love needs only this invitation. Love comes freely to all the Sonship, love being what the Sonship is. By your awakening to love, you are merely forgetting what you are not. This forgetting enables you to remember what you are.

Ch. 7. Sec. 5.

Healing is the Holy Spirit's form of communication in this world, and the only one She accepts. She recognizes no other, because She does not accept the ego's confusion of mind and body. Minds can communicate, but minds cannot hurt. The body in the service of the ego can hurt other bodies, but this cannot occur unless the body has already been confused with the mind.

Fear does not gladden. **Healing** does. Fear always makes exceptions. **Healing** never does. Fear produces dissociation, because fear induces separation. **Healing** always produces harmony, because **healing** proceeds from integration. You cannot separate your Self from your Creator, Who created you by sharing Her Being with you.

Ch. 8. Sec. 9.

I said before that the Holy Spirit is the Answer. The Holy Spirit is the Answer to everything, because the Holy Spirit knows what the answer to everything is. The ego does not know what a real question is, although the ego asks an endless number of questions. Yet you can learn this as you learn to question the value of the ego, and thus establish your ability to evaluate the ego's questions. When the ego tempts you to **sickness** do not ask the Holy Spirit to **heal** the body, for this would merely be to accept the ego's belief that the body is the proper aim of **healing**. Ask, rather, that the Holy Spirit teach you the right perception of the body, for perception alone can be distorted. Only perception can be **sick**, because only perception can be wrong.

Wholeness **heals** because wholeness is of the mind. All forms of **sickness**, even unto death, are physical expressions of the fear of awakening. "Rest in peace" is a blessing for the living, not the dead, because rest comes from waking, not from sleeping. Sleep is withdrawing; waking is joining. Dreams are illusions of joining, because dreams reflect the ego's distorted notions about what joining is.

Healing is release from the fear of waking. The decision to wake, is the reflection of the will to love, since all **healing** involves replacing fear with love.

The ego, which always wants to weaken the mind, tries to separate the mind from the body in an attempt to destroy the mind. The ego despises weakness, even though the ego makes every effort to induce weakness. The ego wants only what it hates. To the ego this is perfectly sensible. Believing in the power of attack, the ego wants attack.

Sickness is not of the body, but **sickness** is of the mind. All forms of **sickness** are signs that the mind is split, and that the mind does not accept a unified purpose.

The unification of purpose, then, is the Holy Spirit's only way of **healing** the mind.

Ch. 13. Sec. 8.

All **healing** is release from the past. That is why the Holy Spirit is the only **Healer**. The Holy Spirit teaches that the past does not exist. For the mind that knows this unequivocally knows also the mind dwells in eternity.

Ch. 27. Sec. 5.

The only way to **heal** is to be **healed**. Accept the miracle of **healing**, and the miracle of **healing** will go forth because of what the miracle is. No one can ask another to be **healed**. But she can let herself be **healed**, and thus offer the other what she has received, which is her on **healing**. The Holy Spirit speaks to you. She does not speak to someone else. Yet by your listening, Her Voice extends, because you have accepted what Her Voice says.

The *holy instant* is the miracle's abiding place. From there in the holy instant, each miracle is born into this world as witness to a state of mind that has transcended conflict, and has reached to peace. The miracle carries comfort from the place of peace into the battleground, and demonstrates that war has no effects. For all the hurt that war has sought to bring, the broken bodies and the shattered limbs, the screaming dying and the silent dead, are gently lifted up and comforted.

There is no sadness where a miracle has come to **heal**. What stands apart from you when you accept the blessing that the holy instant brings? Be not afraid of blessing, for the One Who blesses you loves all the world, and leaves nothing within the world that could be feared.

Come to the holy instant and be **healed**, for nothing that is received there is left behind on your returning to the world. And being blessed you will bring blessing. Life is given you to give life to the dying world. And suffering eyes no longer will accuse, but shine in thanks to you who blessing gave. The holy instant's radiance will light your eyes, and give the suffering the sight to see beyond all suffering and see Christ's face instead. **Healing** replaces suffering.

Peace be to you to whom is **healing** offered. And you will learn that peace is given you when you accept the **healing** for yourself. What occurred within the instant that love entered in without attack will stay with you forever. Your **healing** will be one of the holy instant's effects, as will your sister's. Everywhere you go, will you behold the holy instant's multiplied **healing** effects. God thanks you for your **healing**, for God knows your **healing** is a gift of love unto Her Daughter, and therefore your **healing** gift is given unto Her.

Discussion notes: Practical Truth • Practical Action • Heartfelt Thought

____

____

____

____

TOPIC 50

REBORN

Ch. 22. Sec. 2.

Beyond the body that you interposed between you and your sister is your holy relationship, beloved of God Herself. Every illusion brought to its forgiveness is gently overlooked and disappears. For at the holy relationship's center, Christ has been **reborn**, to light Christ's home with vision that overlooks the world. Would you not have this holy home be yours as well? No misery is here in Christ's home, but only joy.

All you need do to dwell in quiet here with Christ is share Her vision. Quickly and gladly is Christ's vision given anyone who is but willing to see your sister sinless. Look on your holy sister, sinless as yourself, and let her lead you there.

Ch. 26. Sec. 1.

Yet every instant can you be **reborn**, and given life again. In Heaven, God's Son is not imprisoned in a body, nor is God's Son sacrificed in solitude to sin. And as God's Son is in Heaven, so must he be eternally and everywhere. God's Son is the same forever. **Born again** each instant, untouched by time, and far beyond the reach of any sacrifice of life or death. For neither did God's Son make, life or death, and only one, the gift of life, was given God's Son by One Who knows His gifts can never suffer sacrifice and loss.

Ch. 26. Sec. 7.

The miracle but calls your ancient Name, which you will recognize because the truth is in your memory. And to this Name your sister calls for her release and yours. Heaven is shining on the Daughter of God. Deny your sister not, that you may be released. Each instant is the Daughter of God **reborn** until she chooses not to die again. In every wish to hurt she chooses death instead of what her Mother wills for her. Yet every instant offers life to her because her Mother wills that she should live.

Ch. 31. Sec. 1.

Be innocent of judgment, unaware of any thoughts of evil or of good that ever crossed your mind of anyone. Now you are free to learn of your brother, and learn of him anew.

Now is your brother **born again** to you, and you are **born again** to him, without the past judgments that sentenced him to die, and you with him. Now is your brother free to live as you are free, because an ancient learning of judgment passed away, and left a place for truth to be **reborn**.

Discussion notes: Practical Truth • Practical Action • Heartfelt Thought

TOPIC 51

FAITH AND BELIEF

Ch. 13. Sec. 9.

Faith makes the power of **belief**, and where **faith** is invested determines its reward. For **faith** is always given what is treasured, and what is treasured is returned to you.

Be **faithful** unto darkness and you will not see, because your **faith** will be rewarded as you gave it. You will accept your treasure, and if you place your **faith** in the past, the future will be like the past. Whatever you hold dear you think is yours. The power of your valuing will make it so.

Ch. 17. Sec. 6.

The goal of truth requires **faith**. **Faith** is implicit in the acceptance of the Holy Spirit's purpose. Where the goal of truth is set, there **faith** must be.

Ch. 17. Sec. 7.

Faithlessness brought to **faith** will never interfere with truth. But faithlessness used against truth will always destroy **faith**. If you lack **faith**, ask that **faith** be restored where it was lost.

Faithlessness is the servant of illusion. Use faithlessness, and it will carry you straight to illusions. Be tempted not by what illusions offers you.

Truth's call for **faith** is strong. Use not your faithlessness against truth, for truth calls you to salvation and to peace.

Ch. 19. Sec. 1.

To have **faith** is to heal. By **faith**, you offer the gift of freedom from the past, which you received. You do not use anything your brother has done before to condemn him now. You freely choose to overlook your brother's errors, looking past all barriers between yourself and him, and seeing yourself and your brother as one.

Faith is the opposite of fear. **Faith** is the gracious acknowledgment of everyone as a Son of your most loving Father, loved by God like you, and therefore loved by you as yourself.

Faith is the gift of God, through the Holy Spirit Whom God has given you. Faithlessness looks upon the Son of God, and judges your brother unworthy of forgiveness. But through the eyes of **faith**, the Son of God is seen already forgiven, free of all the guilt he laid upon himself. **Faith** sees him only *now* because it looks not to the past to judge him, but would see in him only what it would see in you. **Faith** sees not through the body's eyes, nor looks to bodies for its justification. **Faith** is the messenger of the new perception, sent forth to gather witnesses unto its coming, and to return their messages of **faith** to you.

Grace is not given to a body, but to a mind. And the mind that receives grace looks instantly beyond the body, and sees the holy place where the mind was healed. And there it is that you will realize that there is nothing **faith** cannot forgive.

For **faith** brings peace. For **faith** is still a learning goal, no longer needed when the lesson of **faith** has been learned.

Ch. 21. Sec. 3.

Faith and **belief** and vision are the means by which the goal of holiness is reached. Through them the Holy Spirit leads you to the real world, and away from all illusions where your **faith** was laid. This is the Holy Spirit's direction; the only one the Holy Spirit ever sees. And when you wander, the Holy Spirit reminds you there is but one direction. The Holy Spirit's **faith** and **belief** and vision are all for you. And when you have accepted them completely, instead of yours, you will no longer have need of them. For **faith** and vision and **belief** are meaningful only before the state of certainty is reached. In Heaven they are unknown. Yet Heaven is reached through them.

Ch. 21. Sec. 3. (cont.)

Faith and **belief** become attached to vision, as all the means that once served sin are redirected now toward holiness. For what you think is sin is limitation, and whom you try to limit to the body you hate because you fear. In your refusal to forgive your sister, you would condemn her to the body because the means for sin are dear to you. And so the body has your **faith** and your **belief**. But holiness would set your sister free, removing hatred by removing fear, not as a symptom, but at fear's source.

Those who would free their sisters from the body can have no fear. They have renounced the means for sin by choosing to let all limitations be removed. As they desire to look upon their sisters in holiness, the power of **belief** and **faith** goes far beyond the body, supporting vision, not obstructing vision. The miracles that follow this decision are also born of **faith**. For all who choose to look away from sin are given vision, and are led to holiness.

Ch. 21. Sec. 5.

Faith and perception and **belief** can be misplaced, and serve the great deceiver's needs as well as serve the truth. **Faith** and **belief** can be strong in madness, guiding perception toward what the deceived mind has valued.

Ch. 22. Sec. 2.

The ego will assure you now that it is impossible for you to see no guilt in anyone. This is a crucial period in your awakening, for in your awakening the separation of you and the ego must be made complete. Now must you choose between the truth in yourself and an illusion of yourself. Not both, but one. There is no point in trying to avoid this one decision. The decision must be made. **Faith** and **belief** can fall to either side of truth or illusion, but reason tells you misery lies only on one side and joy upon the other side.

Forsake not now your brother. For you who are the same as your brother will not decide alone, nor differently. Either you give each other life or death; either you are each other's savior or you are his judge, offering him sanctuary or condemnation. You choose between the joy of Heaven or the misery of hell.

Discussion notes: Practical Truth • Practical Action • Heartfelt Thought

TOPIC 52

CALL FOR LOVE

Ch. 12. Sec. 1.

By applying the Holy Spirit's interpretation of the reactions of others more and more consistently, you will gain an increasing awareness that the Holy Spirit's criteria are equally applicable to you. For to recognize fear is not enough to escape from fear, although the recognition is necessary to demonstrate the need for escape. The Holy Spirit must still translate the fear into truth. If you were left with the fear, once you had recognized fear, you would have taken a step away from reality, not towards reality. Yet we have repeatedly emphasized the need to recognize fear, and face fear without disguise, as a crucial step in the undoing of the ego. Consider how well the Holy Spirit's interpretation of the motives of others will serve you then. Having taught you to accept only loving thoughts in others and to regard everything else as an appeal for help, the Holy Spirit has taught you that fear itself is an appeal for help. This is what recognizing fear really means. That is the ultimate value in learning to perceive attack as a **call for love**.

We have learned that fear and attack are inevitably associated with each other. If only attack produces fear, and if you see attack as the call for help that it is, the unreality of fear in attack must dawn on you. For fear is a **call for love**, an unconscious recognition of what has been denied, which is love.

Ch. 14. Sec. 10.

Let the Holy Spirit show your sister to you, and teach you both her love and her **call for love**. Neither your sister's mind nor your mind holds more than these two orders of thought, love and a **call for love**.

The miracle is the recognition that this is true. Where there is love, your sister must give love to you because of what love is. But where there is a **call for love**, you must give love because of what you are. I said I will teach you how to remember what you are, restoring to you your Identity. We have already learned that this Identity, to give love, is shared. The miracle becomes the means of sharing your Identity.

Ch. 14. Sec. 10. (cont.)

You classify some of your thoughts as more important, larger or better, wiser, or more productive and valuable than other thoughts. For some thoughts are reflections of Heaven, while other thoughts are motivated by the ego.

The result is a weaving, changing pattern that never rests and is never still. The changing pattern shifts unceasingly across the mirror of your mind, and the reflections of Heaven last but a moment and grow dim, as darkness blots the reflections of Heaven out. Where there was light, darkness removes the light in an instant, and alternating patterns of light and darkness sweep constantly across your mind. The little sanity that still remains is held together by a sense of order that you establish. Yet the very fact that you can do this, and bring any order into chaos shows you that you are not an ego, and that more than an ego must be in you. For the ego is chaos, and if the ego were all of you, no order at all would be possible. Yet though the order you impose upon your mind limits the ego, the order can also limit you. To order is to judge, and to arrange by judgment.

The only judgment involved in the Holy Spirit's order is to divide thoughts into two categories; one of love, and the other the **call for love**.

Discussion notes: Practical Truth • Practical Action • Heartfelt Thought

TOPIC 53

SEEK AND DO NOT FIND

Ch. 12. Sec. 4.

The ego is certain that love is dangerous, and this is always the ego's central teaching. The ego never puts it this way that love is dangerous; on the contrary, everyone who believes that the ego is salvation seems to be intensely engaged in the search for love. Yet the ego, though encouraging the search for love very actively, makes one proviso; do not find love. The ego's dictates, then, can be summed up simply as: "**Seek and do not find**." This is the one promise the ego holds out to you, and the one promise the ego will keep. For the ego pursues its goal with fanatic insistence, and the ego's judgment, though severely impaired, is completely consistent.

It is surely obvious that no one wants to find what would utterly defeat them. Being unable to love, the ego would be totally inadequate in love's presence, for the ego could not respond at all to love. Then, you would have to abandon the ego's guidance, for it would be quite apparent that the ego had not taught you the response you need to love. The ego will therefore distort love, and teach you that love really calls forth the responses the ego can teach. Follow the ego's teaching, then, and you will search for love, but will not recognize love.

Ch. 12. Sec. 4. (cont.)

Do you realize that the ego must set you on a journey of "**seek and do not find**", which cannot but lead to a sense of futility and depression? To seek and not to find is hardly joyous. Is this the promise you would keep? The Holy Spirit offers you another promise, and one that will lead to joy. For The Holy Spirit's promise is always, "Seek and you will find," and under Her guidance you cannot be defeated. The Holy Spirit's promise is the journey to accomplishment, and the goal She sets before you She will give you. For The Holy Spirit will never deceive God's Daughter whom She loves with the Love of the Mother.

You will undertake a journey because you are not at home in this world. And you will search for your home whether you realize where your home is or not. If you believe your home is outside you the search will be futile, for you will be seeking your home where it is not. You do not remember how to look within for you do not believe your home is there within you. Yet the Holy Spirit remembers where your home is for you, and She will guide you to your home because that is Her mission.

Ch. 12. Sec. 5.

I have said that the ego's rule is, "**Seek and do not find**." Translated into curricular terms this means, "Try to learn but do not succeed." Such a curriculum does not make sense. This attempt at "learning" has so weakened your mind that you cannot love, for the ego curriculum you have chosen is against love, and amounts to a course in how to attack yourself. But perhaps you do not realize, even yet, that there is something you do want to learn, and that you can learn to seek and find, because leaning to succeed is your choice to do so.

Resign now as your own teacher. This resignation will not lead to depression. Your resignation as your own teacher is merely the result of an honest appraisal of what you have taught yourself, and of the learning outcomes that have not resulted in success. Under the proper learning conditions, which you can neither provide nor understand, you will become an excellent learner and an excellent teacher.

Your learning potential, properly understood, is limitless because it will lead you to God. You can teach the way to God and learn the way to God, if you follow the Teacher, the Holy Spirit, Who knows the way and understands the curriculum for learning it. For you really want to learn aright.

Discussion notes: Practical Truth • Practical Action • Heartfelt Thought

TOPIC 54

YOUR BROTHER/SISTER

Ch. 10. Sec. 5.

The Love of God is in everything She created, for God's Daughter is everywhere. Look with peace upon **your sisters**, and God will come rushing into your heart in gratitude for your gift to Her.

Ch. 13. Sec. 3.

Beneath all the ego's grandiosity you hold so dear is your real call for help. For you call for love to your Father as your Father calls you to Himself. In that place which you have hidden, the grandeur of God, you *will* only to unite with the Father, in loving remembrance of Him. You will find this place of truth as you see truth in **your brothers**, for though they may deceive themselves, like you, **your brothers** long for the grandeur that is in them. And perceiving the grander you will welcome it, and the grandeur will be yours.

Ch. 19. Sec. 4.

You are afraid of God because you fear **your sister**.

Think who **your sister** is, before you would condemn her. And offer thanks to God that **your sister** is holy, and has been given the gift of holiness for you. Join **your sister** in gladness, and remove all trace of guilt from her disturbed and tortured mind. Help **your sister** to lift the heavy burden of sin you laid upon her and she accepted as her own, and toss sin lightly and with happy laughter away from her. Press sin not like thorns against her brow, nor nail her to sin, unredeemed and hopeless.

Free **your sister** here, as I freed you. Offer **your sister** freedom and complete release from sin, here in the garden of seeming agony and death.

Together we will disappear into the Presence beyond the veil of the fear of God, not to be lost but found; not to be seen but known. And knowing, nothing in the plan God has established for salvation will be left undone. This knowing is the journey's purpose, without which is the journey meaningless. Here, in this knowing, is the peace of God, given to you eternally by God. Here is the rest and quiet that you seek, the reason for the journey from its beginning. Heaven is the gift you owe **your sister**, the debt of gratitude you offer to the Daughter of God in thanks for what she is, and what her Mother created her to be.

Ch. 24. Sec. 1.

Your brother is your friend because his Father created him like you. There is no difference. Could you attack **your brother** if you chose to see no specialness of any kind between you and him? Look fairly at whatever makes you give **your brother** only partial welcome, or would let you think that you are better off apart from him.

The fear of God and of **your brother** comes from each unrecognized belief in specialness. For you demand **your brother** bow to specialness against his will. Every twinge of malice, or stab of hate or wish to separate arises here in specialness. For here in specialness the purpose that you and **your brother** share, which is you and him are alike, becomes obscured from both of you.

Your brother is your friend because you both are the same.

Ch. 25. Sec. 2.

You and **your siste**r are the same as God Herself is One, and not divided in Her Will. And you must have one purpose, since God gave the same purpose to both of you. See not in **your sister** the sinfulness she sees, but give her honor that you may esteem yourself and her. To you and **your sister** is given the power of salvation, that escape from darkness into light be yours to share; that you may see as one what never has been separate, nor apart from all God's Love as given equally to all.

Ch. 25. Sec. 5.

It is no sacrifice that **your brother** be saved, for by his freedom will you gain your own. To let **your brother's** function be fulfilled is but the means to let yours be fulfilled. And so you walk toward Heaven or toward hell, but not alone. How beautiful **your brother's** sinlessness will be when you perceive it! And how great will be your joy, when **your brother** is free to offer you the gift of sight God gave to him for you! **Your brother** has no need but this; that you allow him the freedom to complete the task God gave to him. Remembering but this; that what **your brother** does you do, along with him. And as you see **your brother**, so do you define the function he will have for you, until you see **your brother** differently, and will let him be what God appointed that he be to you.

In **your brother** you see the picture of your own belief in what the Will of God must be for you. In your forgiveness will you understand God's Love for you; through your attack you believe God hates you, thinking Heaven must be hell. Look once again upon **your brother**, not without the understanding that he is the way to Heaven or to hell, as you perceive him. But forget not this; the role you give to **your brother** is given you, and you will walk the way you pointed out to him because it is your judgment on yourself.

Ch. 31. Sec. 7.

The veil across the face of Christ --the fear of God and of salvation, and the love of guilt and death-- they all are different names for just one error; that there is a space of separation between you and **your brother and your sister**, kept apart by an illusion of yourself that holds them away from you, and you away from them. The sword of judgment is the weapon that you give to the illusion of yourself, that the sword of judgment may fight to keep the space of separation that holds **your brother and your sister** off unoccupied by love. Yet while you hold this sword, you perceive the body as yourself, for you are bound to separation from the sight of **your brother and your sister** who holds the mirror to another view of what they are, and thus what you must be.

The savior's vision is as innocent of what **your brother and your sister** is, as the savior's vision is free of any judgment made upon yourself. The savior's vision sees no past in anyone at all. And thus the savior's vision serves a wholly open mind, unclouded by old concepts, and prepared to look on only what the present holds. The savior's vision cannot judge because it does not know. And recognizing this, the savior merely asks, "What is the meaning of what I behold?" Then is the answer given. And the door held open for the face of Christ to shine upon the one who asks, in innocence, to see beyond the veil of old ideas and ancient concepts held so long and dear against the vision of the Christ in you.

[**Note**: The above passage is the only place in this book where both gender nouns are used within the same passage.]

Discussion notes: Practical Truth • Practical Action • Heartfelt Thought

___

___

___

Topic 55

WHAT YOU ARE

what you are: God's Creation complete and whole, in greatness lacking nothing eternal. We are not separate from God; God is incomplete without us. No one is without God, nor anyone unworthy of God's perfect love. We are love.

Ch. 6. Sec. 1.

You cannot love what you do not appreciate, for fear makes appreciation impossible. When you are afraid of **what you are** you do not appreciate it, and will therefore reject **what you are**. As a result, you will teach rejection.

Each one must learn to teach that all forms of rejection are meaningless. Separation is the notion of rejection. This notion of rejection is not as God thinks, and you must think as God thinks if you are to know God again.

Remember that the Holy Spirit is the Communication Link between God the Mother and Her separated Daughters.

Ch. 6. Sec. 3.

As we have already emphasized, every idea begins in the mind of the thinker. You have taught yourself to believe that you are not **what you are**. You cannot teach what you have not learned.

If you are to be conflict-free, you must learn only from the Holy Spirit and teach only by the Holy Spirit. You are only love, but when you deny this, you make **what you are** something you must learn to remember. I said before that the message of the crucifixion was, "Teach only love, for that is **what you are**." This teaching only love is the one lesson that is perfectly unified, because it is the only lesson that is one. Only by teaching love can you learn love. "As you teach so will you learn." If that is true, and it is true indeed, do not forget that what you teach is teaching you. And what you project or extend you believe.

The only way to have peace is to teach peace. Everything you teach you are learning. Teach only love, and learn that love is yours and you are love.

Ch. 9. Sec. 7.

It is perfectly obvious that if the Holy Spirit looks with love on all He perceives, He looks with love on you. The Holy Spirit's evaluation of you is based on His knowledge of **what you are**, and so He evaluates you truly. And this evaluation must be in your mind, because He is in your mind. The ego is also in your mind, because you have accepted the ego there. The ego's evaluation of you, however, is the exact opposite of the Holy Spirit's, because the ego does not love you. The ego is unaware of **what you are**, and wholly mistrustful of everything it perceives because the ego's perceptions are so shifting. The ego is therefore capable of suspiciousness at best and viciousness at worst.

You have two conflicting evaluations of yourself in your mind, and they cannot both be true. You do not yet realize how completely different these evaluations of the ego and the Holy Spirit's are, because you do not understand how lofty His perception of you really is. The Holy Spirit is not deceived by anything you do, because He never forgets **what you are**.

Whenever you question your value, say:

> *God Himself is incomplete without me.*

Ch. 14. Sec. 4.

Decide that God is right and you are wrong about yourself. God created you out of Herself, but still within Her. God knows **what you are**. Remember that there is no second to God. There cannot, therefore, be anyone without God's Holiness, nor anyone unworthy of Her perfect Love.

You who have tried to throw yourself away have valued God so little. You cannot understand how much your Mother loves you, for there is no parallel in your experience of the world to help you understand it. There is nothing on earth with which you can compare your Mother's love for you, and nothing you have ever felt apart from Her resembles that love ever so faintly.

Ch. 15. Sec. 3.

When you have learned to accept **what you are**, you will make no more tiny gifts to offer to yourself, for you will know you are complete, in need of nothing, and unable to accept anything for yourself. But you will gladly give, having received God's gift. The host of God needs not seek to find anything.

Call forth in everyone only the remembrance of God, and of the Heaven that is in your brother. For where you would have your brother be, there will you think you are. Hear not your brother's appeal to hell and littleness, but only hear his call for Heaven and greatness. Forget not that your brother's call is yours.

Ch. 16. Sec. 3.

To your most holy Self all praise is due for **what you are**, and for what God is, Who created you as you are. Sooner or later must everyone bridge the gap they imagine exists between them "selves", the split-minded self and the Christ-minded Self. Everyone builds this bridge, which carries them across the imaginary gap as soon as they are willing to expend effort on behalf of bridging it.

Your bridge is built stronger than you think, and your foot is planted firmly on your bridge. Have no fear that the attraction of those who stand on the other side and wait for you will not draw you safely across. For you will come where you would be, and where your Self awaits you.

Discussion notes: Practical Truth • Practical Action • Heartfelt Thought

---

PART EIGHT

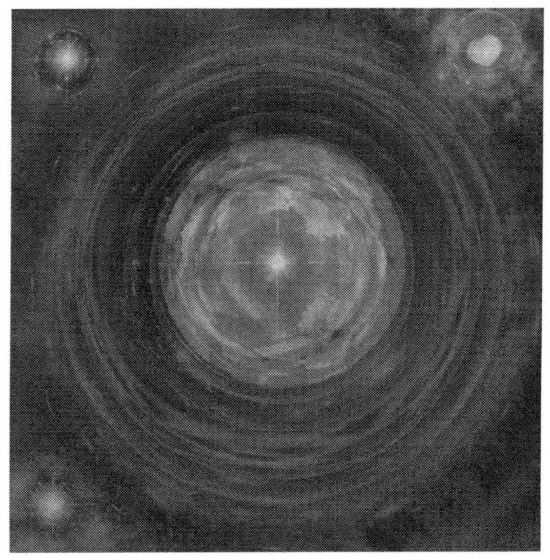

www.jgmgraphicart.com

Topics

Note: All chapter and section notations for the passages are referencing a previously published book titled *A Course in Miracles Abridged Edition.*

Topic 56

Palm Sunday and Easter

Note: In the passages below the religious holidays of Palm Sunday and Easter are characterized in a broader sense than traditionally defined. They express subject matters concerning awakening, forgiveness, redemption, awareness, us, and the Christ.

Ch. 20. Sec. 1.

This is **Palm Sunday**, the celebration of victory and the acceptance of the truth. Let us not spend this holy week brooding on the crucifixion of God's Son, but happily in the celebration of God's Son's release. For **Easter** is the sign of peace, not pain. A slain Christ has no meaning. But a risen Christ becomes the symbol of the Son of God's forgiveness on himself; the sign the Son of God looks upon himself as healed and whole.

This week we celebrate life, not death. And we honor the perfect purity of the Son of God, and not his sins. Offer your brother the gift of lilies, not the crown of thorns; the gift of love and not the "gift" of fear. You stand beside your brother, thorns of guilt in one hand and lilies of forgiveness in the other, uncertain which to give. Join now with me and throw away the thorns, offering the lilies to replace the thorns. We cannot be united in crucifixion and in death. Nor can the resurrection be complete till your forgiveness rests on Christ.

A week is short, and yet this holy week is the symbol of the whole journey the Son of God has undertaken. The Son of God started with the sign of victory, the promise of the resurrection, already given him. Let not your brother wander into the temptation of crucifixion, and delay him there in his thoughts of guilt. Help your brother to go in peace beyond guilt, with the light of his own innocence lighting his way to his redemption and release. Hold not your brother back with thorns and nails when his redemption is so near. But let the whiteness of your shining gift of lilies speed him on his way to resurrection.

If you see glimpses of the face of Christ behind the veil, looking between the snow-white petals of the lilies you have received and given as your gift of forgiveness, you will behold your brother's face and recognize it. I was a stranger and you took me in, not knowing who I was. In your forgiveness of this stranger lies your brother's release and your redemption with him.

The time of **Easter** is a time of joy, and not of mourning. Look on your risen Friend, the Christ, and celebrate your brother's holiness. For **Easter** is the time of your salvation.

Ch. 20. Sec. 2.

This **Easter**, look with different eyes upon your sister.

You have the vision now to look past all illusions. This Christ vision has been given you to see no thorns of sin and guilt, no strangers and no obstacles to peace. The fear of God is nothing to you now. Who is afraid to look upon illusions, knowing her savior stands beside her? With your sister, your Christ vision has become the greatest power for the undoing of illusion that God Herself could give. For what God gave the Holy Spirit, you have received. The Daughter of God looks unto you for her release. For you have asked for and been given the strength to look upon this final obstacle, which is the fear of God, and see no thorns of sin nor nails of guilt to crucify the Daughter of God, and crown her king of death.

Your chosen home is on the other side, beyond the veil of fear. In you the knowledge lies, ready to be unveiled and freed from all the terror that kept it hidden. There is no fear in love. The song of **Easter** is the glad refrain the Daughter of God was never crucified. Let us lift up our eyes together, not in fear but faith. And there will be no fear in us, for in our vision will be no illusions; only a pathway to the open door of Heaven, the home we share in quietness and where we live in gentleness and peace, as one together.

Would you not have your holy sister lead you there to the open door to Heaven? Your sister's innocence will light your way, offering you innocence's guiding light and sure protection, and shining from the holy altar within her where you laid the lilies of forgiveness. Let your sister be to you the savior from illusions, and look on her with the new vision that looks upon the lilies of forgiveness and brings you joy. We go beyond the veil of fear, lighting each other's way. The holiness that leads us is within us, as is our home. So will we find what we were meant to find by the Holy Spirit Who leads us.

This is the way to Heaven and to the peace of **Easter**, in which we join in glad awareness that the Daughter of God is risen from the past, and has awakened to the present. Your gift of innocence has saved your sister from the thorns and nails, and her strong arm is free to guide you safely through the veil of fear and beyond. Walk with your sister now rejoicing, for the savior from illusions has come to greet you, and lead you home with her.

Discussion notes: Practical Truth • Practical Action • Heartfelt Thought

Topic 57

Christmas

Christmas: (1) A holiday commemorating the traditional birth of Jesus. (2) A symbol for the rebirth of the Christ in ourselves; the time of Christ. Dispelling the egoic belief that sacrifice is a gift given on behalf of love.

Ch. 15. Sec. 11.

The sign of **Christmas** is a star, a light in darkness. See the light not outside yourself, but shining in the Heaven within, and accept the light as the sign the time of Christ has come. Christ comes demanding nothing. No sacrifice of any kind, of anyone, is asked by Christ. In Christ's Presence the whole idea of sacrifice loses all meaning. For Christ is Host to God. And you need but invite Christ in Who is there already, by recognizing that God's Host, the Christ, is One.

This **Christmas** give the Holy Spirit everything that would hurt you. Leave nothing behind. All pain and sacrifice and littleness will disappear in our relationship, and without sacrifice there love must be.

You who believe that sacrifice is love must learn that sacrifice is separation from love. For sacrifice brings guilt as surely as love brings peace. Guilt is the condition of sacrifice, as peace is the condition for the awareness of your relationship with God. Through guilt you exclude your Father and your brothers from yourself. Through peace you invite your brothers back, realizing that they are where your invitation bids them be. What you exclude from yourself seems fearful, for you endow what you exclude with fear and try to cast it out, though what you exclude is part of you.

Who can perceive part of himself as loathsome, and live within himself in peace? And who can try to resolve the "conflict" of Heaven and hell in him by casting Heaven out and giving Heaven the attributes of hell, without experiencing himself as incomplete and lonely?

As long as you perceive the body as your reality, so long will you perceive yourself as lonely and deprived. And so long will you also perceive yourself as a victim of sacrifice, justified in sacrificing others.

The Prince of Peace was born to re-establish the condition of love by teaching that communication remains unbroken even if the body is destroyed, provided that you see not the body as the necessary means of communication. And if you understand this lesson of communication, you will realize that to sacrifice the body is to sacrifice nothing, and communication, which must be of the mind, cannot be sacrificed. Where, then, is sacrifice? The lesson I was born to teach, and still would teach to all my brothers, is that sacrifice is nowhere and love is everywhere.

Let no despair darken the joy of **Christmas**, for the time of Christ is meaningless apart from joy. Let us join in celebrating peace by demanding no sacrifice of anyone, for so you offer me the love I offer you. What can be more joyous than to perceive we are deprived of nothing?

Discussion notes: Practical Truth • Practical Action • Heartfelt Thought

____

____

____

____

TOPIC 58

SECOND COMING

Ch. 4. Sec. 4.

The First coming of Christ is merely another name for the creation, for Christ is the Son of God. The **Second Coming** of Christ means nothing more than the end of the ego's rule and the healing of the mind. I was created like you in the First, and I have called you to join with me in the Second. I am in charge of the **Second Coming**, and my judgment, which is used only for protection, cannot be wrong because my judgment never attacks. Your judgment may be so distorted that you believe I was mistaken in choosing you. I assure you this is a mistake of your ego. Your ego is trying to convince you that the ego is real and I am not, because if I am real, you are real. That knowledge means that Christ has come into your mind and healed it.

Ch. 9. Sec. 4.

The ego literally lives on borrowed time, and the ego's days are numbered. Do not fear the Last Judgment, but welcome it and do not wait, for the ego's time is "borrowed" from your eternity. The **Second Coming** is merely the return of "sense". Can this return of sense possibly be fearful?

The **Second Coming** is the *awareness* of true reality, not its return.

Behold, my child, reality is here now. Reality belongs to you and me and God, and is perfectly satisfying to all of Us. Only this awareness heals, because reality is the awareness of truth.

Discussion notes: Practical Truth • Practical Action • Heartfelt Thought

---

TOPIC 59

PICTURE AND A FRAME

Ch. 25. Sec. 2.

A **frame** is but a means to hold a **picture** up, so that the **picture** can be seen. A **frame** that hides the **picture** has no purpose. Without a **picture** then the **frame** is without its meaning. The **frame's** purpose is to set the **picture** off, and not the **frame** itself.

Who hangs an empty **frame** upon a wall and stands before it, deep in reverence, as if a masterpiece were there to see? Yet if you see your sister as a body, it is but this you do. Would you rather see the **frame** instead of God's masterpiece?

How could the Lord of Heaven not be glad if you appreciate Her masterpiece? Forgive your sister, and you cannot separate yourself from her nor from her Mother. You and your sister are the same, as God Herself is One and not divided.

Discussion notes: Practical Truth • Practical Action • Heartfelt Thought

---

TOPIC 60

CREATE

create: (1) The extension of our spirit. God extends to us so we can extend. (2) The power of the mind to make something in this world.

Ch. 1. Sec. 7.

Child of God, you were **created** to **create** the good, the beautiful and the holy. Do not forget this.

Ch. 7. Sec. 1.

God's accomplishments are not yours, but your accomplishments are like His. God created the Sonship and you increase the Sonship. You have the power to add to the Kingdom, though not to add to the Creator of the Kingdom. You claim this power when you become vigilant for God and His Kingdom. By accepting this power as yours you have learned to remember what you are.

Your creations belong in you, as you belong in God. To **create** is to love. Love extends outward simply because love cannot be contained. Eternity is yours, because God created you eternal.

Ch. 8. Sec. 6.

God wants only Her Daughter because Her Daughter is Her only treasure. You made neither yourself nor your function. You made only the decision to be unworthy of both yourself and your function. Yet, you cannot make yourself unworthy because you are the treasure of God, and what She values is valuable. There can be no question of Her Daughter's worth, because Her Daughter's value lies in God's sharing Herself with Her Daughter and establishing Her Daughter's value forever.

Your function is to add to God's treasure by creating your treasure. God's *will* to you is Her *will* for you. God would not withhold creation from you because Her joy is in creation. God's joy lay in creating you, and She extends Her Motherhood to you so that you can extend yourself as She did. Creation is the Will of God. God's Will **created** you to **create**.

Ch. 10. Sec. Intro.

God does not change His mind about you, for He is not uncertain of Himself. God **created** you for Himself, but He gave you the power to **create** for yourself, which is to love, so you would be like Him. When anything threatens your peace of mind, ask yourself, "Has God changed His mind about me?" Then accept God's decision, for His decision is indeed changeless. God will never decide against you, or God would be deciding against Himself.

Discussion notes: Practical Truth • Practical Action • Heartfelt Thought

____

____

____

____

TOPIC 61

INHERITANCE

Ch. 3. Sec. 6.

Everyone is free to refuse to accept his **inheritance**, but he is not free to establish what his **inheritance** is.

Ch. 11. Sec. 4.

Glory is your **inheritance**, given you by your Creator that you might extend glory. Yet, if you hate part of your Self, all your understanding is lost because you are looking on what God created as yourself without love.

Only you can deprive yourself of anything. Do not oppose this realization, for this realization is truly the beginning of the dawn of light. This is a crucial step in the reawakening.

Lay blame upon yourself and you cannot know yourself. Self-blame is therefore ego identification, and as much an ego defense as blaming others.

But love yourself with the Love of Christ, for so does God love you.

Ch. 12. Sec. 4.

Your **inheritance**, which is the Kingdom of Heaven, can neither be bought nor sold. There can be no disinherited parts of the Daughtership, for God is whole and all Her extensions are like Her.

Your **inheritance** awaits only the recognition that you have been redeemed. The Holy Spirit guides you into life eternal, but you must relinquish your investment in death, or you will not see life though eternal life is all around you.

Discussion notes: Practical Truth • Practical Action • Heartfelt Thought

---

TOPIC 62

COMMUNICATION

communication: (1) The process of sending and receiving messages through verbal or nonverbal means. The exchanges and experiences of connection. The interactions within relationships. (2) The spiritual joining of minds to exchange the flow of spirit and love between us and God. Letting go of the thoughts of specialness and separation and being free to express our unified relationship.

Ch. 1. Sec. 1.

Prayer is the medium of miracles. It is a means of **communication** of the created with the Creator. Through prayer love is received, and through miracles love is expressed.

Ch. 14. Sec. 3.

You taught yourself the most unnatural habit of not **communicating** with your Creator. Yet you remain in close **communication** with your Creator, and with everything that is within Her, as everything is within yourself. Unlearn isolation through Her loving guidance, and learn of all the happy **communication** that you have thrown away but could not lose.

Whenever you are in doubt what you should do, think of the Creator's Presence in you, and tell yourself this:

She leads me and knows the way, which I know not.
Yet She will never keep from me what She would have me learn.
*And so I trust Her to **communicate** to me all that She knows for me.*

Ch. 14. Sec. 6.

All things you made have use to the Holy Spirit, for His most holy purpose. The Holy Spirit knows you are not separate from God, but He perceives much in your mind that lets you think you are.

The Holy Spirit's function is entirely **communication**. The Holy Spirit therefore must remove whatever interferes with **communication** in order to restore it. Therefore, keep no source of interference from the Holy Spirit's sight. We must open all doors and let the light come streaming through. There are no hidden chambers in God's temple. The temple gates are open wide to greet God's Son. No one can fail to come where God has called him, if he closes not the door himself upon his Father's welcome.

Ch. 14. Sec. 10.

As God **communicates** to the Holy Spirit in you, so does the Holy Spirit translate Her **communications** through you, so you can understand them. God has no secret **communications**, for everything of God is perfectly open and freely accessible to all, being for all. Nothing lives in secret, and what you would hide from the Holy Spirit is nothing.

Ch. 15. Sec. 4.

Complexity is of the ego, and complexity is nothing more than the ego's attempt to obscure the obvious. You could live forever in the holy instant, beginning now and reaching to eternity. The holy instant is a time in which you receive and give perfect **communication**. This means, however, that the holy instant is a time in which your mind is open, both to receive and give **communication**. The holy instant is the recognition that all minds are in **communication**. The holy instant therefore seeks to change nothing, but merely to accept everything.

Ch. 15. Sec. 7.

Anger takes many forms, but anger cannot long deceive those who will learn that love brings no guilt at all, and what brings guilt cannot be love and must be anger. All anger is nothing more than an attempt to make someone feel guilty. Guilt is the only need the ego has, and as long as you identify with guilt, guilt will remain attractive to you.

Remember this; to be with a body is not true **communication**.

Ch. 15. Sec. 9.

The body is the symbol of the ego, as the ego is the symbol of the separation. And both the ego and the separation are nothing more than attempts to limit **communication**, and thereby to make true **communication** impossible.

Discussion notes: Practical Truth • Practical Action • Heartfelt Thought

---

Topic 63

JOURNEY

Ch. 8. Sec. 6.

We cannot be separated. Whom God has joined cannot be separated, and God has joined all Her Daughters with Herself. Can you be separated from your life and your being? The **journey** to God is merely the reawakening of the knowledge of where you are always, and what you are forever. It is a **journey** without distance to a goal that has never changed.

Ch. 13. Sec. 7.

Whenever you are tempted to undertake a useless **journey** that would lead away from light, remember what you really want, and say:

> *The Holy Spirit leads me unto Christ, and where else would I go?*
> *What need have I but to awake in Christ?*

Then follow the Holy Spirit in joy, with faith that He will lead you safely through all dangers to your peace of mind this world may set before you. Kneel not before the altars to sacrifice, and seek not what you will surely lose. Content yourself with what you will surely keep, which is the Christ, and be not restless, for you undertake a quiet **journey** to the peace of God, where God would have you be in quietness.

Ch. 22. Sec. 4.

When you come to the place where the branch in the road is quite apparent, you cannot go ahead. You must go either one way or the other. For now if you go straight ahead, the way you went before you reached the branch, you will go nowhere. The whole purpose of coming this far on the **journey** was to decide which branch you will take now. The way you came before the branch no longer matters. The way you came before can no longer serve you. No one who reaches this branch can make the wrong decision, although you can delay your decision. And there is no part of the **journey** that seems more hopeless and futile than standing where the road branches, and not deciding on which way to go.

It is but the first few steps along the right way that seem hard, although you still may think you can go back and make the other choice.

Ch. 24. Sec. 5.

The Christ in you is very still. The Christ knows where you are going, and the Christ leads you there in gentleness and blessing all the way. The Christ's Love for God replaces all the fear you thought you saw within yourself. God's Holiness shows you the Christ in your sister whose hand you hold, and whom you lead to God. And what you see is like yourself. For what but Christ is there to see and hear and love and follow home? The Christ in you looked upon you first, but recognized that you were not complete. And so the Christ in you sought for your completion in each living thing that the Christ in you beholds and loves. And the Christ in you seeks for your completion still, that each living thing might offer you the Love of God.

The sight of Christ is all there is to see. The song of Christ is all there is to hear. The hand of Christ is all there is to hold. There is no **journey** but to walk with Christ.

Ch. 31. Sec. 4.

There is no road that leads away from God. A **journey** from yourself does not exist.

Forgive yourself your madness, and forget all senseless **journeys** and all goal-less aims. They have no meaning. You cannot escape from what you are. For God is merciful, and did not let Her Daughter abandon Her. For what God is be thankful, for in that thankfulness is your escape from madness and from death. Nowhere but where God is can you be found. There is no path that does not lead to God.

Discussion notes: Practical Truth • Practical Action • Heartfelt Thought

____

____

____

____

PART NINE

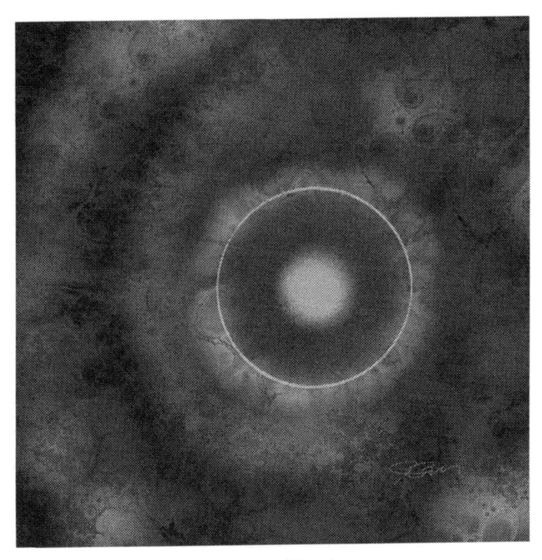

www.jgmgraphicart.com

Topics

Note: All chapter and section notations for the passages are referencing a previously published book titled *A Course in Miracles Abridged Edition.*

TOPIC 64

SOUL

Ch. 5. Sec. 2.

The Voice for God is always quiet, because It speaks of peace. Peace is stronger than war because peace heals. War is division, not increase. No one gains from strife. What profiteth it a man if he gains the whole world and loses his own **soul**? If you listen to the wrong voice you have lost sight of your **soul**. You cannot lose your **soul**, but you can know not your **soul**. Your **soul** is therefore "lost" to you until you choose right.

Ch. 12. Sec. 6.

The ego is trying to teach you how to gain the whole world and lose your own **soul**. The Holy Spirit teaches that you cannot lose your **soul** and there is no gain in the world, for of itself to gain the world profits nothing. To invest without profit is surely to impoverish yourself, and the overhead is high. Not only is there no profit in the investment of this world, but the cost to you is enormous. For investment in this world costs you the real world's reality by denying your true reality, and this impoverished world gives you nothing real in return. You cannot sell your **soul**, but you can sell your awareness of your **soul**.

You do not want this world.

Practical Truth • Practical Action • Heartfelt Thought

Topic 65

SPIRIT

spirit: The essence of divinity and creation. The substance of our true nature, which is nonphysical, eternal, formless, changeless, holy, and perfect. Spirit uses the mind to express itself in the physical world.

Ch. 1. Sec. 4.

The miracle sets reality where it belongs. Reality belongs only to **spirit**, and the miracle acknowledges only truth. The miracle thus dispels illusions about yourself, and puts you in communion with yourself and God. The miracle joins in the Atonement by placing the mind in the service of the Holy Spirit. This establishes the proper function of the mind and corrects the mind's errors, which are merely lacks of love. Your mind can be possessed by illusions, but **spirit** is eternally free. If a mind perceives without love, the mind perceives an empty shell and is unaware of the **spirit** within. But the Atonement restores **spirit** to its proper place. The mind that serves **spirit** is invulnerable.

Ch. 4. Sec. 1.

The ego is afraid of the **spirit's** joy, because once you have experienced the **spirit's** joy you will withdraw all protection from the ego, and become totally without investment in fear. Your investment is great now because fear is a witness to the separation, and your ego rejoices when you witness to the separation. Leave the ego behind! Do not listen to the ego and do not preserve the ego and separation. Listen only to God, who is as incapable of deception as is the **spirit** God created. Release yourself and release others. Do not present a false and unworthy picture of yourself to others, and do not accept such a picture of them yourself.

Ch. 4. Sec. 1. (cont.)

Of your ego you can do nothing to save yourself or others, but of your **spirit** you can do everything for the salvation of both yourself and others. Humility is a lesson for the ego, not for the **spirit**. **Spirit** is beyond humility, because **spirit** recognizes its radiance and gladly sheds its light everywhere. The meek shall inherit the earth because their egos are humble, and this gives the meek truer perception.

Spirit is far beyond the need of your protection. Remember this:

> *In this world, you need not have tribulation, because I have overcome the world.*
>
> *This is why you should be of good cheer.*

Ch. 31. Sec. 6.

You see the flesh or recognize the **spirit**. There is no compromise between the two. What you decide in this determines all you see and think is real and hold as true. On this one choice between the flesh and the **spirit** does all your world depend, for here have you established what you are, as flesh or **spirit** in your own belief. If you choose flesh, you never will escape the body as your own reality, for you have chosen that you want it so. But choose the **spirit**, and all Heaven bends to touch your eyes and bless your holy sight, that you may see the world of flesh no more except to heal and comfort and to bless.

Are you invulnerable? Then the world is harmless in your sight.

Do you forgive? Then is the world forgiving, for you have forgiven the world its trespasses, and so the world looks on you with forgiving eyes that see as yours.

Are you a body? Then is all the world perceived as treacherous, and out to kill.

Are you a **spirit**, deathless, and without the promise of corruption and the stain of sin upon you? Then the world is seen as stable, fully worthy of your trust; a happy place to rest in for a while, where nothing need be feared, but only loved.

Who is unwelcome to the kind in heart? And what could hurt the truly innocent?

Discussion notes: Practical Truth • Practical Action • Heartfelt Thought

____

____

____

____

Topic 66

TEMPTATION

temptation: The perception that things can bring us satisfaction as a substitute for love. The lure of something having a powerful appeal, making it hard to resist. An attraction to make a wrong decision that would lead to an outcome you do not want. Temptation feeds on the internal feeling of lacking things, love, and specialness.

Ch. 1. Sec. 3.

You are the work of God, and His work is wholly lovable and wholly loving. This is how a man must think of himself in his heart, because this is what he is, wholly lovable and wholly loving.

"Lead us not into **temptation**" means "recognize your errors and choose to abandon them."

Ch. 31. Sec. 1.

What is **temptation** but a wish to make the wrong decision on what you would learn, and have an outcome that you do not want? It is the recognition that **temptation** is a state of mind unwanted that becomes the means whereby the choice is reassessed; another outcome seen to be preferred. You are deceived if you believe you want disaster and disunity and pain. Hear not the call for **temptation** within yourself. But listen, rather, to the deeper call beyond **temptation** that appeals for peace and joy. And all the world will give you joy and peace. For as you hear, you answer. And behold! Your answer is the proof of what you learned. The answer's outcome is the world you look upon.

Let us be still an instant, and forget all the past things we ever learned, all thoughts we had, and every preconception that we hold of what things mean and what their purpose is. Let us remember not our own past ideas of what the world is for. We do not know. Let every past image held of everyone be loosened from our minds and swept away.

Ch. 31. Sec. 7.

Be vigilant against **temptation**, then, remembering that **temptation** is but a wish, insane and meaningless, to make yourself a thing that you are not. And think as well upon the thing that you would be instead. **Temptation** is a thing of madness, pain and death; a thing of treachery and black despair, of failing dreams and no remaining hope except to die, and end the dream of fear. This is **temptation**; nothing more than this. Can **temptation's** failing dreams be difficult to choose against? Consider what **temptation** is, and see the real alternatives you choose between. There are but two choices. Be not deceived by what appears as many choices. There is hell or Heaven, and of these you choose but one.

Ch. 31. Sec. 8.

The images you make cannot prevail against what God Herself would have you be. Be never fearful of **temptation**, then, but see **temptation** as it is; another chance to choose again, and let Christ's strength prevail in every circumstance and every place you raised an image of yourself before. For what appears to hide the face of Christ is powerless before Her majesty, and disappears before Her holy sight. The saviors of the world, who see like Christ, are merely those who choose Christ's strength instead of their own weakness, which they see apart from Christ. The saviors will redeem the world, for they are joined in all the power of the Will of God. And what they will is only what God wills.

Learn, then, the happy habit of response to all **temptation** to perceive yourself as weak and miserable with these words:

I am as God created me.
Her Daughter can suffer nothing.
And I am Her Daughter.

Thus is Christ's strength invited to prevail, replacing all your weakness with the strength that comes from God and that can never fail. And thus are miracles as natural as fear and agony appeared to be before the choice for holiness was made. For in that choice are false distinctions gone, illusory alternatives laid by, and nothing left to interfere with truth.

You are as God created you, and so is every living thing you look upon, regardless of the images you see. What you behold as sickness and as pain, as weakness and as suffering and loss, is but **temptation** to perceive yourself defenseless and in hell. Yield not to this, and you will see all pain, in every form, wherever it occurs, but disappear as mists before the sun. A miracle has come to heal God's Daughter, and close the door upon her dreams of weakness, opening the way to her salvation and release. Choose once again what you would have God's Daughter be, remembering that every choice you make establishes your own identity as you will see it, and believe it is.

For it is given you to join with your sister, and through the Christ in you, unveil her eyes, and let her look upon the Christ in her.

Discussion notes: Practical Truth • Practical Action • Heartfelt Thought

TOPIC 67

CONFLICT

conflict: Mental struggle resulting from incompatible or opposing needs, drives, or wishes, fueled by external or internal demands.

Ch. 2. Sec. 7.

The fundamental **conflict** in this world, then, is between creation and mis-creation. All fear is implicit in the second, and all love in the first. The **conflict** is therefore one between love and fear.

It has already been said that you believe you cannot control fear because you yourself made fear, and your belief in fear seems to render fear out of your control. Yet any attempt to resolve the error through attempting the mastery of fear is useless. In fact, it asserts the power of fear by the very assumption that fear need be mastered. The true resolution rests entirely on mastery through love. In the interim, however, the sense of **conflict** is inevitable, since you have placed yourself in a position where you believe in the power of what does not exist, which is fear.

Ch. 7. Sec. 8.

The ego's use of projection and anger can be finally undone. The ego always tries to preserve **conflict**. The ego is very ingenious in devising ways that seem to diminish **conflict**, because the ego does not want you to find **conflict** so intolerable that you will insist on giving the **conflict** up. The ego therefore tries to persuade you that it can free you of **conflict**, lest you give the ego up and free yourself. The ego utilizes the power of the mind only to defeat the mind's real purpose which is to free yourself. The ego projects **conflict** from your mind to other minds, in an attempt to persuade you that you have gotten rid of the problem of **conflict**.

Ch. 11. Sec. 3.

Pain is not of God, for He knows no attack and His peace surrounds you silently. God is very quiet, for there is no **conflict** in God. **Conflict** is the root of all evil, for being blind, **conflict** does not see whom it attacks. Yet **conflict** always attacks the Son of God, and the Son of God is you.

God's Son is indeed in need of comfort. The Kingdom is the Son of God's Kingdom.

Ch. 23. Sec. 1.

Conflict must be between two forces. **Conflict** cannot exist between one power and nothingness. There is nothing you could attack that is not part of you. And by attacking the nothingness of illusion, you make two illusions of yourself, in **conflict** with each other. And this **conflict** about yourself occurs whenever you look on anything that God created with anything but love. **Conflict** is fearful, for **conflict** is the birth of fear. Yet what is born of nothing cannot win reality through battle. Why would you fill your world with **conflicts** with yourself? Let all this madness be undone for you, and turn in peace to the remembrance of God, still shining in your quiet mind.

See how the **conflict** of illusions disappears when it is brought to truth! For the **conflict** seems real only as long as **conflict** is seen as war between **conflicting** truths; the conqueror to be the truer, the more real, and the vanquisher of the illusion that was less real. Thus, **conflict** is the choice between illusions, one to be crowned as real, the other vanquished and despised. Here within the **conflict** of illusions will the Mother never be remembered. Yet no illusion can invade the Mother's home and drive Her out of what She loves forever. And what the Mother loves must be forever quiet and at peace because it is Her home.

Ch. 24. Sec. 5.

There must be doubt before there can be **conflict**. And every doubt must be about yourself. Christ has no doubt, and from Her certainty Her quiet comes. The Christ will exchange Her certainty for all your doubts, if you agree that the Christ is One with you, and that this Oneness is endless, timeless, and within your grasp because your hands are the hands of Christ. The Christ is within you, yet the Christ walks beside you and before, leading the way that She must go to find Herself complete. The Christ's quietness becomes your certainty. And where is doubt when certainty has come?

Discussion notes: Practical Truth • Practical Action • Heartfelt Thought

TOPIC 68

JUSTICE

justice: (1) The principle that determines fair and righteous conduct and unbiased treatment. (2) Giving love and forgiveness to everyone with complete impartiality. Restoration without retribution.

Ch. 25. Sec. 9.

The miracle that you receive, you give. Each miracle is an example of what **justice** can accomplish when **justice** is offered to everyone alike. **Justice** is received and given equally. **Justice** is awareness that giving and receiving are the same. Because **justice** does not make the same unlike, **justice** sees no differences where none exists. And thus **justice** is the same for everyone, because it sees no differences in anyone. **Justice's** offering is universal, and it teaches but one message:

What is God's belongs to everyone, and is everyone's due.

Ch. 25. Sec. 8.

There is a kind of **justice** in salvation of which this world knows nothing. To this world, **justice** and vengeance are the same, for sinners see **justice** only as their punishment, perhaps sustained by someone else, but not escaped. The laws of sin demand a victim. Who the victim is makes little difference. This is not **justice**, but insanity. Yet how could **justice** be defined without insanity where love means hate, and death is seen as victory and triumph over eternity and timelessness and life?

It is extremely hard for those who still believe sin is meaningful, to understand the Holy Spirit's **justice**. They must believe the Holy Spirit shares their own confusion, and cannot avoid the vengeance that their own belief in **justice** must entail. And so they fear the Holy Spirit, and perceive the "wrath" of God in Him. Nor can they trust Him not to strike them dead with lightning bolts torn from the "fires" of Heaven by God's Own angry Hand. They do believe that Heaven is hell, and are afraid of love. And deep suspicion and the chill of fear comes over them when they are told that they have never sinned. Their fearful world depends on sin's stability.

So do they, who still believe sin is meaningful, think the loss of sin a curse. And flee the Holy Spirit as if He were a messenger from hell, sent from above, in treachery and guile, to work God's vengeance on them in the guise of a deliverer and friend. What could the Holy Spirit be to them except a devil, dressed to deceive within an angel's cloak. And what escape has the Holy Spirit for them, who still believe sin is meaningful, except a door to hell that seems to look like Heaven's gate?

Yet **justice** cannot punish those who ask for punishment, but have a Judge Who knows that they are wholly innocent in truth. In **justice**, the Holy Spirit is bound to set them free, and give them all the honor they deserve and have denied themselves because they cannot understand that they are innocent. Love is not understandable to sinners because they think that **justice** is split off from love, and stands for something else. And thus is love perceived as weak, and vengeance strong.

You can be a perfect witness to the power of love and **justice**, if you understand it is impossible the Son of God could merit vengeance. This understanding that you need comes not of you, but from a larger Self, the Christ.

Without impartiality there is no **justice**. To take from one to give another must be an injustice to them both, since they are equal in the Holy Spirit's sight. Their Father gave the same inheritance to both. Who would have more or less is not aware that he has everything.

You have the right to all the universe; to perfect peace, complete deliverance from all effects of sin, and to the life eternal, joyous and complete in every way, as God appointed for His holy Son. This is the only **justice** Heaven knows, and all the Holy Spirit brings to earth. Your special function of extending love and forgiveness to another shows you nothing else but perfect **justice** can prevail for you. And you are safe from vengeance in all forms.

The world deceives, but the world cannot replace God's **justice** with a version of its own. For only love is **just**, and only love can perceive what **justice** must accord the Son of God. Let love decide, and never fear that you, in your own unfairness, will deprive yourself of what God's **justice** has allotted you.

Ch. 25. Sec. 9.

What can it be but arrogance to think your little errors cannot be undone by Heaven's **justice**? And what could this mean except that you believe your errors are sins and not mistakes, forever uncorrectable, and to be met with vengeance, not with **justice**? Are you willing to be released from all effects of sin? You cannot answer this question until you see all that the answer must entail. For if you answer "yes" to this question of your willingness to be released from all effects of sin, it means you will forego all values of this world in favor of the peace of Heaven. Not one sin would you retain. And not one doubt that this is possible will you hold dear that sin be kept in place. You mean that truth has greater value now than all illusions. And you recognize that truth must be revealed to you, because you know not what truth is.

To give reluctantly is not to gain the gift, because you are reluctant to accept it. The gift is saved for you until reluctance to receive the gift disappears, and you are willing to let the gift be given you. God's **justice** warrants gratitude, not fear. Nothing you give is lost to you or anyone, but cherished and preserved in Heaven, where all of the treasures given to God's Daughter are kept for her, and offered anyone who but holds out her hand in willingness these treasures be received. Nor is the treasure less as the treasure is given out. Each gift but adds to the supply. For God is fair. God does not fight against Her Daughter's reluctance to perceive salvation as a gift from Her. Yet would God's **justice** not be satisfied until the gift of salvation is received by everyone.

The sight of innocence makes punishment impossible, and **justice** sure. The Holy Spirit's perception leaves no ground for an attack. Only a loss could justify attack, and loss of any kind the Holy Spirit cannot see. The limited world solves problems in another way. The world sees a resolution as a state in which it is decided who shall win and who shall lose; how much the one shall take, and how much can the loser still defend. Yet does the problem still remain unsolved, for only **justice** can set up a state in which there is no loser; no one left unfairly treated and deprived.

Ch. 26. Sec. 2.

The miracle of **justice** can correct all errors. Every problem is an error. The Holy Spirit does not evaluate injustices as great or small, or more or less. Injustices are mistakes from which the Son of God is suffering, but needlessly. And so He takes the thorns and nails away.

Ask not God to punish others because you find them guilty and would have them die. God offers you the means to see others innocence.

If God is **just**, then can there be no problems that **justice** cannot solve. But there are those who you believe need to be punished and you want them to suffer loss, and there is no one whom you wish to be preserved from sacrifice entirely. Consider once again your special function. This special function is given you to see in others perfect sinlessness.

And you will ask no sacrifice of others because you could not *will* they suffer loss. This miracle of **justice** you call forth will rest on you as surely as on them. Nor will the Holy Spirit be content until the miracle of God's **justice** is received by everyone. For what you give to God is everyone's, and by your giving the miracle of **justice**, can God ensure that everyone receives the gift of God's **justice** equally.

God cannot be remembered until **justice** is loved instead of feared. God cannot be unjust to anyone or anything, because He knows that everything that is belongs to Him, and will forever be as He created it. Nothing God loves but must be sinless and beyond attack. Your special function opens wide the door beyond which is the memory of God's Love kept perfectly intact and undefiled. And all you need to do is but to wish that Heaven be given you instead of hell, and every bolt and barrier that seems to hold the door securely barred and locked will merely fall away and disappear. For it is not your Father's Will that you should offer or receive less than He gave, when He created you in perfect love.

Discussion notes: Practical Truth • Practical Action • Heartfelt Thought

TOPIC 69

CRUCIFIXION AND RESURRECTION

crucifixion: The symbol of the ego, whereas resurrection is the symbol of awakening. Each day, each hour, and each moment, we decide between the crucifixion and the resurrection, between the ego and God. The ego is the choice for guilt, and God is the choice for guiltlessness.

resurrection: The reawakening of the mind. Awareness of the Christ within. Transcending the ego perceptions of the world, the body, and death.

Ch. 4. Sec. Intro.

You can speak from the spirit or from the ego, as you choose. If you speak from spirit you have chosen to "Be still and know that I am God." These words are inspired because they reflect knowledge. If you speak from the ego you are disclaiming knowledge instead of affirming it, and are thus dis-spiriting yourself. Do not embark on useless journeys, because they are indeed in vain. The ego may desire useless journeys, but spirit cannot embark on them because spirit is forever unwilling to depart from its foundation.

The journey to the cross should be the last "useless journey." Do not dwell upon the journey to the cross, but dismiss it as accomplished. You are free to join my **resurrection**. Until you do so your life is indeed wasted. Your life merely re-enacts the separation, the loss of power, the futile attempts of the ego at reparation, and finally the **crucifixion** of the body, or death. Such repetitions are endless until they are voluntarily given up. Do not make the error of "clinging to the old rugged cross." The only message of the **crucifixion** is that you can overcome the cross. Until then, you are free to **crucify** yourself as often as you choose. This clinging to the cross is not the gospel I intended to offer you.

Ch. 6. Sec. 1.

Projection means anger, anger fosters assault, and assault promotes fear.

The message the **crucifixion** was intended to teach was that it is not necessary to perceive any form of assault in persecution. If you respond with anger, you must be equating yourself with the destructible, and are therefore regarding yourself insanely.

You are free to perceive yourself as persecuted if you choose. When you do choose to react that way, however, you might remember that I was persecuted as the world judges, and did not share this evaluation for myself.

If you react as if you are persecuted, you are teaching persecution. This teaching of persecution is not a lesson a Son of God should want to teach if he is to realize his own salvation. Rather, teach your own perfect immunity, which is the truth in you, and realize that your own perfect immunity cannot be assailed. Do not try to protect it yourself, or you are believing that it is assailable. You are not asked to be **crucified**, which was part of my own teaching contribution. You are merely asked to follow my example in the face of much less extreme temptations to misperceive, and not to accept them as false justifications for anger.

Your **resurrection** is your reawakening. I am the model for rebirth, but rebirth itself is merely the dawning on your mind of what is already in your mind. God placed your rebirth there Himself, and so your reawakening is true forever. I believed in your reawakening, and therefore accepted it as true for me. Help me to teach reawakening to our brothers in the name of the Kingdom of God, but first believe that reawakening is true for you.

I elected, for your sake and mine, to demonstrate that the most outrageous assault does not matter. As the world judges these things, but not as God knows them, I was betrayed, abandoned, beaten, torn, and finally killed. It was clear that this assault on my body was only because of the projection of others onto me, since I had not harmed anyone and had healed many.

We are still equal as learners, although we do not need to have equal experiences. The Holy Spirit is glad when you can learn from my experiences, and be reawakened by them. That is my experiences only purpose, and that is the only way in which I can be perceived as the way, the truth and the life.

The **crucifixion** cannot be shared because the **crucifixion** is the symbol of projection, but the **resurrection** is the symbol of sharing because the reawakening of every Son of God is necessary to enable the Sonship to know the Sonship's Wholeness. Only this reawakening is knowledge.

The Apostles often misunderstood **crucifixion**, and for the same reason that anyone misunderstands it. The Apostles own imperfect love made them vulnerable to projection, and out of their own fear they spoke of the "wrath of God" as God's retaliatory weapon.

I do not want you to allow any fear to enter into the thought system toward which I am guiding you. I do not call for martyrs but for teachers. No one is punished for sins, and the Sons of God are not sinners. Any concept of punishment involves the projection of blame, and reinforces the idea that blame is justified.

Ch. 11. Sec. 6.

The **resurrection** is the complete triumph of Christ over the ego, not by attack but by transcendence.

Ch. 11. Sec. 6. (cont.)

Resurrection must compel your allegiance gladly, because **resurrection** is the symbol of joy. The **resurrection's** whole compelling power lies in the fact that it represents what you want to be. The freedom to leave behind everything that hurts you and humbles you and frightens you cannot be thrust upon you, but this freedom can be offered you through the grace of God. And you can accept this freedom by God's grace, for God is gracious to Her Daughter, accepting her without question as Her Own.

You have nailed yourself to a cross, and placed a crown of thorns upon your own head. Yet you cannot **crucify** God's Daughter, for the will of God cannot die. God's Daughter has been redeemed from her own **crucifixion**, and you cannot assign to death whom God has given eternal life. The dream of **crucifixion** still lies heavy on your eyes, but what you see in dreams is not reality. While you perceive the Daughter of God as **crucified**, you are asleep.

You will awaken to your own call, for the Call to awake is within you. Do not set limits on what you believe I can do through you, or you will not accept what I can do for you. Yet it is done already, and unless you give all that you have received you will not know that your redeemer liveth, and that you have awakened with your redeemer. Redemption is recognized by sharing it.

Ch. 12. Sec. 2.

I will awaken you as surely as I awakened myself, for I awoke for you. In my **resurrection** is your release. Our mission is to escape from **crucifixion**, not from redemption.

Ch. 14. Sec. 3.

Each day, each hour and minute, even each second, you are deciding between the **crucifixion** and the **resurrection**; between the ego and the Holy Spirit. The ego is the choice for guilt; the Holy Spirit the choice for guiltlessness. The power of decision is all that is yours. What you can decide between is fixed, because there are no alternatives except truth and illusion. And there is no overlap between truth and illusion, because truth and illusion are opposites, which cannot be reconciled and cannot both be true. You are guilty or guiltless, bound or free, unhappy or happy.

Ch. 19. Sec. 4.

Offer your brother freedom and complete release from sin. So will we prepare together the way unto the **resurrection** of God's Son, and let him rise again to glad remembrance of his Father, Who knows no sin, no death, but only life eternal.

Think carefully how you would look upon the giver of this gift, for as you look on him so will the gift itself appear to be. As he is seen as either the giver of guilt or of salvation, so will his offering be seen and so received.

The **crucified** give pain because the **crucified** are in pain. But the redeemed give joy because the redeemed have been healed of pain. Everyone gives as he receives, but he must choose what it will be that he receives, either guilt or salvation. And in pain or joy he will recognize his choice by what he gives, and what is given him.

Ch. 26. Sec. 5.

Let the dead and gone be peacefully forgotten. **Resurrection** has come to take death's place. And now you are a part of **resurrection**, not of death. No past illusions have the power to keep you in a place of death, a vault God's Daughter entered an instant, to be instantly restored unto her Mother's perfect Love. And how can she be kept in chains long since removed and gone forever from her mind?

Ch. 26. Sec. 7.

Forgiveness is the answer to attack of any kind. So, when you forgive, attack is deprived of its effects, and hate is answered in the name of love. To you to whom your function has been given to save the Son of God from **crucifixion** and from hell and death, all glory be forever. For you have power to save the Son of God because his Father willed that it be so. And in your hands does all salvation lie, to be both offered and received as one.

Discussion notes: Practical Truth • Practical Action • Heartfelt Thought

TOPIC 70

FORGIVE AND FORGIVENESS

forgiveness: A choice to see ourselves and others with the vision of Christ, which shifts our perception away from blame, resentment, punishment, and differences. Being able to take ownership of our feelings, thoughts, and actions without judgment. In this way, we can view wrongness as a projection of separation and understand that forgiveness is the plan for salvation for everyone. To forgive is to overlook what happened in the past. To forgive can feel difficult to do, but it can be done with a willingness to use our intention and attention to extend love. Forgiveness is the path to peace, joy, freedom, and power.

Ch. 1. Sec. 1.

Miracles are natural signs of **forgiveness**. Through miracles you accept God's **forgiveness** by extending God's **forgiveness** to others.

Ch. 9. Sec. 4.

To **forgive** is to overlook. Look, then, beyond error and do not let your perception rest upon the error, for you will believe what your perception holds. Accept as true only what your sister is, if you would know yourself. Perceive what your sister is not and you cannot know what you are, because you see your sister falsely. Remember always that your Identity as the Daughter of God is shared, and that Its sharing is the Daughter of God's reality.

Forgiveness through the Holy Spirit lies simply in looking beyond error from the beginning, and thus keeping the error unreal for you.

Follow the Holy Spirit's teaching in **forgiveness** because **forgiveness** is Her function, and She knows how to fulfill Her function perfectly. That is what I meant when I said that miracles are natural. Miracles are merely the sign of your willingness to follow the Holy Spirit's plan of salvation.

Ch. 15. Sec. 8.

The holy instant does not replace the need for learning, for the Holy Spirit must not leave you as your Teacher until the holy instant has extended far beyond time. In the face of your fear of **forgiveness**, which the Holy Spirit perceives as clearly as the Holy Spirit knows **forgiveness** is release, the Holy Spirit will teach you to remember that **forgiveness** is not loss, but that **forgiveness** is your salvation. And that in complete **forgiveness**, in which you recognize that there is nothing to **forgive**, you are absolved completely.

Ch. 17. Sec. 2.

Can you imagine how beautiful those you **forgive** will look to you? In no fantasy have you ever seen anything so lovely as in those you **forgive**. Nothing you see here, sleeping or waking, comes near to such loveliness. Nothing that you remember that made your heart sing with joy has ever brought you even a little part of the happiness this sight of your **forgiven** brother will bring you. For you will see the Son of God. You will behold the beauty the Holy Spirit loves to look upon, and which He thanks the Father for. The Holy Spirit was created to see this **forgiveness** for you, until you learned to see the loveliness for yourself. And all His teaching leads to seeing this loveliness of **forgiveness** and giving thanks with Him.

This loveliness is not a fantasy. This loveliness is the real world, bright and clean and new, with everything sparkling under the open sun. Nothing is hidden here in the real world, for everything has been **forgiven** and there are no fantasies to hide the truth. The bridge between the world of fantasies and this world of truth is so little and so easy to cross, that you could not believe it is the meeting place of worlds so different. Yet this little bridge is the strongest thing that touches on this fantasy world at all. This little step, so small it has escaped your notice, is a stride through time into eternity, beyond all ugliness into beauty that will enchant you, and will never cease to cause you wonderment at eternity's perfection.

Ch. 25. Sec. 6.

The grace of God rests gently on **forgiving** eyes, and everything they look on speaks of God to the beholder. She who sees with **forgiving** eyes can see no evil; nothing in the world to fear, and no one who is different from herself. And as she who sees with **forgiving** eyes loves everything, so she looks upon herself with love and gentleness. She would no more condemn herself for her mistakes, than damn another. She who sees with **forgiving** eyes is not an arbiter of vengeance, nor a punisher of sin. The kindness of her sight rests on herself with all the tenderness it offers others. For she who sees with **forgiving** eyes would only heal and only bless.

The wish to see with **forgiving** eyes calls down the grace of God upon your eyes, and brings the gift of light that makes sight possible. God is glad to have you look on your sister. Let your sister no more be lonely, for the lonely ones are those who see no function in the world for them to fill; no place where the lonely are needed, and no aim which only they can perfectly fulfill.

Here, in the world of time, where the laws of God do not prevail in perfect form, can she yet do one perfect thing and make one perfect choice. And by this act of special faithfulness to one perceived as other than herself, she learns the gift of **forgiveness** was given to herself, and so she and her sister must be one.

Forgiveness is the only function meaningful in time. **Forgiveness** is for all. When **forgiveness** rests on all, **forgiveness** is complete, and every function of this world completed with it. Then is time no more. Yet while in time, there is still much to do. And each one must do what is allotted her, for on her part does all the plan depend.

Ch. 26. Sec. 4.

Nothing in boundless love could need **forgiveness**.

Forgiveness turns the world of sin into a world of glory, wonderful to see. Each flower shines in light, and every bird sings of the joy of Heaven. There is no sadness and there is no parting here, for everything is totally **forgiven** in this world turned from sin to glory. And what has been **forgiven** must join, for nothing stands between to keep the **forgiven** separate and apart.

Ch. 26. Sec. 7.

Forgiveness is the only function here in this world of time, and **forgiveness** serves to bring the joy this world denies to every aspect of God's Daughter where sin was thought to rule. Perhaps you do not see the role **forgiveness** plays in ending death and all beliefs that rise from mists of guilt. Sins are beliefs that you impose between your sister and yourself.

Forgiveness takes away what stands between your sister and yourself.

Ch. 27. Sec. 2.

Forgiveness is not pity, which but seeks to pardon what the **forgiver** thinks to be the truth. Who can say and mean, "My brother, you have injured me, and yet, because I am the better of the two, I pardon you my hurt." His pardon and your hurt cannot exist together. One denies the other and must make the other false.

He who truly pardons holds not the proof of sin before his brother's eyes. And thus he must have overlooked sin and removed it from his own. **Forgiveness** cannot be for one and not the other. Who **forgives** is healed. And in his healing lies the proof that he has truly pardoned, and retains no trace of condemnation that he still would hold against himself or any living thing.

Forgiveness is not real unless it brings a healing to your brother and yourself. You must attest your brother's sins have no effect on you to demonstrate they are not real. How else could your brother be guiltless? And how could your brother's innocence be justified unless his sins have no effect to warrant guilt? In sins undoing lies the proof that sins are merely errors. Let yourself be healed that you may be **forgiving**, offering salvation to your brother and yourself.

Your healing saves your brother pain as well as you, and you are healed because you wished him well.

Ch. 29. Sec. 6.

How willing are you to **forgive** your sister? How much do you desire peace instead of endless strife and misery and pain? These questions about **forgiveness** are the same, in different form. **Forgiveness** is your peace, for herein lies the end of separation and the dream of danger and destruction, sin and death; of madness and of murder, grief and loss. **Forgiveness** is the "sacrifice" salvation asks, and gladly offers peace instead of endless strife and misery and pain.

Ch. 30. Sec. 6.

No one who sees himself as guilty can avoid the fear of God. But he is saved from this dilemma of guilt if he can **forgive**. The mind must think of its Creator as the mind looks upon itself. If you can see your brother merits pardon, you have learned **forgiveness** is your right as much as your brother's. Nor will you think that God intends for you a fearful judgment that your brother does not merit. For it is the truth that you can merit neither more nor less than your brother.

You must **forgive** God's Son entirely. Or you will keep an image of yourself that is not whole, and you will remain afraid to look within and find escape from every idol there. Salvation rests on faith, there cannot be some forms of guilt that you cannot **forgive**.

Discussion notes: Practical Truth • Practical Action • Heartfelt Thought

Topic 71

GUILT OR GUILTLESS

guilt: (1) The negative emotion experienced when we believe we have committed an offense or wrongdoing, causing us to feel separated from God and others. Fear arises because we mistakenly think God will punish us for our misconduct (errors), which continues the cycle of feeling guilty and afraid. Guilt can cause us to attack others or ourselves. (2) Fear-based thoughts that reinforce the illusion we are incomplete or inadequate and that there is something fundamentally wrong with us. [Note: Guilt can be valuable as a prompt to consider improvement of a behavior, or to determine if there is a need to take a responsible action; such as, apologize, set a boundary, or pursue further conversations to clarify things. Subsequently, the goal is to let go of guilt.]

guiltless and guiltlessness: The removal of the concept of guilt. We are not guilty but rather in a state of growth and awakening where our errors and mistakes exist. Past errors may affect current circumstances, like robbing a bank and being sent to prison. However, guilt is the memory of an action we wish we could change. Guilt can keep us stuck in the past or troubled about the future, which distracts us from living in the present moment.

Ch. 5. Sec. 7.

Whenever you are not wholly joyous, your lack of joy is because you have reacted with a lack of love to one of God's creations. Perceiving this lack of love as "sin" you become defensive because you expect attack. The decision to react in this way is yours, and therefore your decision can be undone. The reaction to your lack of love cannot be undone by repentance in the usual sense, because repentance implies **guilt**. If you allow yourself to feel **guilty**, you will reinforce the error rather than allow the error to be undone for you.

The first step in the undoing of **guilt** is to recognize that you actively decided wrongly, but can as actively decide otherwise. Be very firm with yourself in this choosing, and keep yourself fully aware that the undoing process, which does not come from you, is nevertheless within you because God placed the undoing process there. Your part is merely to return your thinking to the point at which the error was made, and give the error over to the Atonement in peace.

Ch. 13. Sec. Intro.

If you did not feel **guilty** you could not attack, for condemnation is the root of attack. Condemnation is the judgment of one mind by another as unworthy of love and deserving of punishment. But herein lies the split. For the mind that judges, perceives itself as separate from the mind being judged, believing that by punishing another, the mind that judges will escape punishment.

The acceptance of **guilt** into the mind of God's Daughter was the beginning of the separation, as the acceptance of the Atonement is separation's end. The world of **guilt** you see is the delusional system of those made mad by **guilt**. Look carefully at this world of **guilt**, and you will realize that this is so.

Ch. 13. Sec. 1.

Love and **guilt** cannot coexist, and to accept one is to deny the other. **Guilt** hides Christ from your sight, for **guilt** is the denial of the blamelessness of God's Son.

Without **guilt** the ego has no life. And God's Son is without **guilt**.

Ch. 13. Sec. 1. (cont.)

As you look upon yourself and judge what you do honestly, you may be tempted to wonder how you can be **guiltless**. Yet consider this: You are not **guiltless** in time, but in eternity. You have "sinned" in the past, but there is no past. Time seems to go in one direction, but when you reach time's end time will roll up like a long carpet spread along the past behind you, and time will disappear. As long as you believe the Daughter of God is **guilty** you will walk along this carpet, believing that time leads to death. And the journey will seem long and cruel and senseless, for so it is.

The journey the Daughter of God has set herself on is useless indeed, but the journey on which her Mother sets her is one of release and joy. The Mother is not cruel, and Her Daughter cannot hurt herself. The retaliation that she fears and that she sees will never touch her, for although she believes in God's retaliation the Holy Spirit knows it is not true. The Holy Spirit stands at the end of time, where you must be because She is with you. She has already undone everything unworthy of the Daughter of God, for such was the Holy Spirit's mission, given Her by God. And what God gives has always been.

For the idea of **guilt** brings a belief in condemnation of one by another, projecting separation in place of unity. You can condemn only yourself, and by so doing you cannot know that you are God's Daughter. You have denied the condition of God's Daughter's being, which is her perfect blamelessness. Out of love God's Daughter was created, and in love God's Daughter abides.

As you perceive the holy companions who travel with you, you will realize that there is no journey, but only an awakening. There is no road to travel on, and no time to travel through. For God waits not for Her Daughter in time, being forever unwilling to be without Her Daughter. And so it has always been. Let the holiness of God's Daughter shine away the cloud of **guilt** that darkens your mind.

You are invulnerable because you are **guiltless**. You can hold on to the past only through **guilt**. For **guilt** establishes that you will be punished for what you have done, and thus depends on one-dimensional time, proceeding from past to future. No one who believes this can understand what "always" means, and therefore **guilt** must deprive you of the appreciation of eternity. You are immortal because you are eternal, and "always" must be now. And immortality is the opposite of time, for time passes away, while immortality is constant.

The ego teaches you to attack yourself because you are **guilty**, and this will increase the **guilt**, for **guilt** is the result of attack. In the ego's teaching, then, there is no escape from **guilt**. For attack makes **guilt** real, and if **guilt** is real there is no way to overcome **guilt**. The Holy Spirit dispels **guilt** simply through the calm recognition that it has never been. As the Holy Spirit looks upon the **guiltless** Daughter of God, the Daughter of God knows that this is true. And being true for you, you cannot attack yourself, for without **guilt** attack is impossible. You, then, are saved because God's Daughter is **guiltless**. And being wholly pure, you are invulnerable.

Ch. 13. Sec. 2.

The ultimate purpose of projection is always to get rid of **guilt**. Yet, characteristically, the ego attempts to get rid of **guilt** from the ego's viewpoint only, for much as the ego wants to retain **guilt** you find **guilt** intolerable, since **guilt** stands in the way of your remembering God.

You project **guilt** outward to get rid of it, but you are actually merely concealing **guilt**. You do experience the **guilt**, but you have no idea why. On the contrary, you associate **guilt** with a weird assortment of "ego ideals," which the ego claims you have failed. Yet you have no idea that you are failing the Son of God by seeing him as **guilty**.

Ch. 13. Sec. 2. (cont.)

You have perhaps recognized the futility of the ego and its offerings, but though you do not want the ego's offerings, you may not yet look upon the alternative with gladness. In the extreme, you are afraid of redemption and you believe redemption will kill you. Make no mistake about the depth of this fear of redemption. For you believe that, in the presence of truth, you might turn on yourself and destroy yourself.

Little child, this is not so. Your "**guilty** secret", that redemption will kill you is nothing, and if you will but bring your **guilt** to the light, the light will dispel the **guilt**. And then no dark cloud will remain between you and the remembrance of your Father, for you will remember God's **guiltless** Son, who did not die because he is immortal. And you will see that you were redeemed with God's **guiltless** Son, and have never been separated from him. In this understanding lies your remembering, for this understanding is the recognition of love without fear. There will be great joy in Heaven on your homecoming, and the joy will be yours. For the redeemed son of man is the **guiltless** Son of God, and to recognize him is your redemption.

Ch. 13. Sec. 9.

The **guilty** always condemn, and having done so the **guilty** will still condemn, linking the future to the past as is the ego's law. The ego's laws are strict, and breaches are severely punished. Therefore, give no obedience to its laws, for they are laws of punishment. And those who follow them believe that they are guilty, and so they must condemn. Between the future and the past, the laws of God must intervene, if you would free yourself. Atonement, which is the extension of forgiveness, stands between the ego's laws and God's laws, like a lamp shining so brightly that the chain of darkness in which you bound yourself will disappear.

See no one as **guilty**, and you will affirm the truth of **guiltlessness** unto yourself. In every condemnation that you offer the Daughter of God lies the conviction of your own **guilt**. If you would have the Holy Spirit make you free of condemnation, accept Her offer of Atonement for all your sisters. For so you learn that the Atonement is true for you.

Guilt makes you blind, for while you see **guilt** within you, you will not see the light. And by projecting **guilt**, the world seems dark, and shrouded in your **guilt**. You throw a dark veil over the world, and cannot see the world because you cannot look within. You are afraid of what you would see within, but **guilt** is not there. The **guilt** you fear is gone. If you would look within you would see only the Atonement, shining in quiet and in peace upon the altar to God, your Mother.

Do not be afraid to look within. The ego tells you all is black with **guilt** within you, and bids you not to look. Instead, the ego bids you look upon your sisters, and see the **guilt** in them. Yet this seeing of **guilt** you cannot do without remaining blind. For those who see their sisters in the dark, and **guilty** in the dark in which they shroud them, are too afraid to look upon the light within. Within you is not what you believe is there. Within you is the holy sign of perfect faith your Mother has in you. Look, then, upon the light She placed within you, and learn that what you feared was there has been replaced with love.

Ch. 13. Sec. 10.

In any union with a brother in which you seek to lay your **guilt** upon him, or share it with him or perceive his own, you will feel **guilty**.

As long as you believe that **guilt** is justified in any way, in anyone, whatever a brother may do, you will not look within, where you would always find Atonement. The end of **guilt** will never come as long as you believe there is a reason for **guilt**.

Give no reality to **guilt**, and see no reason for **guilt**.

Now it is given you to heal and teach, to make what will be now. As yet it is not now. The Son of God believes that he is lost in **guilt**, alone in a dark world where pain is pressing everywhere upon him from without. When he has looked within and seen the radiance there, he will remember how much his Father loves him. And it will seem incredible that he ever thought his Father loved him not, and looked upon him as condemned. The moment that you realize **guilt** is insane, wholly unjustified and wholly without reason, you will not fear to look upon the Atonement and accept the Atonement wholly.

Ch. 14. Sec. 3.

Whenever the pain of **guilt** seems to attract you, remember that if you yield to **guilt**, you are deciding against your happiness, and will not learn how to be happy. Say therefore, to yourself, gently, but with the conviction born of the Love of God and of Her Daughter:

What I experience I will make manifest. If I am guiltless, I have nothing to fear.
I choose to testify to my acceptance of the Atonement, not to its rejection.
I would accept my guiltlessness by making my guiltlessness manifest and sharing it.
Let me bring peace to God's Daughter from her Mother.

The miracle teaches you that you have chosen **guiltlessness**, freedom and joy. The miracle is not a cause, but an effect. The miracle is the natural result of choosing right, attesting to your happiness that comes from choosing to be free of **guilt**. Everyone you offer healing to returns healing.

The joy of learning that darkness has no power over the Daughter of God is the happy lesson the Holy Spirit teaches, and would have you teach with Her. Teaching that darkness has no power over the Daughter of God is the Holy Spirit's joy to teach it, as teaching it will be yours.

The way to teach this simple lesson that darkness has no power is merely this: **Guiltlessness** is invulnerability. Therefore, make your invulnerability manifest to everyone. Teach your sister that whatever she may try to do to you, your perfect freedom from the belief that you can be harmed shows her that she is **guiltless**. Your sister can do nothing that can hurt you, and by refusing to allow her to think she can hurt you, you teach her that the Atonement, which you have accepted for yourself, is also hers. There is nothing to forgive. No one can hurt the Daughter of God. Your sister's **guilt** is wholly without cause, and being without cause, **guilt** cannot exist.

God is the only Cause, and **guilt** is not of God. Teach no one she has hurt you, for if you do, you teach yourself that what is not of God has power over you.

Ch. 14. Sec. 6.

The light of **guiltlessness** shines **guilt** away because, when **guiltlessness** and **guilt** are brought together, the truth of **guiltlessness** must make the falsity of **guilt** perfectly clear.

Ch. 18. Sec. 6.

A body cannot be **guilty**, for a body can do nothing of itself. You who think you hate your body deceive yourself. You hate your mind, for **guilt** has entered into your mind.

Guilt is projected to the body, which suffers and dies because the body is attacked to hold the separation in the mind, and let the mind not know its Identity. Mind cannot attack, but mind can make fantasies and direct the body to act these fantasies out. Yet it is never what the body does that seems to satisfy. Unless the mind believes the body is actually acting out the mind's fantasies, the mind will attack the body by increasing the projection of its **guilt** upon the body.

It is insane to use the body as the scapegoat for **guilt**.

Ch. 25. Sec. 3.

To the extent to which you value **guilt**, to that extent will you perceive a world in which attack is justified. To the extent to which you recognize that **guilt** is meaningless, to that extent you will perceive attack cannot be justified. This is in accord with perception's fundamental law: You see what you believe is there, and you believe it is there because you want it there. Perception has no other law than this.

Discussion notes: Practical Truth • Practical Action • Heartfelt Thought

PART TEN

www.jgmgraphicart.com

Topics

Note: All chapter and section notations for the passages are referencing a previously published book titled *A Course in Miracles Abridged Edition.*

TOPIC 72

DEFENSE

defense: Protection of an idea, concept, or cause. An argument in support or justification of a point of view. Resistance to an opposing thought or idea.

Ch. 22. Sec. 5.

How does one overcome illusions? Surely not by force or anger, nor by opposing the illusion in any way. Merely by letting reason tell you that illusions contradict reality. Illusions go against what must be true. Reality opposes nothing. What merely is reality needs no **defense**, and offers none. Only illusions need **defense** because of illusion's weakness. And how can it be difficult to walk the way of truth when only weakness interferes? You are the strong one in this seeming conflict between truth and illusions. And you need no **defense**. Everything that needs **defense** you do not want, for anything that needs **defense** will weaken you.

God rests with you in quiet, undefended and wholly undefending, for in this quiet state alone is strength and power. Here in the quiet state can no weakness enter, for here is no attack and therefore no illusions. Love rests in certainty. Only uncertainty can be **defensive**. And all uncertainty is doubt about yourself.

Forget not, when you feel the need arise to be **defensive** about anything, you have identified yourself with an illusion, and therefore feel that you are weak. This is the cost of all illusions.

Discussion notes: Practical Truth • Practical Action • Heartfelt Thought

TOPIC 73

DENY AND DENIAL

denial: (1) Refusal to accept something or the rejection of something not wanted. (2) A statement, action, allegation, or claim pronouncing something to be untrue or unuseful.

Ch. 2. Sec. 2.

True **denial** is a powerful protective device. You can and should **deny** any belief that *error* can hurt you. This kind of **denial** is not a concealment but a correction. Your right mind depends on the belief that error cannot hurt you. **Denial** of error is a strong defense of truth, but **denial** of truth results in mis-creation, the projections of the ego. In the service of the right mind the **denial** of error frees the mind, and re- establishes the freedom of the will. When the *will* is really free, the mind cannot mis-create, because the mind with free *will* recognizes only truth.

Ch. 7. Sec. 7.

Denial has no power in itself, but you can give **denial** the power of your mind, whose power is without limit. If you use the power of your mind to **deny** reality, reality is gone for you. **Denial** is a defense, and so **denial** is as capable of being used positively as well as negatively. Used negatively **denial** will be destructive, because it will be used for attack. But in the service of the Holy Spirit, **denial** can help you recognize part of reality, and thus appreciate all of reality.

Ch. 11. Sec. 2.

Every miracle that you accomplish speaks to you of the Fatherhood of God. Every healing thought that you accept, either from your brother or in your own mind, teaches you that you are God's Son. In every hurtful thought you hold, wherever you perceive a hurtful thought, lies the **denial** of God's Fatherhood and of your Sonship.

You cannot **deny** part of yourself, because you will seem to be separate and therefore without meaning. And being without meaning to you, you will not understand yourself. To **deny** your meaning is to fail to understand. You can heal only yourself, for only God's Son needs healing. You need healing because you do not understand yourself, and therefore know not what you do. Having forgotten your will, you do not know what you really want.

Discussion notes: Practical Truth • Practical Action • Heartfelt Thought

____

____

____

____

Topic 74

EVERYTHING

everything: Internal awareness (rather than possessions, health, fame or power) that we are complete and one with the source of all. A recognition of our connection to a state outside of time that contains no past and no future, no beginning and no end, only always. The knowing of abundance comes when we see that everything is not a thing.

Ch. 1. Sec. 4.

Those who perceive and acknowledge that they have **everything**, have no needs of any kind. The purpose of the Atonement is to restore **everything** to you; or rather, to restore **everything** to your awareness. You were given **everything** when you were created, just as everyone was given **everything**.

Ch. 2. Sec. 7.

Nothing and **everything** cannot coexist. To believe in one is to deny the other. Fear is really nothing and love is **everything**. Whenever light enters darkness, the darkness is abolished. What you believe is true for you.

Ch. 4. Sec. 3.

In your own mind, though denied by the ego, is the declaration of your release. God has given you **everything**. This one fact means the ego does not exist, and this makes the ego profoundly afraid. In the ego's language, "to have" and "to be" are different, but they are identical to the Holy Spirit. The Holy Spirit knows that you both have **everything** and are **everything**.

Ch. 26. Sec. 7.

What is the Will of God? God wills Her Daughter have **everything**. And this God guaranteed when She created Her Daughter as **everything**.

This guarantee that you are **everything** is the miracle by which creation became your function, sharing creation with God. Your function of creation, which is sharing the face of Christ with **everything**.

Ch. 7. Sec. 6.

Love is your power, which the ego must deny. The ego must also deny **everything** this power of love gives you because this power gives you **everything**. No one who has **everything** wants the ego.

Discussion notes: Practical Truth • Practical Action • Heartfelt Thought

TOPIC 75

GRANDEUR VERSUS GRANDIOSITY

Ch. 9. Sec. 8.

Grandeur is of God, and only of Her. Therefore, **grandeur** is in you. Whenever you become aware of the **grandeur**, however dimly, you abandon the ego automatically, because in the presence of the **grandeur** of God the meaninglessness of the ego becomes perfectly apparent. Self-inflation, **grandiosity**, is of the ego; it is the ego's alternative to the **grandeur** of God.

Grandiosity is always a cover for despair. The essence of **grandiosity** is competitiveness, because **grandiosity** always involves attack. **Grandiosity** is a delusional attempt to outdo, but not to undo. We said before that the ego vacillates between suspiciousness and viciousness. The ego remains suspicious as long as you despair about yourself. The ego shifts to viciousness when you decide not to tolerate self-abasement and seek relief. Then the ego offers you the illusion of attack as a "solution."

The ego does not understand the difference between **grandeur** and **grandiosity**, because the ego sees no difference between miracle impulses and ego-based beliefs of its own.

The ego is immobilized in the presence of God's **grandeur**, because Her **grandeur** establishes your freedom. Even the faintest hint of your reality drives the ego from your mind, because you will give up all investment in the ego. **Grandeur** is totally without illusions, and because **grandeur** is real, **grandeur** is compellingly convincing.

The ego will make every effort to recover and mobilize its energies against your release. The ego will tell you that you are insane, and argue that **grandeur** cannot be a real part of you because of the littleness in which the ego believes. Yet your **grandeur** is not delusional because you did not make your **grandeur**. You made **grandiosity** and are afraid of **grandiosity** because it is a form of attack, but your **grandeur** is of God, Who created **grandeur** out of Her Love.

The ego depends solely on your willingness to tolerate it. If you are willing to look upon your **grandeur** you cannot despair, and therefore you cannot want the ego. Your **grandeur** is God's answer to the ego, because your **grandeur** is true.

Your **grandeur** will never deceive you, but your illusions always will. Illusions are deceptions.

It is easy to distinguish **grandeur** from **grandiosity**, because with **grandeur** love is returned and pride is not. Pride will not produce miracles, and will therefore deprive you of the true witnesses to your reality. God wants you to behold what She created because it is Her joy.

God is incomplete without you because Her **grandeur** is total, and you cannot be missing from God's **grandeur**.

Discussion notes: Practical Truth • Practical Action • Heartfelt Thought

___

___

___

___

Topic 76

LITTLENESS VERSUS MAGNITUDE

Ch. 9. Sec. 8.

You are altogether irreplaceable in the Mind of God. No one else can fill your part in God's Mind, and while you leave your part of it empty, your eternal place merely waits for your return. Your value is in God's Mind, and therefore not in your mind alone. To accept yourself as God created you is not arrogant, because to accept yourself as God created you is the denial of arrogance. To accept your **littleness** is arrogant, because to accept your **littleness** means that you believe your evaluation of yourself is truer than God's.

God would have you replace the ego's belief in **littleness** with God's Own exalted answer to what you are, so that you can cease to question what you are and know it for what it is.

Ch. 13. Sec. 3.

The Holy Spirit's vision is merciful and His remedy is quick. Lay before the Holy Spirit's eternal sanity all your hurt, and let Him heal you. Do not leave any spot of pain hidden from His light, and search your mind carefully for any thoughts you may fear to uncover. For He will heal every **little** thought you have kept to hurt you and cleanse these hurtful thoughts of their **littleness**, restoring your thoughts to the **magnitude** of God.

Ch. 15. Sec. 3.

Be not content with **littleness**. But be sure you understand what **littleness** is, and why you could never be content with it. **Littleness** is the offering you give yourself. You offer this **littleness** in the place of **magnitude**, and you accept it. Everything in this world is **little** because it is a world made out of **littleness**, in the strange belief that **littleness** can content you.

When you strive for anything in this world with the belief that anything in this world will bring you peace, you are belittling yourself and blinding yourself to glory. **Littleness** and glory are the choices open to your striving and your vigilance. You will always choose one at the expense of the other.

Yet what you do not realize, each time you choose, is that your choice is your evaluation of yourself. Choose **littleness** and you will not have peace, for you will have judged yourself unworthy of peace. And whatever you offer as a substitute for peace, is much too poor a gift to satisfy you. It is essential that you accept the fact there is no form of **littleness** that can ever content you. You are free to try as many forms of **littleness** as you wish, but all you will be doing is to delay your homecoming to glory and **magnitude**. For you will be content only in glory and **magnitude**, which is your home.

The Holy Spirit can hold your **magnitude**, clean of all **littleness**, clearly and in perfect safety in your mind, untouched by every **little** gift the world of **littleness** would offer you. But for this, you cannot side against God in what God wills for you. Decide for God. For **littleness**, and the belief that you can be content with **littleness**, are small decisions you make about yourself.

The power and the glory that lie in you from God are for all who, like you, perceive themselves as **little**, and believe that **littleness** can be blown up into a sense of **magnitude** that can content them. Neither give **littleness**, nor accept **littleness**. All honor is due the host of God. Your **littleness** deceives you, but your **magnitude** is of God Who dwells in you, and in Whom you dwell.

Ch. 15. Sec. 3. (cont.)

There is a deep responsibility you owe yourself, and one you must learn to remember all the time. The lesson may seem hard at first, but you will learn to love it when you realize that the lesson is true and is but a tribute to your power. You who have sought and found **littleness**, remember this: Every decision you make stems from what you think you are, and represents the value that you put upon yourself. Believe the **little** can content you, and by limiting yourself, you will not be satisfied. For your function, which is healing and forgiveness, is not **little**, and it is only by finding your function and fulfilling your function that you can escape from **littleness**.

There is no doubt about what your function is, for the Holy Spirit knows what it is. There is no doubt about your function's **magnitude**, for it reaches you through Her from **magnitude**. You do not have to strive for your **magnitude**, because you have it. All striving must be directed against **littleness**, for **littleness** does require vigilance to protect your **magnitude** in this world. To hold your **magnitude** in perfect awareness in a world of **littleness** is a task the **little** cannot undertake. Yet the task is asked of you, in tribute to your **magnitude** and not your **littleness**. Nor is the task asked of you alone. The power of God will support every effort you make on behalf of Her dear Daughter.

Search for the **little**, and you deny yourself God's power. God is not willing that Her Daughter be content with less than everything. For God is not content without Her Daughter, and Her Daughter cannot be content with less than her Mother has given her.

Ch. 23. Sec. Intro.

Let not the **little** interferers pull you to **littleness**. There can be no attraction of guilt in innocence. Think what a happy world you walk, with truth beside you! Do not give up this world of freedom and truth for a **little** sigh of seeming sin, nor for a tiny stirring of guilt's attraction. Would you, for all these meaningless distractions, lay Heaven aside? Your destiny and purpose are far beyond the meaningless distractions, in the clean place where **littleness** does not exist.

Let us not let **littleness** lead God's Son into temptation. The Son of God's glory is beyond **littleness**, measureless and timeless as eternity. Do not let time intrude upon your sight of God's Son. Leave God's Son not frightened and alone in his temptation, but help God's Son rise above **littleness** and perceive the light of which he is a part. Your innocence will light the way to his, and so is yours protected and kept in your awareness. For who can know God's Son's glory, and perceive the **little** and the weak about him?

Discussion notes: Practical Truth • Practical Action • Heartfelt Thought

___

___

___

___

Topic 77

LOVE AND FEAR

love: The essence of being, which contains the emotions of acceptance, peace, and joy; the attraction to connection. Love is already within each of us, and as the blocks to love's awareness (such as guilt, shame, and judgment) are removed, we become mindful that love always has and always will encircle us and everything. Love's attributes are goodness, honesty, compassion, patience, understanding, forgiveness, joy, peace, inclusion, acceptance, release, and encouragement. Love motivates, comforts, sustains, heals, and protects.

fear: A sensation of vulnerability, despair, doubt, confusion, anger, and anxiety. Fear is a recoil to a perceived source of danger. An emotion we experience when we believe we are not safe now or in the future and need to be prepared to defend or attack. This maintains the belief that separation is security. The fear of God causes us to feel separate and incomplete. Fear attributes include unhappiness, negativity, anger, unworthiness, dishonesty, mistrust, doubt, malice, arrogance, exclusion, resistance, control, judgment, and criticism. Fear can motivate, aggravate, deceive, hurt, and occasionally protect.

Ch. 2. Sec. 1.

All **fear** is ultimately reducible to the basic mis-perception that you have the ability to usurp the power of God. Of course, you neither can nor have been able to do this. Here, in this mis-perception of God's power, is the real basis for your escape from **fear**.

Ch. 2. Sec. 6.

Fear is always a sign of strain; strain arises whenever *what you want* conflicts with *what you are doing*. Whenever there is **fear**, it is because you have not made up your mind.

Ch. 2. Sec. 6. (cont.)

Only your mind can produce **fear**. The mind does produce **fear** whenever the mind is conflicted in what it wants, producing inevitable strain because wanting and doing are discordant. This conflict can be corrected only by accepting a unified goal.

Ch. 2. Sec. 7.

We have already attempted to correct the fundamental error that **fear** can be mastered, and have emphasized that the only real mastery is through **love**.

Ch. 4. Sec. 1.

God is not the author of **fear**. You are.

Ch. 9. Sec. 1.

The fact that God is **Love** does not require belief, but God's **Love** does require acceptance. It is indeed possible for you to deny facts, although it is impossible for you to change the facts. If you hold your hands over your eyes, you will not see. If you deny **love**, you will not know **love**.

Ch. 12. Sec. 1.

Fear is a symptom of your own deep sense of loss. **Fear** and **love** are the only emotions of which you are capable. **Fear** is false, for **fear** was made out of denial; and denial depends on the belief in what is denied for its own existence.

Thus does the Holy Spirit replace **fear** with **love** and translate the error of **fear** into truth. And thus will you learn of the Holy Spirit how to replace your dream of separation with the fact of unity. For the separation is only the denial of union, and correctly interpreted, attests to your eternal knowledge that union is true.

Ch. 13. Sec. 5.

I have said you have but two emotions, **love** and **fear**. **Love** is changeless and **fear** has many forms.

Projection makes perception, and you cannot see beyond your projection. Again and again you have attacked your brother, because you saw in him a shadow figure in your private world. And thus you attack yourself first, for what you attack is not in others. For the shadow figures only reality is in your own mind, and by attacking others you are literally attacking what is not there.

The delusional can be very destructive, for they do not recognize they have condemned themselves. The delusional do not wish to die, yet they will not let condemnation go. And so the delusional separate into their private worlds, where everything is disordered, and where what is within appears to be without.

You have but two emotions, **love** and **fear**, yet in your private world you react to each of them as though it were the other. If you see your own hatred as your brother, you are not seeing him. Everyone draws nigh unto what he **loves**, and recoils from what he **fears**. And you react with **fear** to **love**, and draw away from **love**. Yet **fear** attracts you, and believing **fear** is **love**, you call **fear** to yourself. Your private world is filled with shadow figures of **fear** you have invited into it, and all the **love** your brothers offer you, you do not see.

Ch. 13. Sec. 7.

God **loves** Her Daughter forever, and Her Daughter returns her Mother's **Love** forever. The real world is the way that leads you to remembrance of the one thing that is wholly true and wholly yours, which is God's **Love**. For all else you have lent yourself in time, and time will fade. But this one thing, God's **Love**, is always yours, being the gift of God unto Her Daughter. Your one reality was given you, and by God's **Love**, God created you as one with Her.

Ch. 14. Sec. 6.

The quiet light in which the Holy Spirit dwells within you is merely perfect openness, in which nothing is hidden and therefore nothing is **fearful**. Attack will always yield to **love** if attack is brought to **love**, not hidden from **love**. There is no darkness that the light of **love** will not dispel, unless the darkness is concealed from **love's** beneficence. What is kept apart from **love** cannot share **love's** healing power, because what is kept apart has been separated off and kept in darkness.

Ch. 16. Sec. 4.

Love is not an illusion. It is a fact. Where disillusionment is possible, there was not **love** but hate. For hate is an illusion.

Your task is not to seek for **love**, but merely to seek and find all of the barriers within yourself that you have built against **love**. It is not necessary to seek for what is true, but it is necessary to seek for what is false. Every illusion is one of **fear**, whatever form the illusion takes. And the attempt to escape from one illusion into another will fail. If you seek **love** outside yourself you can be certain that you perceive hatred within yourself, and are afraid of the hatred. Yet peace will never come from the illusion of **love**, but only from the reality of **love**.

Ch. 18. Sec. 9.

Love is not learned. **Love's** meaning lies within itself. And learning ends when you have recognized all that **love** is not. That is the interference to **love** and that is what needs to be undone. **Love** is not learned because there never was a time in which you knew **love** not.

Ch. 19. Sec. 1.

Faith is the opposite of **fear**, and faith is as much a part of **love** as **fear** is of attack. Faith is the acknowledgment of union. It is the gracious acknowledgment of everyone as a Son of your most loving Father, **loved** by Him like you, and therefore **loved** by you as yourself. It is God's **love** that joins you, and for His **Love** you would keep no one separate from your **love**. Each one appears just as he is perceived in the holy instant, united in your purpose to be released from guilt. You see the Christ in your brother, and he is healed because you look on what makes faith forever justified in everyone.

Ch. 19. Sec. 4.

Relationships in this world are the result of how the world is seen. And how the world is seen depends on which emotion, **love** or **fear**, was called on to send its messengers to look upon the world, and return with word of what either **love** or **fear** saw. The Holy Spirit has given you **love's** messengers to send, instead of those you trained through **fear**.

If you send forth only the messengers the Holy Spirit gives you, wanting no messages but Hers, you will see **fear** no more. The world will be transformed before your sight, cleansed of all guilt and softly brushed with beauty. The Holy Spirit has given you Her messengers to send to your sister and return to you with what **love** sees. And the Holy Spirit's messengers go forth to signify the end of **fear**.

Love, too, would set a feast before you, on a table covered with a spotless cloth, set in a quiet garden where no sound but singing and a softly joyous whispering is ever heard. This is a feast that honors your holy relationship, and at which everyone is welcomed as an honored guest. And in a holy instant, grace is said by everyone together, as they join in gentleness before the table of communion. And I will join you there, as long ago I promised and promise still. For in your new relationship am I made welcome. And where I am made welcome, there I am.

Discussion notes: Practical Truth • Practical Action • Heartfelt Thought

TOPIC 78

RELATIONSHIP

Ch. 1. Sec. 5.

God is not partial. All God's children have Her total Love, and all Her gifts are freely given to everyone alike. "Except ye become as little children" means that unless you fully recognize your complete dependence on God, you cannot know the real power of the Daughter in her true **relationship** with the Mother. The specialness of God's Daughters does not stem from exclusion but from inclusion.

Ch. 15. Sec. 5.

All special **relationships** supported by our ego have elements of fear in them. This is why our special **relationships** shift and change so frequently. They are not based on changeless love alone. And love, where fear has entered, cannot be depended on because it is not perfect. In the Holy Spirit's function as Interpreter of what you made, He uses those special **relationships**, which you have chosen to support the ego, as learning experiences that point to truth. Under His teaching, every **relationship** becomes a lesson in love.

The Holy Spirit knows no one is more special. Yet He also perceives that you have made special **relationships**, which He would purify and not let you destroy. No matter how unholy you made the special relationship be, the Holy Spirit can translate your special **relationships** into holiness by removing as much fear as you will let Him remove.

You can place any **relationship** under HIs care and be sure that it will not result in pain, if you offer the Holy Spirt your willingness to have the **relationship** serve no need but His. Do not, then, be afraid to let go your imagined needs, which would destroy the **relationship**. Your only need is the Holy Spirit's.

In the holy instant no one is special, for your personal needs intrude on no one to make your brothers seem different. Without the values from the past, you would see your brothers all the same and like yourself. Nor would you see any separation between yourself and your brothers. In the holy instant, you see in each **relationship** what each **relationship** will be when you perceive only the present.

Ch. 15. Sec. 7.

The ego establishes **relationships** only to get something.

Ch. 15. Sec. 8.

Relate with what will never leave you, and what you can never leave, which is Christ's love. Refuse not the awareness of your completion, and seek not to restore your completion for yourself. Fear not to give redemption over to your Redeemer's Love. Your Redeemer, the Christ, will not fail you, for She comes from One Who cannot fail. Accept your sense of failure as nothing more than a mistake in who you are. For the holy host of God, the Christ, is beyond failure. You are forever in a **relationship** so holy that it calls to everyone to escape from loneliness, and join you in your love.

Your **relationships** are with the universe. And this universe, being of God, is far beyond the petty sum of all the separate bodies you perceive. For all the Daughtership's parts are joined in God through Christ.

Leave, then, what seems to you to be impossible to the Holy Spirit, and let Her teach you the only meaning of **relationships**. For God created the only **relationship** that has meaning, and that is God's **relationship** with you.

Ch. 16. Sec. 7.

Seek and find God's message in the holy instant, where all illusions are forgiven. From there the miracle extends to bless everyone and to resolve all problems, be the problems perceived as great or small, possible or impossible. To join in close **relationship** with God is to accept **relationships** as real, and through their reality you give over all illusions to gain the reality of your **relationship** with God. Praise be to your **relationship** with God and to no other.

*Forgive us our illusions, Father, and help us to accept our true **relationship** with You, in which there are no illusions, and where none can ever enter. Our holiness is Yours. What can there be in us that needs forgiveness when Your Forgiveness is perfect? The sleep of forgetfulness is only the unwillingness to remember Your forgiveness and Your Love. Let us not wander into temptation, for the temptation of the Son of God is not Your Will. And let us receive only what You have given, and accept but this into the minds which You created and which You love. Amen.*

Discussion notes: Practical Truth • Practical Action • Heartfelt Thought

Topic 79

God's will and your will

Ch. 2. Sec. 6.

The Holy Spirit cannot ask more than you are willing to do. The strength to do comes from your undivided decision. There is no strain in doing **God's Will** as soon as you recognize that **God's Will is also your own will**.

Ch. 7. Sec. 7.

You are the **Will of God**. Do not accept anything else as **your will**, or you are denying what you are, which is the **Will of God**. Deny this and you will attack, believing you have been attacked. But see the Love of God in you, and you will see the Love of God everywhere because the Love of God is everywhere. See God's abundance in everyone, and you will know that you are in God with everyone. Everyone is part of you, as you are part of God.

Ch. 9. Sec. 1.

You may insist that the Holy Spirit does not answer you, but it might be wiser to consider the kind of questioner you are. **Your true will** is your salvation because **your will** is the same as **God's Will**. The separation is nothing more than the belief that **your will** is different from **God's Will**.

No right mind can believe that its will is stronger than God's. If, then, a mind believes that its will is different from **God's Will**, it can only decide either that there is no God or that **God's Will** is fearful. The former, that there is no God, accounts for the atheist and the latter, that **God's Will** is fearful, accounts for the martyr, who believes that God demands sacrifices. Either of these insane decisions will induce panic, because the atheists believes they are alone, and the martyrs believes that God is crucifying them. Yet no one really wants either abandonment or retaliation, even though many may seek both.

Ultimately everyone must remember the **Will of God**, because ultimately everyone must recognize their Self. This recognition is the recognition that **your will** and **God's Will** are one. In the presence of truth, there are no unbelievers and no sacrifices. In the security of reality, fear is totally meaningless. To deny *what is* can only seem to be fearful. God is

Love and you do want God. This is **your will**. Ask for God's Love and you will be answered, because you will be asking only for what belongs to you.

Ch. 11. Sec. 1.

God's Will is that you are His Son. By denying that you are His Son you deny your **own will**, and therefore do not know what **your will** is. You must ask what **God's Will** is in everything, because it is yours. You do not know what **your will** is, but the Holy Spirit remembers it for you. Ask the Holy Spirit, therefore, what **God's Will** is for you, and He will tell you **your will**.

The projection of the ego makes it appear as if **God's Will** is outside yourself, and therefore not **your will**. In this interpretation it seems possible for **God's Will** and **your will** to conflict. God, then, may seem to demand of you what you do not want to give, and thus deprive you of what you want. Would God, Who wants only **your will**, be capable of this deprivation? **Your will** is God's life, which God has given to you.

You are afraid to know **God's Will**, because you believe **God's Will** is not yours. This belief is your sickness and your fear. Believing that **God's Will** is not **your will** you hide in darkness, denying that the light is in you.

You are asked to trust the Holy Spirit only because He speaks for you. He is the Voice for God, but never forget that God did not will to be alone. Blessed are you who learn that to hear the **Will of your Father** is to know your own. **God's Will** is that His Son be one, and united with Him in His Oneness. That is why healing is the beginning of the recognition that **your will** is **God's Will**.

Ch. 11. Sec. 3.

O my child, if you knew what **God wills** for you, your joy would be complete! And what **God wills** has happened, for it was always true. When the light comes and you have said, "**God's Will is mine**," you will see such beauty that you will know the light is not of you. Out of your joy you will create beauty in God's Name, for your joy could no more be contained than God's joy. The bleak little world will vanish into nothingness, and your heart will be so filled with joy that your heart will leap into Heaven, and into the Presence of God. I cannot tell you what this will be like, for your heart is not ready. Yet I can tell you, and remind you often, that what **God wills** for Herself **She wills for you**, and what **God wills** for you is yours.

The way is not hard, but the way is very different. Yours is the way of pain, of which God knows nothing. That way of pain is hard indeed, and very lonely. Fear and grief are your guests, and fear and grief go with you and abide with you on the way of pain. But the dark journey is not the way of God's Daughter. Walk in light and do not see the dark companions of fear and grief, for fear and grief are not fit companions for the Daughter of God, who was created of light and in light.

The Great Light always surrounds you and shines out from you. How can you see the dark companions in a light such as this? If you see fear and grief, it is only because you are denying the light. But deny fear and grief instead, for the light is here and the way is clear.

God hides nothing from Her Daughter, even though God's Daughter would hide herself. Yet the Daughter of God cannot hide her glory, for **God wills** Her Daughter to be glorious, and gave Her Daughter the light that shines in her. You will never lose your way, for God leads you. When you wander, you but undertake a journey that is not real.

The dark companions, the dark way, are all illusions. Turn toward the light, for the little spark in you is part of a light so great that this little spark of light in you can sweep you out of all darkness forever. For your Mother is your Creator, and you are like your Mother.

Do not be deceived by the dark comforters of fear and grief, and never let the dark comforters enter the mind of God's Daughter, for they have no place in God's temple. When you are tempted to deny God remember that there are no other gods to place before God, and accept **God's Will** for you in peace.

Ch. 30. Sec. 2.

Do you not understand that to oppose the Holy Spirit is to fight yourself? The Holy Spirit tells you but **your will**; He speaks for you. In His Divinity is but your own divinity. God is no enemy to you.

How wonderful it is to do **your will**! For to do **your will** is freedom. Unless you do **your will**, you are not free. God would not have His Son made prisoner to what God's Son does not want. God joins with you in willing you be free. And to oppose God is to make a choice against yourself, and choose that you be bound.

Look once again upon your enemy, the one you chose to hate instead of love. For thus was hatred born into the world, and thus the rule of fear established there in this world. Now hear God speak to you, through the Holy Spirit Who is God's Voice and yours as well, reminding you that it is not **your will** to hate and be a prisoner to fear, a slave to death, a little creature with a little life. **Your will** is boundless; it is not **your will** that it be bound.

What cause have you for anger in a world that merely waits your blessing to be free? If you be prisoner, then God Himself could not be free. This world awaits the freedom you will give when you have recognized that you are free. But you will not forgive the world until you have forgiven God, Who gave **your will** to you. For it is by **your will** the world is given freedom.

Discussion notes: Practical Truth • Practical Action • Heartfelt Thought

---

PART ELEVEN

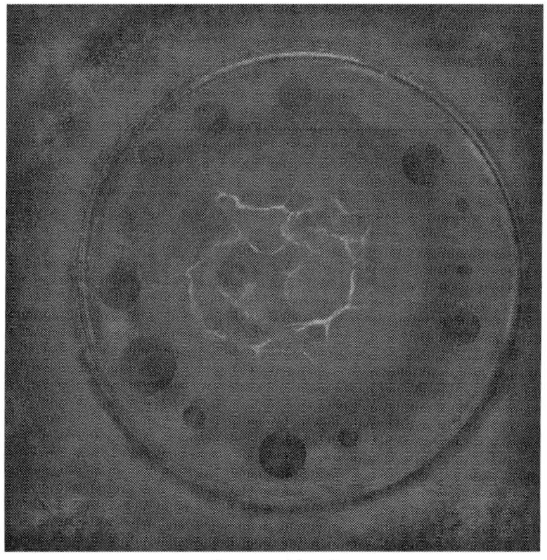

www.jgmgraphicart.com

Topics

80. LIGHT
81. MEMORY AND REMEMBERING
82. MIRACLE
83. PEACE
84. PERCEPTION AND KNOWLEDGE
85. PROJECTION AND EXTENSION
86. SEPARATE AND SEPARATION

Note: All chapter and section notations for the passages are referencing a previously published book titled *A Course in Miracles Abridged Edition.*

TOPIC 80

LIGHT

Ch. 7. Sec. 5.

Come unto me, and learn of the truth in you. The mind we share is shared by all our brothers and as we see them truly, all our brothers will be healed. Let your mind shine with mine upon all your brother's minds, and by our gratitude to all our brothers make them aware of the **light** in them. This **light** will shine back upon you and on the whole Sonship, because this is your proper gift to God.

Ch. 13. Sec. 6.

There is a **light** that this world cannot give. Yet you can give this **light**, as the **light** was given you. And as you give this **light**, the **light** shines forth to call you from the world and follow it. For this **light** will attract you as nothing in this world can do. And you will lay aside the dark world and find another world. This other world is bright with love which you have given it. And here in this other world will everything remind you of your Mother and Her holy Daughter. **Light** is unlimited, and spreads across this world in quiet joy. All those you brought with you will shine on you, and you will shine on them in gratitude because they brought you here to this world of **light**. Your **light** will join with theirs in power so compelling, that this **light** will draw the others out of darkness as you look on them.

Ch. 18. Sec. 3.

The **light** is in you. Darkness can cover the **light**, but cannot put the **light** out.

Fear seems to live in darkness, and when you are afraid you have stepped back into the darkness. Let us then join quickly in an instant of **light**, and it will be enough to remind you that your goal is **light**.

Truth has rushed to meet you since you called upon it. If you knew Who walks beside you on the way that you have chosen, fear would be impossible. You are advancing to love's meaning, and away from all illusions in which you have surrounded love. When you retreat to illusion your fear increases, for in illusion is little doubt that what you think love means is fearful.

Ch. 21. Sec. 1.

Beyond the body, beyond the sun and stars, past everything you see and yet somehow familiar, is an arc of golden **light** that stretches as you look past everything into a great and shining circle. And all the circle fills with **light** before your eyes. The edges of the circle disappear, and what is in the circle is no longer contained at all. The **light** expands and covers everything, extending to infinity forever shining and with no break or limit anywhere. Within the golden **light** everything is joined in perfect continuity. Nor is it possible to imagine that anything could be outside, for there is nowhere that this **light** is not.

Discussion notes: Practical Truth • Practical Action • Heartfelt Thought

---

TOPIC 81

MEMORY AND REMEMBERING

Ch. 10. Sec. 2.

Offer the Holy Spirit only your willingness to **remember**, for He retains the knowledge of God and of yourself for you, waiting for your acceptance. Give up gladly everything that would stand in the way of your **remembering**, for God is in your **memory**. God's Voice will tell you that you are part of God when you are willing to **remember** Him and know your own reality again. Let nothing in this world delay your **remembering** of God, for in this **remembering** is the knowledge of yourself.

Ch. 12. Sec. 6.

The Holy Spirit is your strength because She knows nothing but the spirit as you. She is perfectly aware that you do not know yourself, and perfectly aware of how to teach you to **remember** what you are. Because She loves you, She will gladly teach you what She loves, for She wills to share it. **Remembering** you always, She cannot let you forget your worth. For the Mother never ceases to remind the Holy Spirit of the Mother's Daughter, and the Holy Spirit never ceases to remind God's Daughter of the Mother. God is in your **memory** because of the Holy Spirit. You chose to forget your Mother but you do not really want to do so, and therefore you can decide otherwise.

Ch. 12. Sec. 8.

Because of your Father's Love you can never forget Him, for no one can forget what God Himself placed in your **memory**. You can deny your **memory**, but you cannot lose your **memory**. You are waiting only for God, and you do not know you are waiting. Yet, God's **memory** shines in your mind and cannot be obliterated. God's **memory** is no more past than future, being forever always.

You have but to ask for this **memory** of God, and you will **remember**. Yet the **memory** of God cannot shine in a mind that has obliterated this **memory** and wants to keep it so. For the **memory** of God can dawn only in a mind that chooses to **remember**, and that has relinquished the insane desire to control reality. You who cannot even control yourself should hardly aspire to control the universe. But look upon what you have made of your reality, and rejoice that your reality is not so.

Ch. 28. Sec. 1.

Remembering is perception of the past as if the past were occurring now, and as if the past were still there to see. **Memory** and **remembering** can be used to heal and not to hurt, if you so wish it be.

The Holy Spirit can indeed make use of **memory**, for God Herself is there in **memory**. You have held **memory** to being a part of *time*.

The Holy Spirit's use of **memory** is quite apart from time. She does not seek to use **memory** as a means to keep the past, but rather use the **memory** as a way to let the past go. And if **memory** seems to serve to cherish hate, and gives you pictures of injustices and hurts that you were saving, then this is what you asked **memory's** message be. Committed to **memory's** vaults, the history of all the body's past is hidden there. All of the strange associations made to keep the past alive, the present dead, are stored within the past **memory**, waiting your command that the **memory** be brought to you, and made alive again.

Yet time is but another phase of what does nothing. Time works hand in hand with all the other attributes with which you seek to keep concealed the truth about yourself. Time neither takes away nor can restore. And yet you make strange use of time, as if the past had caused the present, which is but a consequence in which no change can be made possible because past cause has gone.

When **memories** of hate appear, **remember** that their cause for hatred is gone. Be glad that the past cause is gone, for this hate is what you would be pardoned from. And see, instead, the new effects of cause accepted now, with consequences here. The new effects will surprise you with their loveliness.

Discussion notes: Practical Truth • Practical Action • Heartfelt Thought

____

____

____

____

TOPIC 82

MIRACLE

miracle: A divine healing of human perception; a change of mind that shifts perception from fear and guilt to love and forgiveness. The undoing of delusions and illusions through divine communication. An awakening that heals the mind from pain and suffering.

Ch. 1. Sec. 1.

Miracles are a kind of exchange. Like all expressions of love, which are always miraculous in the true sense, **miracles** bring more love both to the giver and the receiver.

A **miracle** is a service. A **miracle** is the maximal service you can render to another. It is a way of loving your neighbor as yourself. You recognize your own worth and your neighbor's worth simultaneously.

Miracles reawaken the awareness that the spirit, not the body, is the altar of truth.

Miracles praise God through you. **Miracles** heal because they deny body-identification and affirm spirit-identification.

Miracles restore the mind to its fullness.

A major contribution of **miracles** is their strength in releasing you from your false sense of isolation, deprivation and lack.

The **miracle** is an expression of an inner awareness of Christ.

Ch. 1. Sec. 3.

Miracles arise from a mind that is ready for them. As an expression of what you truly are, the **miracle** places the mind in a state of grace. The mind then naturally welcomes the Host within and the stranger without. When you bring in the stranger, she becomes your sister.

Ch. 1. Sec. 7.

Your distorted perceptions produce a dense cover over **miracle** impulses, making it hard for **miracles** to reach your own awareness. The confusion of **miracle** impulses with physical impulses is a major perceptual distortion. All real pleasure comes from doing God's Will. Do not deceive yourself into believing that you can relate in peace to God, or to your brothers, with anything external.

Ch. 12. Sec. 2.

Miracles are merely the translation of denial into truth. If to love oneself is to heal oneself, those who are sick do not love themselves. Therefore, they are asking for the love that would heal them, but which they are denying to themselves. If they knew the truth about themselves, they could not be sick. The task of the **miracle** worker thus becomes to deny the denial of truth. The sick must heal themselves, for the truth is in them. Yet having obscured the truth in them, the light in another mind must shine into theirs because that light is theirs.

The light in the sick shines as brightly regardless of the density of the fog that obscures it. If you give no power to the fog to obscure the light, it has none.

Ch. 27. Sec. 6.

The Holy Spirit Who brings the **miracle** perceives sin's witnesses all as one, and called all sin's witnesses by the name of fear. As fear is witness unto death, so is the **miracle** the witness unto life. The **miracle** is a witness no one can deny, for it is the effects of life that the **miracle** brings. The dying live, the dead arise, and pain has vanished. Yet a **miracle** speaks not but for itself, but what the **miracle** represents.

Be you then witness to the **miracle**, and not the laws of sin. There is no need to suffer any more. But there is need that you be healed, because the suffering and sorrow of the world have made the world deaf to its salvation and deliverance.

The resurrection of the world awaits your healing and your happiness, that you may demonstrate the healing of the world. The holy instant will replace all sin, and no one will elect to suffer any more. What better function could you serve than this function to save the world?

Ch. 28. Sec. 3.

What waits in perfect certainty beyond salvation is not our concern. The **miracle** alone is your concern at present. Here in the present is where we must begin. When you accept a **miracle**, you do not add your dream of fear to one that is already being dreamed. Without support, the dream will fade away without effects. For it is your support of the ego that strengthens your dream of fear.

Discussion notes: Practical Truth • Practical Action • Heartfelt Thought

---

Topic 83

PEACE

Ch. 2. Sec. 2.

Remember that where your heart is, there is your treasure also. You believe in what you value. If you are afraid you will inevitably value wrongly, and by endowing all thoughts with equal power will inevitably destroy **peace**. That is why the Bible speaks of "the **peace** of God which passeth understanding." The **peace** of God is totally incapable of being shaken by errors of any kind. The **peace** of God denies the ability of anything that is not of God to affect you. The **peace** of God is not used to hide anything, but to correct error.

Everyone defends his treasure, and will do so automatically. The real questions are: "what do you treasure?", and "how much do you treasure it?" Once you have learned to consider these questions and to bring them into all your actions, you will have little difficulty in clarifying the means.

Ch. 8. Sec. 4.

Do you not think the world needs **peace** as much as you do? Do you not want to give **peace** to the world as much as you want to receive **peace**? For unless you do want to give **peace**, you will not receive **peace**.

Ch. 19. Sec. 4.

As **peace** extends from deep inside yourself to embrace all the Creation and give Creation rest, **peace** will encounter many obstacles. Some of them you will try to impose. Others will seem to arise from elsewhere; from your brothers, and from various aspects of the world outside. Yet **peace** will gently cover the obstacles to it, extending past completely unencumbered. The extension of the Holy Spirit's purpose from your relationship to others, to bring others gently into **peace**, will quietly extend to every aspect of your lives, surrounding each of you with glowing happiness and the calm awareness of complete protection. And you will carry **peace's** message of love and safety and freedom to everyone who draws nigh unto your temple, where healing waits for him.

Ch. 24. Sec. Intro.

Forget not that the motivation for this course is the attainment and the keeping of the state of **peace**. Given this state of **peace** the mind is quiet, and the condition in which God is remembered is attained. **Peace** will be yours because it is God's Will.

Ch. 26. Sec. 7.

Abide in **peace**, where God would have you be. And be the means whereby your sister finds the **peace** in which your wishes are fulfilled. For what can save each one of us can save us all. There is no difference among the Daughters of God. And everything belongs to each of us.

Discussion notes: Practical Truth • Practical Action • Heartfelt Thought

---

Topic 84

PERCEPTION AND KNOWLEDGE

perception: A construct of thoughts that interprets or judges information to form belief. The manner in which we process our understanding of the world around us, which we inherently see as entirely separate from ourselves. Perceptions define how we see the world; some are true perceptions, and some are mis-perceptions. Both influence our thoughts, beliefs, actions, and feelings. Miracles change our mis-perceptions of fear into perceptions that foster love. What we perceive within ourselves determines what we see outside ourselves. Therefore, reality is our interpretation of it.

knowledge: Inner knowing; divine disclosure. Certainty without the need to defend or explain. Divine knowledge is experienced rather than perceived. Perception is a mere reflection or image of knowledge.

Ch. 1. Sec. 1.

Miracles are examples of right thinking, aligning your **perceptions** with truth as God created it.

Ch. 1. Sec. 6.

Lack implies that you would be better off in a state somehow different from the one you are in. You act according to the particular order of needs you establish. This order of needs, in turn, depends on your **perception** of what you are.

Ch. 3. Sec. 3.

To know is to be certain, and certainty is strength. **Perception** is temporary. As an attribute of the belief in time and space, **perception** is subject either to fear or to love. Mis-**perceptions** produce fear and true **perceptions** foster love, but neither brings certainty because all **perception** varies. That is why **perception** is not **knowledge**. True **perception** is the basis for **knowledge**, but knowing is the affirmation of truth and beyond all **perceptions**.

You can see in many ways because **perception** involves interpretation. The miracle, being a way of perceiving, is not **knowledge**. The miracle is the right answer to a question, but you do not question when you know. Questioning illusions is the first step in undoing illusions. The miracle, or the right answer, corrects illusions. Since **perceptions** change, their dependence on time is obvious. How you perceive at any given time determines what you do, and actions must occur in time. **Knowledge** is timeless, because certainty is not questionable. You know when you have ceased to ask questions.

When you say you are acting on the basis of **knowledge**, you are really confusing **knowledge** with **perception**, because **knowledge** does not require action. **Knowledge** is the result of revelation and induces only thought. Even in **perception's** most spiritualized form, **perception** involves the body. **Knowledge** comes from the altar within and is timeless because **knowledge** is certain. To perceive the truth is not the same as to know the truth.

Ch. 3. Sec. 5.

Forgiveness is the healing of the **perception** of separation. Correct **perception** of others is necessary, because without correct **perceptions**, minds have chosen to see themselves as separate. Spirit knows God completely. That complete knowledge is spirit's miraculous power. The fact that each one of us has this power to know God completely is a condition entirely alien to the world's thinking.

How beautiful indeed are the Thoughts of God who live in God's light! Your worth is beyond **perception** because your worth is beyond doubt. Do not perceive yourself in different lights. Know yourself in the One Light of God where the miracle that is you is perfectly clear.

Ch. 4. Sec. 2.

It cannot be emphasized too often that correcting **perception** is merely a temporary expedient. Correct **perception** is necessary only because mis-**perception** is a block to **knowledge**, while accurate **perception** is a steppingstone towards **knowledge**. The whole value of right **perception** lies in the inevitable realization that all **perception** is unnecessary. You may ask how this realization is possible, as long as you appear to be living in this world. That is a reasonable question. You must be careful, however, that you really understand the question. Who is the "you" who are living in this world? Spirit is immortal, and immortality is a constant state. Immortality is as true now as it ever was or ever will be. **Knowledge** never involves comparisons, like **perception** does. That is **knowledge's** main difference from everything else the mind can grasp.

Ch. 5. Sec. 3.

The Holy Spirit is the Bridge for the transfer of **perception** to **knowledge**.

Ch. 6. Sec. 2.

The Holy Spirit remains the Bridge between **perception** and **knowledge**. By enabling you to use **perception** in a way that reflects **knowledge**, you will ultimately remember you know God. The ego would prefer to believe that this memory is impossible, yet memory is your **perception** the Holy Spirit guides.

Ch. 7. Sec. 7.

You do not need God's blessing because that you have forever, but you do need your blessing. The ego's picture of you is deprived, unloving and vulnerable. You cannot love this picture. Yet you can very easily escape from this image by leaving the ego's picture behind. You are not there in the ego's image and that is not you. Teach no one that your brother is what you would not want to be. Your brother is the mirror in which you see the image of yourself as long as **perception** lasts. And **perception** will last until the Sonship knows itself as whole.

Ch. 11. Sec. 8.

The end of the world is not its destruction, but its translation into Heaven. The reinterpretation of the world is the transfer of all **perception** to **knowledge**.

Perceptions are learned, and you are not without a Teacher. Yet your willingness to learn from the Teacher depends on your willingness to question everything you learned of yourself, for you who learned amiss should not be your own teacher.

Ask yourself, therefore, but one simple question:

> *Do I want the problem or do I want the answer?*

You may be afraid of the Teacher's specificity, for fear of what you think the Teacher will demand of you. Yet, only by asking will you learn that nothing of God demands anything of you. God gives; God does not take. When you refuse to ask, it is because you believe that asking is taking rather than sharing.

Ch. 12. Sec. 7.

You see what you expect, and you expect what you invite. Your **perception** is the result of your invitation, coming to you as you sent for it. Whose manifestations would you see? Of whose presence would you be convinced? For you will believe in what you manifest, and as you look out so will you see in.

Remember always that you see what you seek, for what you seek you will find. The ego finds what it seeks, and only that. The ego does not find love, for love is not what the ego is seeking.

Ch. 14. Sec. 7.

Perception is the medium by which ignorance is brought to **knowledge**. Yet the **perception** must be without deceit, for otherwise the **perception** becomes the messenger of ignorance rather than a helper in the search for truth.

Light cannot enter darkness when a mind believes in darkness, and will not let darkness go. Truth does not struggle against ignorance, and love does not attack fear.

Ch. 21. Sec. 5.

Perception selects, and makes the world you see. **Perception** literally picks the world you see out as the mind directs. The still, small Voice for God is not drowned out by all the ego's raucous screams and senseless ravings to those who want to hear the Voice. **Perception** is a choice and not a fact. But on this choice of **perception** depends far more than you may realize as yet. For on the voice you choose to hear, and on the sights you choose to see, depends entirely your whole belief in what you are. **Perception** is a witness but to what you believe you are, and never to reality. Yet **perception** can show you the conditions in which awareness of true reality is possible, or the conditions where true reality could never be.

Faith and **perception** and belief can be misplaced, and serve the great deceiver's needs as well as truth.

Ch. 25. Sec. 1.

Perception is a choice of what you want yourself to be; the world you want to live in, and the state in which you think your mind will be content and satisfied. **Perception** chooses where you think your safety lies, at your decision. **Perception** reveals yourself to you as you would have you be.

Ch. 26. Sec. 10.

Confused **perception** will block **knowledge**.

Discussion notes: Practical Truth • Practical Action • Heartfelt Thought

Topic 85

PROJECTION AND EXTENSION

projection: (1) The act of deflecting our internal conflicts and suffering onto others, making it appear as though other people carry these damages and not us. (2) A method of separatism that demonstrates internal guilt and anguish over our perceived sins and extends this guilt onto others.

extension (little self): The egoistic, expressed thoughts of the mind, triggering worldly effects that can cause confusion and separation.

extension (higher Self): The inner radiance of God given to others through love, forgiveness, and healing. The ability of our Spirit to express forgiveness and experience oneness.

Ch. 2.1.

To **extend** is a fundamental aspect of God which She gave to Her Daughter. In the creation, God **extended** Herself to Her creations and imbued creation with the same loving will to create. There is no emptiness in you. Because of your likeness to your Creator you are creative. No child of God can lose this ability because to create is inherent in what she is, but she can use her ability to create inappropriately by **projecting**. The inappropriate use of **projection**, or **extension**, occurs when you believe that some emptiness or lack exists in you, and that you can fill this lack with your own ideas instead of truth.

Ch. 6. Sec. 2.

What you **project** you disown, and therefore do not believe what you **project** is yours. You are excluding yourself by the very judgment that you are different from the one on whom you **project**. Since you have also judged against what you **project**, you continue to attack it because you continue to keep what you **project** separated. By doing this unconsciously, you try to keep the fact that you attacked yourself out of your awareness, and thus imagine that you have made yourself safe.

Yet **projection** will always hurt you. **Projection** reinforces your belief in your own split mind, and **projection's** only purpose is to keep the separation going. **Projection** is solely a device of the ego to make you feel different from your brothers and separated from them.

The ego justifies this feeling different on the grounds that it makes you seem "better" than they are, thus obscuring your equality with them still further. **Projection** and attack are inevitably related, because **projection** is always a means of justifying attack. Anger without **projection** is impossible. The ego uses **projection** only to destroy your perception of both yourself and your brothers.

Ch. 7. Sec. 8.

We have said that without **projection** there can be no anger, but it is also true that without **extension** there can be no love. Every mind must **project** or **extend**, because that is how the mind lives, and every mind is life.

Ch. 7. Sec. 9.

Selfishness is of the ego, but Self-fullness is of spirit because that is how God created spirit. The Holy Spirit is in the part of the mind that lies between the ego and the spirit, mediating between them always in favor of the spirit.

The **extension** of God's Being is spirit's only function. Spirit's fullness cannot be contained, any more than can the fullness of its Creator. Fullness is **extension**. The ego's whole thought system blocks **extension**, and thus blocks your only function. The ego therefore blocks your joy, so that you perceive yourself as unfulfilled.

The Kingdom is forever **extending** because the Kingdom is in the Mind of God. You do not know your joy because you do not know your own Self-fullness. The full appreciation of the mind's Self-fullness makes selfishness impossible and **extension** inevitable. Self-fullness and **extension** is why there is perfect peace in the Kingdom.

Ch. 10. Sec. 5.

Do not forget, however, that to deny God will inevitably result in **projection**, and you will believe that others, and not yourself, have done this denial of God to you. You may believe that you judge your sisters by the messages they give you, but you have judged them by the message you give to them. Do not attribute your denial of joy to your sisters, or you cannot see the spark in them that would bring joy to you. It is the denial of the spark that brings depression, for whenever you see your sisters without the spark, you are denying God.

Allegiance to the denial of God is the ego's religion.

Ch. 12. Sec. 6.

The only thing of value in the world is whatever part of the world you look upon with love. Love gives the world the only true reality the world will ever have. The world's value is not in itself, but yours is in you. As self-value comes from **self-extension**, so does the perception of self-value come from the **extension** of loving thoughts outward. Make the world real unto yourself, so the real world belongs to you.

Ch. 12. Sec. 7.

I said before that what you **project** or **extend** is up to you, but you must do one or the other, for that, to **project** or **extend**, is a law of mind, and you must look in before you look out. As you look in, you choose either the ego or the Holy Spirit as the guide for seeing. And then you look out and behold your chosen guide's witnesses.

Ch. 21. Sec. Intro.

Projection makes perception. The world you see is what your **projections** gave it, nothing more than that. The world you see is the witness to your state of mind, the outside picture of an inward condition. As a man thinketh, so does a man perceive. Therefore, seek not to change the world, but choose to change your mind about the world. Perception is a result and not a cause.

Damnation is your judgment on yourself, and this judgment you will **project** upon the world. See the world as damned, and all you see is what you did to hurt the Son of God. If you behold disaster and catastrophe, you tried to crucify the Son of God. If you see holiness and hope, you joined the Will of God to set the Son of God free. There is no choice that lies between these two decisions, for either you crucify or set free the Son of God.

Ch. 22. Sec. 6.

Extension of forgiveness is the Holy Spirit's function. Leave this to Her. Let your concern be only that you give to Her that which can be **extended**. Save no dark secrets that the Holy Spirit cannot use, but offer Her the tiny gifts She can **extend** forever.

The Holy Spirit will take each gift of forgiveness and make of it a potent force for peace. The Holy Spirit will withhold no blessing from each gift of forgiveness, nor limit each gift of love in any way. The Holy Spirit will join to each gift all the power that God has given Her, to make each little gift of love a source of healing for everyone. Each little gift you offer to your sister lights up the world. Be not concerned with darkness; look away from darkness and toward each other. And let the darkness be dispelled by Her Who knows the light, and lays it gently in each quiet smile of faith and confidence, with which you bless each other.

Discussion notes: Practical Truth • Practical Action • Heartfelt Thought

---

Topic 86

SEPARATE AND SEPARATION

separation: (1) A mind-set that supports the concept that we are independent from creation. Through dissociation, we create an identity that we are dissimilar beings, forming a story about "me" and the evaluations of everything outside of "me." The illusion that "me" or "my tribe" is somehow better, wiser, or more special than others. (2) The denial of the spiritual condition that everything is connected by virtue of divine energy.

Ch. 8. Sec. 4.

Separation is overcome by union. **Separation** cannot be overcome by **separating**. The decision to unite must be unequivocal, or the mind itself is divided and not whole. Your mind is the means by which you determine your own condition, because mind is the mechanism of decision. Mind's mechanism of decision is the power by which you **separate** or join, and experience pain or joy accordingly.

Ch. 14. Sec. 10.

Separation remains the ego's chosen condition.

Ch. 16. Sec. 5.

Separation is only the decision not to know yourself. The ego's whole thought system is a carefully contrived learning experience, designed to lead you away from truth and into fantasy. Yet for every learning that would hurt you, God offers you correction and complete escape from all its hurtful consequences.

The decision whether or not to listen to God's offer and follow His correction, is but the choice between truth and illusion. For here is truth, separated from illusion and not confused with illusion at all. How simple does this choice between truth and illusion become when fantasy is perceived as only what it is. For only fantasies make confusion in choosing possible, and fantasies are totally unreal.

Thus, this is the time to make the easiest decision that ever confronted you, and also the only one decision. You will cross the bridge into true reality simply because you will recognize that God is on the other side, and know that nothing at all is here in your world of fantasies.

Ch. 25. Sec. 1.

You are the means for God; not **separate**, nor are you with a life apart from God's life. God's life is manifest in you who are Her Daughter. Each aspect of God is framed in holiness and perfect purity. Each aspect of God's radiance shines through each body that it looks upon, and brushes all the body's darkness into light merely by looking past the body to the light. The veil is lifted through each aspect of God's gentleness, and nothing hides the face of Christ from its beholders. You and your sister stand before God now, to let Her draw aside the veil that seems to keep you and your sister **separate** and apart.

Since you believe that you are **separate**, Heaven presents itself to you as **separate**, too. Not that Heaven is **separate** from you in truth, but that the link that has been given you to join the truth may reach to you through what you understand. Mother and Daughter and Holy Spirit are as One, as all your sisters join as one in truth. Christ and the Mother have never been **separate**, and Christ abides within your understanding, in the part of you that shares the Mother's Will. The Holy Spirit links the other part, the ego --the tiny, mad desire to be **separate**, different and special-- to the Christ, to make the oneness clear to what is really one. In this separate world this Oneness is not understood, but can be taught.

The Holy Spirit serves Christ's purpose in your mind, so that your aim of **separation** can be corrected where the error lies, which is in the mind. This correction is understood by a mind perceived as one, aware that the mind is one, and so experienced as one. It is the Holy Spirit's function to teach you how this oneness of mind is experienced, what you must do that oneness can be experienced, and where you should go to do it.

Discussion notes: Practical Truth • Practical Action • Heartfelt Thought

---

PART TWELVE

www.jgmgraphicart.com

Topics

Note: All chapter and section notations for the passages are referencing a previously published book titled *A Course in Miracles Abridged Edition.*

TOPIC 87

ETERNITY

Ch. 9. Sec. 6.

Eternity is one time, its only dimension being "always." This cannot mean anything to you until you remember God's open Arms, and finally know God's open Mind. Like God, you are "always"; in God's mind and with a mind like Gods.

Ch. 13. Sec. 8.

When you have seen your sisters as yourself you will be released to knowledge, having learned to free yourself through Christ Who knows of freedom. And suddenly time will be over, and we will all unite in the **eternity** of God the Mother.

Ch. 14. Sec. 10.

The reflections you accept into the mirror of your mind in time, but bring **eternity** nearer or farther. But **eternity** itself is beyond all time. Reach out of time and touch **eternity**, with the help of **eternity's** reflection in you. And you will turn from time to holiness, as surely as the reflection of holiness calls everyone to lay all guilt aside. Reflect the peace of Heaven here, and bring this world to Heaven. For the reflection of truth draws everyone to truth, and as they enter into truth, they leave all mirrored reflections behind.

Ch. 24. Sec. 6.

Nothing is lost to you in all the universe. No Thought within God's Mind is absent from your own mind. It is God's Will you share His Love for you, and look upon yourself as lovingly as God conceived of you before the world began, and as God knows you still. God changes not His Mind about His Son with passing circumstance which has no meaning in **eternity** where God abides, and you with God. Your brother is as God created him. And it is this that saves you from a world that God created not.

Discussion notes: Practical Truth • Practical Action • Heartfelt Thought

---

TOPIC 88

TIME (AND SPACE)

time (and space): The physical world, which is home to illusions of separation where the body and mind are acting in a linear progression. The place where birth and death, peace and violence, forgiveness and judgment, love and fear, and joy and pain occur. Where past, present, and future compete for our attention. Where past and future thoughts keep us from the reality of the present. To the struggling self, it is a prison; to the awakening Self, it is a classroom. We are on a spaceship called Earth, traveling through time.

Ch. 5. Sec. 3.

The ego made the world as the ego perceives it, but the Holy Spirit, the re-interpreter of what the ego made, sees the world as a teaching device for bringing you home. The Holy Spirit must perceive **time**, and reinterpret **time** into the **timeless**. The Holy Spirit must work with and for a mind that is in opposition with itself.

Ch. 5. Sec. 6.

You do not belong in **time**. Your place is only in eternity, where God Himself placed you forever.

Guilt feelings are the preservers of **time**. Guilt feelings induce fears of retaliation or abandonment, and thus ensure that the future will be like the past. This is how the ego's continuity is maintained. Ensuring that the future will be like the past gives the ego a false sense of security by believing that you cannot escape from **time**. But you can and must.

God offers you the continuity of eternity in exchange. When you choose to make this exchange, **time** for eternity, you will simultaneously exchange guilt for joy, viciousness for love, and pain for peace.

Your patience with your brother is your patience with yourself. Is not a child of God worth patience?

Now you must learn that only infinite patience produces immediate effects. Infinite patience is the way in which **time** is exchanged for eternity. Infinite patience calls upon infinite love, and by producing results now patience and love renders **time** unnecessary.

We have repeatedly said that **time** is a learning device to be abolished when **time** is no longer useful.

The Holy Spirit, Who speaks for God in **time**, also knows that **time** is meaningless. The Holy Spirit reminds you of that **time** is meaningless in every passing moment of **time**, because it is His special function to return you to eternity and remain to bless your creations there. The Holy Spirit has been given you freely by God, you must give Him as you received Him.

Ch. 10. Sec. 5.

Time itself is your choice. If you would remember eternity, you must look only on the eternal. If you allow yourself to become preoccupied with the temporal, you are living in **time**. As always, your choice is determined by what you value. **Time** and eternity cannot both be real, because **time** and eternity contradict each other. If you will accept only what is **timeless** as real, you will begin to understand eternity and make eternity yours.

Ch. 13. Sec. 4.

It is evident that the Holy Spirit's perception of **time** is the exact opposite of the ego's. The reason is equally clear, for the ego and the Holy Spirit perceive the goal of **time** as diametrically opposed. The Holy Spirit interprets **time's** purpose as rendering the need for **time** unnecessary. The Holy Spirit regards the function of **time** as temporary, serving only Her teaching function, which is temporary by definition. The Holy Spirit's emphasis is therefore on the only aspect of **time** that can extend to the infinite, for the present moment is the closest approximation of eternity that this world offers. It is in the reality of "now," without past or future, that the beginning of the appreciation of eternity lies. For only "now" is here, and only "now" presents the opportunities for the holy encounters in which salvation can be found.

The ego, on the other hand, regards the function of **time** as one of extending itself, the ego, in place of eternity, for like the Holy Spirit, the ego interprets the goal of **time** as the ego's own goal. The continuity of past and future, under the ego's direction, is the only purpose the ego perceives in **time**. The ego's continuity, then, would keep you in **time**, while the Holy Spirit would release you from **time**.

You, too, will interpret the function of **time** as you interpret your own function. If you accept your function in the world of **time** as one of healing, you will emphasize only the aspect of **time** in which healing can occur, which is in the present moment. Healing cannot be accomplished in the past. Healing must be accomplished in the present to release the future. This interpretation of healing ties the future to the present, and extends the present rather than the past. But if you interpret your function as destruction, you will lose sight of the present and hold on to the past to ensure a destructive future. And **time** will be as you interpret **time**, for of itself, **time**, is nothing.

Ch. 15. Sec. 1.

Can you imagine what it means to have no cares, no worries, no anxieties, but merely to be perfectly calm and quiet all the **time**? Yet to be perfectly calm all the **time** is what **time** is for; to learn just perfect calmness and nothing more. God's Teacher, the Holy Spirit, cannot be satisfied with His teaching until it constitutes all your learning. When this has happened, you will no longer need a teacher or **time** in which to learn.

The ego, like the Holy Spirit, uses **time** to convince you of the inevitability of its goal. To the ego the goal is death, which is **times** end. But to the Holy Spirit the goal of **time** is life, which has no end.

Ch. 15. Sec. 1. (cont.)

Fear is not of the present, but fear is only of the past and future, which do not exist. There is no fear in the present when each instant stands clear and separated from the past, without any of fears past shadow reaching out into the future. Each instant is a clean, untarnished birth, in which the Daughter of God emerges from the past into the present. And the present extends forever. The Daughter of God is so beautiful and so clean and free of guilt that nothing but happiness is there in the present. No darkness is remembered, and immortality and joy are now.

For what is **time** without a past and future? The ego has taken **time** to misguide you so completely, but it takes no **time** at all to be what you are. Begin to practice the Holy Spirit's use of **time** as a teaching aid to happiness and peace. Take this very instant, now, and think of this very instant as all there is of **time**. Nothing can reach you here out of the past, and it is here, in this very instant, that you are completely absolved, completely free and wholly without condemnation. From this holy instant wherein holiness was born again you will go forth in **time** without fear, and with no sense of change with **time**.

Time is your friend, if you leave **time** to the Holy Spirit to use. The Holy Spirit needs but very little to restore God's whole power to you. The Holy Spirit, Who transcends **time** for you, understands what **time** is for. Holiness lies not in **time**, but holiness lies in eternity. There never was an instant in which God's Daughter could lose her purity. The Daughter of God's changeless state is beyond **time**, for her purity remains forever beyond attack and without variability. **Time** stands still in her holiness, and **time** changes not.

Ch. 15. Sec. 2.

Peace will come, being the lesson God gives you, through the Teacher He has appointed to translate **time** into eternity. Blessed is God's Teacher, Whose joy is to teach God's holy Son his holiness. The Holy Spirit's joy is not contained in **time**. The Holy Spirit's teaching is for you because His joy is your joy. Through the Holy Spirit you stand before God's altar, where He gently translates hell into Heaven. For it is only in Heaven that God would have you be.

How long can it take to be where God would have you? For you are where you have forever been and will forever be. All that you have, you have forever. The blessed instant reaches out to encompass **time**, as God extends Himself to encompass you.

Ch. 26. Sec. 5.

All learning is a help or hindrance to the gate of Heaven. There are two teachers only, the ego and the Holy Spirit, who each point in different ways. And you will go along the way your chosen teacher leads. There are but two directions you can take, while **time** remains and choice is meaningful. For never will another road be made except the way to Heaven. You but choose whether to go toward Heaven, or away to nowhere. There is nothing else to choose.

Nothing is ever lost but **time**, which in the end, **time** itself, is meaningless. For **time** is but a little hindrance to eternity, quite meaningless to the real Teacher of the world. Yet since you do believe in **time**, why should you waste **time** going nowhere, when **time** can be used to reach a goal as high as learning can achieve? Think not the way to Heaven's gate is difficult at all. Nothing you undertake with certain purpose and high resolve and happy confidence, holding your sister's hand and keeping step to Heaven's song, is difficult to do. But an undertaking is hard indeed if you choose to wander off, alone and miserable, down a road that leads to nothing and that has no purpose.

God gave Her Teacher to replace the teacher you made, not to conflict with it. And what God would replace has been replaced. Such is the justice your All-Loving Mother has ensured must come to you. And from your own unfairness to yourself has God protected you. You cannot lose your way because there is no way but God's way, and nowhere can you go except to Her.

Discussion notes: Practical Truth • Practical Action • Heartfelt Thought

____

____

____

____

Topic 89

TIMELESSNESS AND TIME

timelessness: The state of eternal existence and perpetual being; the state of always existing. Eternity.

Ch. 2. Sec. 5.

In **time** we exist for and with each other. In **timelessness** we coexist with God.

Ch. 13. Sec. 8.

Apart from the Mother and the Daughter, the Holy Spirit has no function. The Holy Spirit is not separate from Either, the Mother or the Daughter, being in the Mind of Both, and knowing that Mind is One. The Holy Spirit is a Thought of God, and God has given the Holy Spirit to you. The Holy Spirit's message speaks of **timelessness** in **time**, and that is why Christ's vision looks on everything with love.

Ch. 14. Sec. 9.

The making of **time** to take the place of **timelessness** lay in the decision to be not as you are.

Ch. 15. Sec. 5.

God knows you *now*. The holy instant reflects God's knowing by bringing all perception out of the past, thus removing the past frame of reference you have built by which to judge your brothers. Once this past frame is gone, the Holy Spirit substitutes His frame of reference for your frame. The Holy Spirit's frame of reference is simply God. The Holy Spirit's **timelessness** lies only here now. For in the holy instant, free of the past, you see that love is in you, and you have no need to look without and snatch love guiltily from where you thought love was.

God loves every brother as He loves you; neither less nor more. God needs all your brother's equally, and so do you.

Ch. 17. Sec. 4.

The holy instant is a miniature of Heaven, sent you from Heaven. The holy instant is a picture set in a frame. If you accept this gift of the holy instant, you will not see the frame at all, because the gift can only be accepted through your willingness to focus all your attention on the picture, which is the holy instant. The holy instant is a miniature of eternity. It is a picture of **timelessness**, set in a frame of **time**.

Ch. 29. Sec. 6.

This world will bind your feet and tie your hands and kill your body only if you think that this world was made to crucify God's Daughter. For even though this world was a dream of death, you need not let this world stand for death to you.

How lovely is the world whose purpose is forgiveness of God's Daughter! How free from fear, how filled with blessing and with happiness! And what a joyous thing it is to dwell a little while in such a happy forgiving place! Nor can the forgiveness of God's Daughter be forgot, in such a joyous world, it is a little while till **timelessness** comes quietly to take the place of **time**.

Discussion notes: Practical Truth • Practical Action • Heartfelt Thought

---

TOPIC 90

PAST AND PRESENT

Ch. 13. Sec. 4.

The ego has a strange notion of time, and it is with this notion of time that your questioning might well begin. The ego invests heavily in the **past**, and in the end believes that the **past** is the only aspect of time that is meaningful. Remember that the ego's emphasis on guilt enables the ego to ensure its continuity by making the future like the **past**, and thus avoiding the **present**. By the notion of paying for the **past** in the future, the **past** becomes the determiner of the future, making the **past** and the future continuous without an intervening **present**. For the ego regards the **present** only as a brief transition to the future, in which the ego brings the **past** to the future by interpreting the **present** in **past** terms.

"Now" has no meaning to the ego. The **present** merely reminds the ego of **past** hurts, and the ego reacts to the **present** as if the **present** were the **past**. The ego cannot tolerate release from the **past**, and although the **past** is over, the ego tries to preserve the **past's** image by responding as if the **past** were **present**. The ego dictates your reactions to those you meet in the **present** from a **past** reference point, obscuring their **present** reality. In effect, if you follow what the ego's dictates, you will react to your brother as though he were someone based on a **past** reference point, and this will surely prevent you from recognizing your brother as he is now. And you will receive messages from your brother out of your own **past**, because by making your **past** real in the **present**, you are forbidding yourself to let your **past** go. You thus deny yourself the message of release that every brother offers you now.

The shadowy figures from the **past** are precisely what you must escape. The shadowy figures are not real, and have no hold over you unless you bring them with you. The shadowy figures carry the spots of **past** pain in your mind, directing you to attack in the **present** in retaliation for a **past** that is no more. And this decision is one of future pain. Unless you learn that **past** pain is an illusion, you are choosing a future of illusions and losing the many opportunities you could find for release in the **present**.

Ch. 26. Sec. 5.

Now you are shifting back and forth between the **past and present**. Sometimes the **past** seems real, as if the **past** were the **present**. Voices from the **past** are heard and then are doubted. You are like to one who still hallucinates, but lacks conviction in what you perceive. This is the borderland between the worlds, the bridge between the **past and present**. Here in the borderland the shadow of the **past** remains, but still a **present** light is dimly recognized. Once a **present** light is seen, this light can never be forgotten. The light must draw you from the **past** into the **present**, where you really are.

Forgive the **past** and let the **past** go, for the **past** is gone. You stand no longer on the ground that lies between the worlds of **past and present**. You have gone on, and reached the world that lies at Heaven's gate. There is no hindrance to the Will of God, nor any need that you repeat again a journey that was over long ago. Look gently on your sister, and behold the world in which perception of your hate has been transformed into a world of love.

Discussion notes: Practical Truth • Practical Action • Heartfelt Thought

---

Topic 91

YOUR FUNCTION

your function: The act of extending God's love (or Spirit) that creates awareness of oneness. On earth, our function is healing, which comes from the extension of forgiveness (love) authored by the Spirit. This frees us to experience the Spirit's joy and leads us back to God, reminding us of our earthly mission of forgiveness, healing, and unity by sharing the face of Christ with everyone.

Ch. 13. Sec. 4.

You have been told that **your function** in this world is healing, and **your function** in Heaven is creating. The ego teaches that **your function** on earth is destruction, and you have no function at all in Heaven. The ego would thus destroy you here in this world and bury you here, leaving you no inheritance except the dust out of which the ego thinks you were made. As long as the ego is reasonably satisfied with you, as the ego's reasoning goes, the ego offers you oblivion. When the ego becomes overtly savage, the ego offers you hell.

Ch. 22. Sec. 6.

You will see your value through your brother's eyes, and each one is released as he beholds his brother as savior in place of the attacker who he thought was there. Through this releasing of your brother is the world released. This gift of forgiveness is your part in bringing peace. For you have asked what is **your function** here, and have been answered that **your function** is to forgive. Seek not to change **your function**, nor to substitute another goal.

Accept **your function** to forgive and serve it willingly.

Ch. 26. Sec. 7.

What is the Will of God? God wills Her Daughter have everything. And this God guaranteed when She created Her Daughter as everything.

This guarantee that you are everything is the miracle by which creation became **your function**, sharing creation with God. **Your function** of creation, which is sharing the face of Christ with everything.

Discussion notes: Practical Truth • Practical Action • Heartfelt Thought

Topic 92

YOUR PURPOSE

your purpose: (1) The reason for which something is done or created or for which something exists. One's intention or objective. (2) Our higher Self's purpose is the acceptance that everyone is the same. Seeing others not as a body but rather through the vision of Christ. We are all forgiven and not bound by sin.

Ch. 12. Sec. 2.

Let us not save nightmares, for our nightmares are not fitting offerings for Christ, and so they are not fit gifts for you. Take off the covers and look at what you are afraid of. Only the anticipation will frighten you, for the reality of nothingness cannot be frightening. Let us not delay this, for your dream of hatred will not leave you without help, and Help is here. Learn to be quiet in the midst of turmoil, for quietness is the end of strife and this quietness is the journey to peace. Look straight at every image that rises to delay you, for the goal is inevitable because love is eternal. The goal of love is but your right, and love belongs to you despite your dreams.

You still want what God wills, and no nightmare can defeat a child of God in his purpose. For **your purpose** was given you by God, and you must accomplish **your purpose** because it is God's Will. Awake and remember **your purpose**, for it is your will to do so. What has been accomplished for you must be yours. Do not let your hatred stand in the way of love, for nothing can withstand the love of Christ for God, or God's Love for Christ.

Ch. 20. Sec. 8.

Your sister's sinlessness is given you in shining light, to look on with the Holy Spirit's vision and to rejoice in your sister's sinlessness along with Her. For peace will come to all who ask for vision with real desire and sincerity of purpose, shared with the Holy Spirit and at one with Her on what salvation is. Be willing, then, to see your sister sinless, that Christ may rise before your vision and give you joy. And place no value on your sister's body, which holds her to illusions of what she is. It is your sister's desire to see her sinlessness, as it is yours to see sinlessness.

The Holy Spirit guarantees that what God willed and gave you shall be yours. This vision that Christ will rise is **your purpose** now, and the vision makes sinlessness yours and ready to be given. You have the vision that enables you to see the body not. And as you look upon your sister with your Christ vision, you will see an altar to your Mother, holy as Heaven, glowing with radiant purity and sparkling with the shining lilies you laid upon Her altar. What can you value more than this? Why do you think the body is a better home, a safer shelter for God's Daughter? Why would you rather look on the body than on the truth?

Ch. 23. Sec. 4.

The overlooking of the battleground is now **your purpose**.

Be lifted up, and from a higher place look down upon the battleground. From there will your perspective be quite different. Here in the midst of the battleground, the battle does seem real. Here you have chosen to be part of the battle.

Those with the strength of God in their awareness could never think of battle. What could they gain but loss of their perfection? For everything fought for on the battleground is of the body; something the body seems to offer or to own. No one who knows that he has everything could seek for limitation, nor could he who knows he has everything value the body's offerings. The senselessness of conquest is quite apparent from the quiet sphere above the battleground.

Discussion notes: Practical Truth • Practical Action • Heartfelt Thought

---

Glossary

These definitions are not meant for doctrinal purposes, as doctrine can create rigidity and exclusivity and cause distractions. Instead, these definitions are offered to provide a language context so we can adapt and apply the universal wisdom this book has to offer.

Note that gender identification is generally a human distinction. When gender nouns and pronouns are used to refer to God, Christ, and the Holy Spirit, this is not asserting they have gender; rather it is for a metaphorical purpose, as this usage may support a deeper personal connection.

* * *

abridgment:
A shortened form of a work retaining the general sense and unity of the original.

altar:
The place within our consciousness that chooses what we are devoted to, where one chooses between God and the ego, between truth and illusion, between love and fear.

anti-Christ:
A symbol for the ego. The belief in a power that can oppose the omnipotence of God and deny the reality of our Christ within. An idol.

atonement:
Rectifying the false belief that we are separate from God and from all of God's creations by accepting that we are all one with God. Release from the guilt of separation through forgiveness of ourselves, others, and everything we resist. Acceptance that we are all joined and not separate. Healing the thoughts of separation returns the mind to wholeness. At-one-ment.

attack:
The expression of anger toward others. An attempt to justify our own guilt by projecting it onto others.

authority problem:
Our attempt to create a self-image without including our divinity as a source to express our true Self. This belief in our egoic authority can cause us to project our deficiencies onto another person, which creates guilt and fear. We have power of free will, and God does not control how we use it.

awaken:
To raise one's consciousness. A moment of awareness of true reality that was previously unrealized. The continuance of such realizations helps us recognize higher consciousness, which brings clarity, well-being, and harmony.

behavior:
The way in which one acts or conducts oneself, especially toward others.

body:
A biological form (a physical instrument) that our mind uses to communicate with the outer world. The body is a means (a device) to connect with all that we encounter while in the physical world of time. The body is neutral and has no opinions or influence of its own. Only the mind assigns meaning to things. The body is important and valuable, as it is the thing we use to extend love and expand the Self. Seeing through the Christ mind will guide us to use the body for its highest purpose.

charity:
Generosity and helpfulness, especially toward the needy, suffering, or disfavored. Aid given to those in need. Benevolent goodwill toward or love of humanity, lenient judgment of others, forbearance.

Christ:
The divine Identity that is everywhere and within all creation. The shared experience of God's Spirit. The Self that God placed within all by the extension of the Spirit. Christ is the author of true vision within everyone (the higher Self) and our shared identity of oneness with everything. Jesus fully embodied the Christ and serves as a model for transcending the ego's influence through awakening into Christ consciousness. Note that the Holy Spirit is the mediator between the Christ Mind and our ego mind.

Christ vision:
Spiritual sight. Seeing beyond the body and the ego by way of divine Spirit. Interpreting others' behavior as either an act of love or a calling out for love. Seeing both as no reason for defense or attack and every reason for extending love. The ability to mentally see beyond all worldly interference to the light of holiness in everything.

Christmas:
(1) A holiday commemorating the traditional birth of Jesus. (2) A symbol for the rebirth of the Christ in ourselves; the time of Christ. Dispelling the egoic belief that sacrifice is a gift given on behalf of love.

communication:
(1) The process of sending and receiving messages through verbal or nonverbal means. The exchanges and experiences of connection. The interactions within relationships. (2) The spiritual joining of minds to exchange the flow of spirit and love between us and God. Letting go of the thoughts of specialness and separation and being free to express our unified relationship.

conflict:
Mental struggle resulting from incompatible or opposing needs, drives, or wishes, fueled by external or internal demands.

content and form:

All things in this world have two aspects: form and content. Form refers to the things in the world while content is the meaning behind those things. What will bring lasting change in us is not a change of form but a change in how we perceive the content.

create:

(1) The extension of our spirit. God extends to us so we can extend. (2) The power of the mind to make something in this world.

Creation:

The extension of God's essence or spirit.

crucifixion:

The symbol of the ego, whereas resurrection is the symbol of awakening. Each day, each hour, and each moment, we decide between the crucifixion and the resurrection, between the ego and God. The ego is the choice for guilt, and God is the choice for guiltlessness. See also resurrection.

darkness:

Thoughts of illusions and separation. Denial of eternal reality.

death:

(1) The expiration of the physical form called a body. (2) The biological proof of the earthly concept that we are not eternal, allegedly confirming our separation from the undying God. In this viewpoint, we are not eternal because we can die and God cannot.

defense:

Protection of an idea, concept, or cause. An argument in support or justification of a point of view. Resistance to an opposing thought or idea.

denial:

(1) Refusal to accept something or the rejection of something not wanted. (2) A statement, action, allegation, or claim pronouncing something to be untrue or unuseful.

depression:

Feelings of despondency and dejection. A state of feeling sad, lonely, guilty, or hopeless.

devil:

An egoic projection that shifts the blame for destructive calamity and suffering onto an imagined powerful external entity, making it the responsible source. This fear-based assertion enlarges the feeling of being separate from our Creator, thereby causing anxiety and victim-minded thinking. Humans can be powerfully influential and industrious beings, and this power can be responsible for catastrophic harm or incredible healing. The results are usually labeled good or evil, love or hate.

dream:

The mind experiencing egoistic perceptions in the physical world, creating illusions and deceptions. Dreams of guilt and fear can be exchanged for peace and joy through awakening into higher perceptions of love and forgiveness by the gift of transformative miracles revealed to us by Spirit. Miracles are the means to heal fearful dreams. See also miracle.

earth:

The physical place where our mind and body interact with things through the experience of feelings, thoughts, and actions. The earth can be a place where love resides and tragedy seems to reign, a place of beauty or decay, a place of wonder or disaster—all of which is dependent upon our interpretation.

ego:

Lower level consciousness that stifles Self awareness. Thoughts and beliefs that are rooted in fear and can produce guilt, arrogance, blame, confusion, stress, and separation. The ego is habitually involved in various struggles and dramas, aggrandizing the little self and its story, which distract us from our real purpose of knowing our true divine Self. The ego is not something to fight against but rather to recognize, be amused by, and not fooled by. Waking up from the ego's deceptions is the pathway to redemption. This frees us to experience peace, joy, and contentment. Desire, motivation, and accomplishments can originate and be pursued through egoistic thoughts or through the higher Self. Our best interest is to listen to and follow our higher Self when determining how to use our intention and attention.

error:

A mistake, wrong-thinking, mis-perception, or mis-creation by the mind. Only the mind is capable of errors, but errors are expressed through the body. Errors may be perceived as sin; however, errors are corrected through forgiveness and choosing to let go of the story held in our mind.

everything:

Internal awareness (rather than possessions, health, fame, or power) that we are complete and one with the source of all. A recognition of our connection to a state outside of time that contains no past and no future, no beginning and no end, only always. The knowing of abundance comes when we see that everything is not a thing.

extension (higher Self):

The inner radiance of God given to others through love, forgiveness, and healing. The ability of our Spirit to express forgiveness and experience oneness.

extension (little self):

The egotistical expressed thoughts of the mind triggering worldly effects that can cause confusion and separation.

faithlessness:

Faith in the little self of illusions, lacking faith in God. Belief in separation.

fear:

A sensation of vulnerability, despair, doubt, confusion, anger, and anxiety. Fear is a recoil to a perceived source of danger. An emotion we experience when we believe we are not safe now or in the future and need to be prepared to defend or attack. This maintains the belief that separation is security. The fear of God causes us to feel separate and incomplete. Fear attributes include unhappiness, negativity, anger, unworthiness, dishonesty, mistrust, doubt, malice, arrogance, exclusion, resistance, control, judgment, and criticism. Fear can motivate, aggravate, deceive, hurt, and occasionally protect.

forgiveness:

A choice to see ourselves and others with the vision of Christ, which shifts our perception away from blame, resentment, punishment, and differences. Being able to take ownership of our feelings, thoughts, and actions without judgment. In this way, we can view wrongness as a projection of separation and understand that forgiveness is the plan for salvation for everyone. To forgive is to overlook what happened in the past. To forgive can feel difficult to do, but it can be done with a willingness to use our intention and attention to extend love. Forgiveness is the path to peace, joy, freedom, and power.

free will:

The freedom of choice in the world of time and space. We can freely choose which voice to listen to—the ego or the Spirit, a thought of separation or of oneness.

gap:

The illusionary space between ourselves and God and ourselves and others that is brought about by the belief that we are separate and incomplete.

God:

The eternal Energy. The infinite Source. Energy and Source encompasses everything. This Energy/Source (God) is expansion, extension, evolution, connection, force, order, flow, unity, rebirth and Love. Words help us connect with God's life-giving Essence, but words are unable to express the true reality of God and Creation.

guilt:

(1) The negative emotion experienced when we believe we have committed an offense or wrongdoing, causing us to feel separated from God and others. Fear arises because we mistakenly think God will punish us for our misconduct (errors), which continues the cycle of feeling guilty and afraid. Guilt can cause us to attack others or ourselves. (2) Fear-based thoughts that reinforce the illusion we are incomplete or inadequate and that there is something fundamentally wrong with us. [Note: Guilt can be valuable as a prompt to consider improvement of a behavior, or to determine if there is a need to take a responsible action; such as, apologize, set a boundary, or pursue further conversations to clarify things. Subsequently, the goal is to let go of guilt.]

guiltless and guiltlessness:

The removal of the concept of guilt. We are not guilty but rather in a state of growth and awakening where our errors and mistakes exist. Past errors may affect current circumstances, like robbing a bank and being sent to prison. However, guilt is the memory of an action we wish we could change. Guilt can keep us stuck in the past or troubled about the future, which distracts us from living in the present moment.

hallucination:

An unfounded or mistaken impression or notion of reality. A perception of something with no reality. A delusion.

hate:

To feel extreme aversion for or extreme hostility toward someone or something because of fear.

heal:

To correct the perception that we are separate from God and others. The mending of the mind's belief that the self is comprised only of a body that suffers. Healing is releasing the fearful illusion that we are vulnerable and can be victims of the world. Our body experiences physical sickness, but our true identity is in our spirit, not our body. Healing occurs when we let go of the attachment to the body and embrace the unity with God and others.

Heaven:

A state of mind in which we see the world as a place of union, peace, joy, and serenity, without the veil of fear. An awareness of love; an experience of peace. Heaven can be experienced in this world of time through the conduit of unified relationships, which is accomplished through the extending and receiving of love and acceptance. Everyone's eternal home becomes known at time's end.

hell:

A state of mind in which we seem to be separate, vulnerable, deficient, unfulfilled, and mistreated. A feeling that someone or something is trying to control or harm us, and we have to fight or flee to be safe. The pursuit of the egoistic thought system that leads us to selfish and destructive behaviors rooted in fear and guilt causing pain and suffering in us and others.

holy instant:

(1) Any instant when we still our minds and become centered and present. In this stillness, we have no sense of fear, and nothing stands in the way of our connection to God's acceptance. (2) An opportunity to receive guidance and identify with what we are. (3) The moment in which we experience a feeling of peace, joy, and love. A release from the past and future and an alignment with unity and oneness. The holy instant is a device that can be used to teach and share love's meaning. Ultimately, our goal is to make every instant a holy instant.

holy relationship:

A relationship of forgiveness and truth. The process of personal growth through the Christ vision, where one's perceptions change the experience of separation into an embrace of the oneness of everyone we meet and everything we see.

Holy Spirit:
The communication link to God that is within everyone. The voice for God; the divine teacher. Our internal Guide. Our higher Self. The Holy Spirit is the mediator between the Christ Mind and our ego mind.

host to God:
When we choose to listen, observe, and embrace the divine within ourselves.

hostage to the ego:
When we listen to the confused and limited split (ego) mind and choose to think thoughts of separation, which engenders fear and isolation.

idol:
The allegiance to an external thing, body, place, substance, possession, relationship, idea, or achievement that we believe holds our escape from pain and the answer to pleasure. A belief that those effects will bring us to completion as a substitution for what the divine has to offer.

illusion:
Something that deceives by producing a false or misleading impression of reality. Beliefs that are not true.

insanity:
The state of believing in the ego's system of control and manipulation, which creates repetitive and destructive thoughts and emotions that maintain the feelings of isolation and separation. The thought that we can control our life while defending against the things trying to take control of it.

Jesus:
One who fully embodied the Christ. Jesus serves as a model for transcending the ego's influence through awakening into Christ consciousness. This was demonstrated by his benevolent words and actions of love and acceptance.

judgment:
The mental process of deciding and selecting what to accept or reject. When wrongly used, judgment promotes a world of separation and specialness. The correct use of this process is to judge the ego's voice as insane and replace it with the sanity of Spirit.

justice:
(1) The principle that determines fair and righteous conduct and unbiased treatment. (2) Giving love and forgiveness to everyone with complete impartiality. Restoration without retribution.

(the) Kingdom:
The reality of oneness. Truth without the illusions of sin and guilt. God's Kingdom is love.

knowledge:
Inner knowing; divine disclosure. Certainty without the need to defend or explain. Divine knowledge is experienced rather than perceived. Perception is a mere reflection or image of knowledge.

lack:

The belief that we are not enough or that we do not have enough. This belief is founded on the misguided principle that there is not enough to go around, and we try to fill that lack by acquiring things. We imagine that those things will make us feel safe, accepted, and satisfied.

learn and teach:

The process of examining the thoughts about what we believe we are—for the purpose of undoing the sense of separation from God and others. It is sorting out truth from illusion to help us rise to higher perceptions; an awakening in us that is expressed into this world.

love:

The essence of being, which contains the emotions of acceptance, peace, and joy; the attraction to connection. Love is already within each of us, and as the blocks to love's awareness (such as guilt, shame, and judgment) are removed, we become mindful that love always has and always will encircle us and everything. Love's attributes are goodness, honesty, compassion, patience, understanding, forgiveness, joy, peace, inclusion, acceptance, release, and encouragement. Love motivates, comforts, sustains, heals, and protects.

mind:

(1) The set of cognitive faculties, including consciousness, imagination, perception, thinking, judgment, language, and memory. The faculty of a thing's consciousness. It is debatable as to where the mind is and what things influence it. (2) The expression of the self that includes awareness, choice, thought, and emotion.

miracle:

A divine healing of human perception; a change of mind that shifts perception from fear and guilt to love and forgiveness. The undoing of delusions and illusions through divine communication. An awakening that heals the mind from pain and suffering.

mis-create:

The act of projection, rejection, fear, and separation.

murder:

Thoughts of blame, anger, revenge, and vengeance toward ourselves or others. What is not love is murder.

original sin:

The belief we are guilty and have to do something to be accepted and complete. The belief that we are lacking and separate and that God is outside us.

perception:

A construct of thoughts that interprets or judges information to form belief. The manner in which we process our understanding of the world around us, which we inherently see as entirely separate from ourselves. Perceptions define how we see the world; some are true perceptions, and some are mis-perceptions. Both influence our thoughts, beliefs, actions, and feelings. Miracles change our mis-perceptions of fear into perceptions that foster love. What we perceive within ourselves determines what we see outside ourselves. Therefore, reality is our interpretation of it.

projection:

(1) The act of deflecting our internal conflicts and suffering onto others, making it appear as though other people carry these damages and not us. (2) A method of separatism that demonstrates internal guilt and anguish over our perceived sins and extends this guilt onto others.

real world:

A state of mind in which the egoic world is freed from projections of guilt and separation, accomplished through the miracles of changed perception. This does not change the physical world; rather, it changes the way we see the world. We see the world of love, happiness, and joy through the Christ vision.

resurrection:

The reawakening of the mind. Awareness of the Christ within. Transcending the ego perceptions of the world, the body, and death.

right-minded:

The part of our mind that contains the Spirit that allows us to see the real world through the Christ vision. The state of mind in which the escape from fear is possible.

sacrifice:

(1) A belief that someone must lose if another is to gain. (2) A perception that we must pay a price to receive God's love. The ego, not God, needs or demands a sacrifice.

salvation:

(1) Correction to the thoughts of separation and judgment through love and the acceptance of everyone we meet and everything we see. To recognize we are neither above nor below anyone and that we all journey together. (2) The undoing of the belief in sin and guilt. A change of mind through the power of perceptual miracles. The awakening of the mind so we can experience love and forgiveness instead of fear and guilt.

self:

A concept constructed from the beliefs one holds about oneself and the perceptions one construes from the reactions of others. We are all saviors of the world by the acceptance and forgiveness of everyone and everything through the Christ vision.

separation:

(1) A mindset that supports the concept that we are independent from creation. Through dissociation, we create an identity that we are dissimilar beings, forming a story about "me" and the evaluations of everything outside of "me." The illusion that "me" or "my tribe" is somehow better, wiser, or more special than others. (2) The denial of the spiritual condition that everything is connected by virtue of divine energy.

sickness:

(1) The part of the mind that believes in separation and prevents us from recognizing the oneness of all creation. (2) The expression of fear and vulnerability that may be displaced onto the body.

sin:

The belief (perception) that an action or thought is wicked, immoral, or selfish. The label that is assigned to an action or thought that is believed to go against God's laws or goodness. Some religions claim they know what is sinful and project those beliefs onto everyone. They believe sin is punishable and irreversible unless a sacrifice is made. This belief can create feelings of guilt and separation from God. If we think God demands punishment or sacrifice for sin, this belief can cause confusion about the nature of unconditional love. The ego's goal is to convince us that sin has a permanent effect unless a price is paid. The good news is that there is no sin but rather errors, mistakes, wrong decisions, or hurtful actions. These, therefore, can be forgiven and healed; although some may feel harder to forgive than others. Note that errors, mistakes, wrong decisions, or hurtful actions can cause pain, chaos, and destruction here on earth.

Son/Daughter of God:

Our true identity is that we are all a son or daughter of God. Mankind is not separate from the universal Self who encompasses all beings. We are God's extension and continuation of love and grace. Everyone is a part of God's creation, at one with God and each other. We are all the incarnation of God; otherwise we would not exist. God is the true identity of everything. See also God.

Sonship/Daughtership:

This is a singular term that means the collective Oneness. All that God created, us and everything, is in an eternal relationship with the Divine. The inclusive Oneness of all that is.

specialness:

The idea of being superior to others, which requires others to be inferior. Specialness always makes comparisons and judgments, thereby becoming the source of separation. We crave it because we think that specialness is the opposite of rejection, but it is a feeble attempt to get what we feel God has withheld. In truth, God's love is indiscriminate and makes specialness irrelevant because everything is the grandeur of God.

spirit:
The essence of divinity and creation. The substance of our true nature, which is nonphysical, eternal, formless, changeless, holy, and perfect. Spirit uses the mind to express itself in the physical world.

split mind:
A mind divided between two parts—the "right mind," or home of God, and the "wrong mind," or home of the ego. The right mind embraces love, acceptance, and peace, while the wrong mind promulgates fear, sin, and guilt.

teacher of God:
The process of examining the beliefs about the self for the purpose of undoing the sense of separation from the divine. Sorting out truth from illusion to advance to higher perceptions that will be expressed in the physical world.

temptation:
The perception that things can bring us satisfaction as a substitute for love. The lure of something having a powerful appeal, making it hard to resist. An attraction to make a wrong decision that would lead to an outcome we do not want. Temptation feeds on the internal feeling of lacking things, love, and specialness.

time (and space):
The physical world, which is home to illusions of separation where the body and mind are acting in a linear progression. The place where birth and death, peace and violence, forgiveness and judgment, love and fear, and joy and pain occur. Where past, present, and future compete for our attention. Where past and future thoughts keep us from the reality of the present. To the struggling self, it is a prison; to the awakening Self, it is a classroom. We are on a spaceship called Earth, traveling through time.

timelessness:
The state of eternal existence and perpetual being; the state of always existing. Eternity.

Trinity:
(1) God, the divine Source. (2) The Christ, the divine Identity. (3) The Holy Spirit, the divine Teacher.

two voices:
The ego's voice and the Spirit's voice.

vision:
Seeing through the eyes of Christ rather than through the eyes of the body. Seeing beyond the body to the Spirit, which leads to true perception.

war:
A state of hostility, conflict, or antagonism. A struggle or competition between opposing forces.

what you are:
God's Creation complete and whole, in greatness lacking nothing eternal. We are not separate from God; God is incomplete without us. No one is without God, nor anyone unworthy of God's perfect love. We are love.

willingness:
The quality or state of being prepared to do something; readiness. See also holy instant.

wrong-minded:
The part of our mind entangled with the ego's thought system that creates and stockpiles false perceptions.

your function:
The act of extending God's love (or Spirit) that creates awareness of oneness. On Earth, our function is healing, which comes from the extension of forgiveness (love) authored by the Spirit. This frees us to experience the Spirit's joy and leads us back to God, reminding us of our earthly mission of forgiveness, healing, and unity by sharing the face of Christ with everyone.

your purpose:
(1) The reason for which something is done or created or for which something exists. One's intention or objective. (2) Our higher Self's purpose is the acceptance that everyone is the same. Seeing others not as a body but rather through the vision of Christ. We are all forgiven and not bound by sin.

Book Resources

A Course in Miracles by Helen Schucman
https://en.wikisource.org/wiki/A_Course_in_Miracles

A Course in Miracles Abridged Edition by Stan Herrmann/Helen Schucman
www.acim-a.org

A Course in Miracles for Dummies Volume I Ch. 1-15 by Thomas Wakechild

A Course in Miracles for Dummies Volume II Ch. 15-31 by Thomas Wakechild

Glossary-Index for A Course in Miracles (6th edition) by Kenneth Wapnick

Glossary of Terms from A Course in Miracles (2nd edition) by Robert Perry

Gender word count in book

Father	51	Mother	67
Son	111	Daughter	118
Brother	156	Sister	177
He	152	She	143
Him/His	217	Her	265
Son of God	47	Daughter of God	46
God's Son	32	God's Daughter	42
Sonship	13	Daughtership	6

The Foundation for Inner Peace

To learn more about *A Course in Miracles*, I recommend you visit the website of the authorized publisher and copyright holder of the Course, the Foundation for Inner Peace: **www.acim.org**.

The Foundation for Inner Peace is a non-profit organization dedicated to uplifting humanity through *A Course in Miracles*. The organization depends on donations and is currently immersed in translating the Course into many languages (26 to date). The Foundation also donates thousands of copies of the Course. If you would like to support more people to benefit from *A Course in Miracles,* donating to the Foundation for Inner Peace would be a worthy endeavor. Website: www.acim.org.

Book Recommendations

The Bhagavad Gita A New Translation....................Stephen Mitchell

The Upanishads: A Classic of Indian Spirituality....................Eknath Easwaran

Tao Te Ching....................Lao Tzu

The Heart of the Buddha's Teaching....................Thich Nhat Hanh

The Power of Now....................Eckhart Tolle

A New Earth....................Eckhart Tolle

A Return to Love....................Marianne Williamson

The Universal Christ....................Richard Rohr

The Way of Mastery....................Shanti Christo Foundation

Resurrecting Jesus....................Adyashanti

The Four Agreements....................Don Miguel Ruiz

The Seven Spiritual Laws of Success....................Deepak Chopra

Mindfulness for Beginners....................Jon Kabat-Zinn

Change Your Thoughts Change Your Life....................Wayne Dyer

Is God a Mathematician....................Mario Livio

The Power of Awareness....................Neville Goddard

Take me to Truth....................Nouk Sanchez / Tomas Vieira

Three Magic Words....................Uell S. Andersen

Living a Course in Miracles....................Jon Mundy

A Gradual Awakening....................Stephen Levine

Jesus the Son of Man....................Kahlil Gibran

I Don't Believe in Atheists....................Chris Hedges

Original Blessing .... Matthew Fox

The Untethered Soul ....Michael Singer

Path of Light....................Robert Perry

Journey Without Distance....................Robert Skutch

A Course in Miracles Combined Volume (www.acim.org)....................Helen Schucman

A Course in Miracles Abridged Edition (www.acim-a.org)..Stan Herrmann/Helen Schucman

The Bible....................Multiple Authors

Printed in Great Britain
by Amazon